Hyperinflation, Currency Board, and Bust
The Case of Argentina

T0316395

# Hohenheimer
# Volkswirtschaftliche Schriften

**Herausgegeben von**
Prof. Dr. Michael Ahlheim, Prof. Dr. Thomas Beißinger, Prof. Dr. Ansgar Belke,
Prof. Dr. Rolf Caesar, Prof. Dr. Harald Hagemann, Prof. Dr. Klaus Herdzina,
Prof. Dr. Walter Piesch, Prof. Dr. Ingo Schmidt, Prof. Dr. Ulrich Schwalbe,
Prof. Dr. Peter Spahn, Prof. Dr. Jochen Streb, Prof. Dr. Gerhard Wagenhals,

## Band 56

# PETER LANG

Frankfurt am Main · Berlin · Bern · Bruxelles · New York · Oxford · Wien

Jutta Maute

# Hyperinflation, Currency Board, and Bust

The Case of Argentina

## PETER LANG

Frankfurt am Main · Berlin · Bern · Bruxelles · New York · Oxford · Wien

**Bibliographic Information published by Die Deutsche Bibliothek**
Die Deutsche Bibliothek lists this publication in the Deutsche Nationalbibliografie; detailed bibliographic data is available in the internet at <http://dnb.ddb.de>.

Zugl.: Hohenheim, Univ., Diss., 2006

Gedruckt mit Unterstützung der
**Stiftung**
Landesbank Baden-Württemberg

LB≡BW

D 100
ISSN 0721-3085
ISBN 3-631-55608-X
US-ISBN 0-8204-8708-2

© Peter Lang GmbH
Europäischer Verlag der Wissenschaften
Frankfurt am Main 2006
All rights reserved.

Printed in Germany 1 2 3 4 5   7

www.peterlang.de

In commemoration of my late friend Sabine

# Overview

# Contents

# Figures

## Abbreviations and Acronyms

| | |
|---|---|
| ALCA | Área de Libre Commercio des las Américas |
| BCRA | Banco Central de la República Argentina |
| BOCON | Bonos de Consolidación de Deudas |
| BONEX | Bonos Externos |
| CBA | Currency Board Arrangement |
| CEPAL | Comisión Económica para América Latina y el Caribe |
| CFA | Communauté Financière d'Afrique |
| CPI | Consumer Price Index |
| DATAFIEL | Statistical Database of FIEL |
| EMBI | Emerging Markets Bond Index |
| EPH | Encuesta Permanente de Hogares |
| EU | European Union |
| FDI | Foreign Direct Investment |
| FIEL | Fundación de Investigaciones Económicas Latinoamericanas |
| FREPASO | Frente País Solidario |
| FTAA | Free Trade Area of the Americas |
| GDP | Gross Domestic Product |
| GNP | Gross National Product |
| IFS | International Financial Statistics of the IMF |
| IMF | International Monetary Fund |
| INDEC | Instituto Nacional de Estadística y Censos |
| LIBOR | London Interbank Offered Rate |
| MECON | Ministerio de Economía y Producción |
| MERCOSUR | Mercado Común del Sur |
| NPV | Net Present Value |
| PJ | Partido Justicialista |
| SBA | Stand-by Arrangement |
| SDR | Special Drawing Right |
| UCEMA | Universidad del CEMA |
| UCR | Unión Cívica Radical |
| US | United States of America |
| UTDT | Universidad Torcuato di Tella |
| VAR | Vector Auto Regression |
| VAT | Value Added Tax |
| WPI | Wholesale Price Index |
| XPI | Export Price Index |

# Acknowledgements

I am deeply indebted to Professors Dr. Harald Hagemann and Dr. Heinz-Peter Spahn, both at Universität Hohenheim, Germany, and especially to Professor Dr. Hans-Michael Trautwein, at Carl von Ossietzky Universität Oldenburg, Germany, who have supported this dissertation with critical discussions and valuable input. Also, I am grateful to the participants in the „Forschungs- und Doktorandenseminar", held at the Institut für Volkswirtschaftslehre, Lehrstühle für Wirtschaftstheorie und Wirtschaftspolitik, Universität Hohenheim, who always were reliable sources of inspiration and critical censors in discourse.

Likewise, I am deeply obliged to Evangelisches Studienwerk e.V. Villigst, Germany, which supported this dissertation within the project "Promotionsschwerpunkt Globalisierung und Beschäftigung", both financially, with a generous stipend enabling me to undertake this dissertation project in the first place, and academically, with the organisation of outstanding pertinent symposia.

Furthermore, this work would not have been possible without the generous scientific and statistical support as well as invaluable anecdotal input given by Professors Daniel Heymann, of CEPAL, Roque Fernández and Jorge Miguel Streb, both of UCEMA, Fernando Navajas, of FIEL, and Pablo Sanguinetti, of UTDT, during my stay in Buenos Aires in the autumn of 2004.

Finally, I am thankful for the firm support given to me by my family, above all my husband who stepped in during the "hot" phase as a "househusband", to my mother who always stood ready to take care of our children when necessary, and, after all, to my children themselves who often rightly asked what bizarre kind of long story it must be Mom is writing up there in the loft. I am glad to prove at last that it is not a never-ending one.

# 1 Introduction

During most of the 1990s, Argentina enjoyed stability and an economic boom such that many Argentines felt that their country had entered the path of catching up with the industrialised countries, and so would finally approach its deserved place in the world. Indeed, the first world was where the country arguably once belonged to: barely a century ago, Argentina, the land of silver[1], ranked among the richest nations in the world: its income per head was on a par with that of Germany and France in 1913[2]. This wealth had been achieved through a textbook process of catching up via productivity-enhancing technological progress, financed largely by foreign investment, in the global free-trade environment of the late 19th and early 20th century[3]: both the new technology of deep freezing and the extensive construction of railways connecting the remote Pampa areas with the Atlantic coast had enabled the country to export its main staples, beef and other agricultural products, on a large scale to Europe. Present-day Buenos Aires, the "Paris of the South", is still, in its grandeur, witness of these golden years, which attracted masses of immigrants[4].

Entering the 21st century, the second-largest South American country with its well-educated population of mainly European descent and its abundance in natural resources has found itself brutally disillusioned. The tragic crisis the country experienced in 2001/02 put not only an end to the expectations of catching up fast but also added the worst recession in the country's history and another bad political turmoil to the series of crises and chronic instability that mark the country's history since the 1930s.

The growth of the 1990s was the result of successful stabilisation via the "Plan Convertibilidad", a currency board arrangement cum escorting economic policies, with the fixed Dollar exchange rate at its core. The currency board's success in putting an end to the previous decades of ever higher inflation, and finally

---

[1]  Argentina's name is derived from "argentum", Latin for silver, due to its erstwhile important silver mines on the territories of present-day Bolivia, the exploits of which were shipped through the port of Buenos Aires.

[2]  See N.N. (2004), p. 4.

[3]  See the seminal paper "Catching Up, Forging Ahead, and Falling Behind" written by Moses Abramovitz in 1986.

[4]  "Etre riche comme un Argentin": this French idiom of the time is further witness of the country's former splendour.

hyperinflation, was nothing less than spectacular. Today, the judgements about "Convertibilidad", seemingly the magic cure of the 1990s, range from "outright poison"[5] to "flagrantly wrongly administered, but potentially beneficial remedy". The Argentine currency board, its justification, its conditionalities, the reasons for its collapse, and finally its evaluation is what this treatise is about.

A thorough analysis of Argentina's currency board requires the detailed identification of the historical, economic, and social context of its implementation, and this not only for the sake of episodical completeness but, above all, for the understanding of the determinants of its choice and configuration. Following this introduction, section 2 will therefore analyze the country's desperate situation, marked by economic decay and high inflation culminating in hyperinflation, at the time when the new government of Carlos Menem took over in mid-1989. The complex and devastating interdependencies of causes and effects that fuel the accelerating inflationary process and lead to a continuing economic erosion over decades, and finally develop into hyperinflation, are analyzed for typical high inflations in general, and examined for the case of Argentina during the 1980s in particular. From this exercise it will get palpable that, having seen so many failed stabilisation attempts before, with the result of ever more eroded policy credibility, the country's remaining options for stabilisation in effect excluded all but the strictest ones.

Section 3 gives a detailed exposition of the theory of currency boards. The currency board idea, its historical roots, its functioning principles, strengths and weaknesses, and the conditionalities a currency board entails with respect to its appropriateness, as well as its duration and termination, will be dealt with in detail. While the informed reader primarily interested in the Argentine case may well skip this section, for any other reader the exercise may well be worth the effort since, all too often, much is said about the dangers of the regime and little about its potentials. This is especially true for the appealing idea of dual currency boards outlined at the end of this section.

Section 4 focuses on the Argentine currency board's implementation and development during the barely 11 years of its existence. Clearly, the two vivid growth phases before and after 1995 were owed to the market oriented reforms embraced with the Convertibility Plan, but also to favourable external conditions, just as the deep recession that started in 1998 was not solely the consequence of

---

[5]   See, e.g., Porzecanski (2003).

negative external shocks but also, and fatally, of inconsistencies between the macroeconomic framework set by the currency board and the concomitant fiscal, but also microeconomic policies. The interactions between these inconsistencies, on the one hand, and the exogenous factors aggravating them, on the other, make an exciting plot in a story that was long thought to be one of success but instead ended as a tragedy. In exploring the plot's determinants, the ground is prepared for the evaluation to follow.

Section 5 summons the main suspects to closer investigation. The spectrum ranges from the country's mainly internal responsibilities, such as fiscal lenience, the overvalued exchange rate, institutional deficiencies in labour markets as well as the industrial and financial sectors, political economy, and, of course, the currency board itself, to the multiple external conditionalities such as the behaviour of international capital markets, policy constellations within MERCOSUR, the IMF's involvement, as well as the economic credo that stood behind the country's economic course of the 1990s (the "Washington Consensus"). This allows for the extraction of the few main factors responsible, as supported by empirical evidence, for the traumatic collapse of Argentina's currency board, which, as will be argued, could have been avoided until early 2001. Though necessarily dotted with a degree of speculation, some inferences are made about potential exit opportunities during different periods of the currency board's existence. They make it seem highly plausible that any of these opportunities, if seized, would have had an outcome entailing less immediate damage than the one actually undergone.

Concluding this investigation will require some lessons to be drawn. The lessons from the Argentine experience are related to the old and central issues of risks specific to hard pegs, of sustainable fiscal policies, and of the importance of these issues increasing with global financial integration. These lessons are hardly new, but, sadly, they seem to need ever new accentuation "by default" to be paid heed to. A concluding assessment of the Argentine currency board experience, from an economist's point of view, will be undertaken. To be sure, political scientists, sociologists, or even psychologists will have additional clues to help explain this recent chapter in Argentina's history, which fits so well into the overall self-perception of many Argentines, and is prone to be interpreted as just another reflex of a tragic socio-economic dynamism[6]. Unfortunately, the post-collapse

---

[6]    See e.g. the popular volume of Jorge Lanata (2004).

developments, despite the fast economic recovery they included, do little so far to prove such fatalism wrong.

# 2 Argentina's Stabilisation Challenge

There is no subtler, no surer means of overturning the existing basis of society than to debauch the currency. The process engages all the hidden forces of economic law on the side of destruction and does it in a manner which not one man in a million can diagnose.
(John Maynard Keynes)[7]

This section describes the factors that led to the adoption of the Argentine currency board arrangement (CBA) in 1991. The central purpose of the currency board was to stop inflation, which had been plaguing Argentina since the middle of the century and particularly during the 1980s (the so-called "lost decade"), and which hit it especially hard with two bouts of hyperinflation in mid-1989 and early 1990.

Most high and hyperinflations share a common set of characteristics and a more or less typical sequence of events[8]. In order to understand the special problems Argentina faced in the late 1980s, these features will be named and qualified for the inflationary bouts that paved the way for the introduction of the currency board. Beforehand, a brief overview over the disinflation attempts that preceded this latest one will be given, as the Argentine history of failed reforms was an overwhelming argument for the adoption of the strict regime of the currency board.

## 2.1 Preceding Stabilisation Attempts since the Days of Perón

Since the Great Depression in the 1920s, Argentina had followed the political strategy of import substitution and closing the economy. This proved initially encouraging, especially during the years of the 2nd World War, when Argentina built up substantial foreign exchange reserves from its agricultural exports that met a high demand worldwide. But the increasing tightness of administrative regulations and capital controls more and more hindered economic efficiency and growth, and produced corruption[9]. The populist policy of Juan Perón (president from 1946 to 1955) included broad nationalisation of enterprises, protection against foreign

---

[7] Keynes (1920), p. 220.

[8] For a comparative analysis of all hyperinflations in history, see Bernholz (2003).

[9] An interesting link between prevailing corruption and left wing ideologies is explored by Di Tella/MacCulloch (2004).

competition, massive state intervention in the economy, and rapid wage growth. After having exhausted the country's foreign exchange reserves, huge losses of nationalised enterprises and fiscal deficits were readily financed by printing money, which produced rising inflation.

Perón's removal in a military putsch in 1955, which reflected popular discontent with inflation, corruption, demagoguery, and oppression, was followed by a period of political instability and further military putsches. High inflation eroded savings and living standards, unemployment rose. A first major stabilisation attempt in 1959 under president Frondizi, including monetary and fiscal discipline and a pronounced devaluation of the currency, proved initially effective but failed to deliver lasting stability. A second attempt in 1967 added heterodox elements of income policy to orthodox fiscal and monetary measures, but equally failed to produce stability in the longer run[10]. A few months after Perón's re-election in 1973, he died unexpectedly, with his wife Isabel following him and continuing in the same protectionist and populist policies. An ephemeral stabilisation attempt, initiated by the Peronist[11] government, collapsed in 1975 after various speculative attacks. Economic deterioration and political instability paved the way for the military junta again seizing power in 1976. The following period, stamped the "guerra sucia" (dirty war), was not only the worst period of Argentina's recent history in political and social terms, but eventually left the country with a deep economic and financial crisis, growing inflation and a rapidly devaluing currency[12].

Another stabilisation effort, the so-called "Tablita", initiated by the military government in 1978, relied on orthodox measures and tried to establish the exchange rate as stabilising instrument, using a pre-announced devaluation schedule to control inflation expectations. This policy initially produced declining inflation rates (although slower than expected) and an improvement of fiscal accounts, but fell apart in 1981 after the resurgence of massive budget deficits, a deteriorated current account due to the massive real appreciation of the currency, and a severe banking crisis[13]. A further stabilisation effort, announced by finance minister Alemann in 1981, was choked by Argentina's invasion of the Falkland

---

[10]  See Kiguel (1992), p. 103.

[11]  The Peronist Party's official name is Partido Justicialista (PJ).

[12]  See Jonas (2002), p. 6.

[13]  Végh cites the failed Tablita attempt as a textbook example for a non-credible, exchange rate-based stabilisation, generating a boom-recession cycle and U-shaped curves for inflation and the real exchange rate. See Végh (1995), pp. 64 ff.

Islands in 1982, itself representing a scarcely masked effort of the military government to divert attention away from the severe domestic problems. Warfare financing via money printing, as well as severely adverse external factors, such as decreasing international commodity prices, increasing foreign interest rates, the world-wide recession, and the world debt crisis, led to a culmination of the crisis in July 1982.

Inflation continued to increase and reached 6,000 percent during 1985. The so-called "Plan Austral", launched by President Alfonsín in 1985, was supported by the International Monetary Fund (IMF) and included orthodox tight fiscal and monetary policy measures as well as price and wage controls. Again, it proved initially effective, but deficits returned massively after the effects of various temporary measures had petered out and the necessary fiscal reform was still not undertaken. Inflation started to rise again, and, as had happened after each of the previous programmes, reached higher levels than before. Two further heterodox programmes followed ("Plan Primavera" in 1988, "Plan Bunge y Born"[14] in 1989, already initiated under president Menem), but they lacked credibility even from the start, as they did not tackle the main cause of inflation, the ongoing monetary financing of the budget deficit. Each of them produced ever higher inflation rates, runs on the currency, and ended with devaluations by several hundred percent[15].

Figure 1 summarises the chronology of the stabilisation programmes preceding the introduction of the currency board in 1991.

**Figure 1: Stabilisation Programmes in Argentina 1959-1990**

| Name of Programme | Date of Start | Date of Crisis/Abandonment |
|---|---|---|
| (Frondizi) | 1959 | n.a. |
| Vasena | 3/1967 | 6/1970 |
| Gelbard | 5/1973 | 3/1975 |
| Tablita | 12/1978 | 4/1981 |
| Alemann | 12/1981 | 7/1982 |
| Austral | 6/1985 | 9/1987 |
| Primavera | 8/1988 | 4/1989 |
| Bunge y Born (BB) | 7/1989 | 2/1990 |

Sources: Choueiri/Kaminsky (1999), and Kiguel (1992), own arrangement.

---

[14] The programme was named after Argentina's largest transnational company, the advisors of which were involved in the programme design.

[15] See Choueiri/Kaminsky (1999), p. 9.

Since the collapse of the "Tablita" in 1981, exchange rate management was highly discretionary and changed between fixing and floating the exchange rate, with dual exchange rates and capital controls prevailing over long periods[16]. In February 1990, the exchange rate was floated and all price controls removed. Currency reserves were nearly exhausted. Argentina approached hyperinflation and a total economic collapse. In the year between March 1989 and March 1990, the price level rose by 20,000 percent. Real GDP fell in 1989 by more than seven and in 1990 by more than two percent. Argentine real per capita income declined by 26 percent during 1980-89[17].

Figure 2 gives an overview of Argentine inflation over the seven decades preceding 1989. Figure 3 concentrates on the decade 1980-1990.

**Figure 2: Inflation in Argentina 1920-1989**[1]

| Period | Average | Maximum |
|--------|---------|---------|
| 1920-29 | -1.7 | 17.1 |
| 1930-39 | -0.3 | 13.0 |
| 1940-49 | 10.6 | 31.1 |
| 1950-59 | 30.3 | 111.6 |
| 1960-69 | 23.3 | 31.9 |
| 1970-79 | 132.9 | 444.4 |
| 1980-89 | 750.4 | 4,923.3 |

(1) CPI change in %, annual basis.
Source: Cavallo (1996).

---

[16]  See Setzer (2001), p. 21 f.
[17]  See Leijonhufvud (1990), p. 2.

Figure 3: Annual Inflation Rates 1980-1990[1]

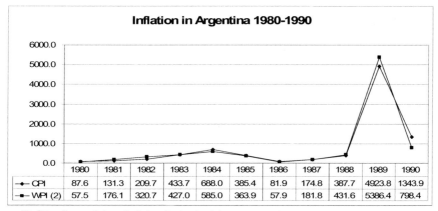

| | 1980 | 1981 | 1982 | 1983 | 1984 | 1985 | 1986 | 1987 | 1988 | 1989 | 1990 |
|---|---|---|---|---|---|---|---|---|---|---|---|
| CPI | 87.6 | 131.3 | 209.7 | 433.7 | 688.0 | 385.4 | 81.9 | 174.8 | 387.7 | 4923.8 | 1343.9 |
| WPI (2) | 57.5 | 176.1 | 320.7 | 427.0 | 585.0 | 363.9 | 57.9 | 181.8 | 431.6 | 5386.4 | 798.4 |

(1)  Rates of increase between the final months of each period.
Source: Oficina de la CEPAL en Buenos Aires, on data of INDEC, BCRA, and other sources.[18]

## 2.2   High and Hyperinflation in Argentina in the 1980s

Inflations occur in different magnitudes. They are generally classified along the three broad categories of moderate inflation, high inflation, and hyperinflation. There is no generally agreed clear delimitation line between moderate and high inflations – though annual price increases between 5 and 10 percent are mostly offered as the limit where high inflations start. A qualitative criterion has been proposed by Bernholz, who defines an economy as moving into high inflation as soon as the (corrected) real stock of money starts to decline[19].

The delimitation between high and hyperinflations is less disputed. Since Philip Cagan's classic study of German post-World War I inflation[20], his definition of hyperinflation as price rises exceeding monthly rates of 50% has become generally accepted. This criterion is in rough accord with the observation that during moderate inflations, a quotation of inflation in percent per year is sufficient for economic agents, whereas in higher inflations, people measure price increases in per cent per month. When the effective time horizon for quoting money prices falls below one

---

[18]   See Heymann (2000), p. 162.
[19]   He defines the corrected real stock of money as the nominal money stock divided by the price level and corrected by the growth of GDP. See Bernholz (2003), p. 2.
[20]   See Cagan (1956).

month, the economy is considered to be in hyperinflation. Thus, we end up with the mentioned approximate numerical delimitation between high inflation (up to 50 percent per month) and hyperinflation (higher than 50 percent per month)[21].

A more qualitative distinction between high and hyperinflation lies in the observation that high inflations can be sustained for years, whereas hyperinflations rapidly lead to economic collapse[22]. It is generally agreed that hyperinflations should be treated as extreme cases of high inflations, since they share the main characteristics of the latter but eventually render financial and economic conditions unsustainable. Therefore, studying hyperinflations implies studying high inflations as the latter deliver the basic insights in the complex interaction of causes and effects of inflation and its persisting detrimental impact on the financial sector and the real economy.

"Inflation is the observable outcome of a complex process of political and economic interaction in society."[23] The observable outcome is an increase of the price level over a certain period as measured by one or several price indices[24]. Such an increase is the result of pricing decisions previously made by innumerable firms and individuals. Obviously, these pricing decisions are the most direct cause of inflation. But behind them lie market and policy signals, and behind them again still other economic and extra-economic causes. Some chains of causation in the complex structure of interaction even loop back on themselves in a way that causes and effects over time become indiscernible – the so-called "price-wage spiral" being the most prominent example. Examining the complete picture of causes and effects in the complex interaction called inflation becomes a near to impossible task.

---

[21] For orientation: a constant monthly inflation rate of 50 percent would result in an annual rate of 12,874 percent. The corresponding weekly and daily rates would be 10.67 and 1.36 percent respectively.

[22] See Végh (1995), p. 38f. He uses the term "chronic" inflation for high inflation more or less constantly persisting over years, and differentiates between cases in which chronic inflation never developed into hyperinflation (as, e.g., in Uruguay), cases where hyperinflation took off without preceding chronic inflation (Bolivia), and cases where chronic inflation eventually accelerated into hyperinflation (Argentina).

[23] Heymann/Leijonhufvud (1995), p. 11.

[24] This is the generally accepted criterion. Other criteria, such as e.g. the expansion of the money supply or of credit, are possible and have in history at times been more at the centre of attention. See Bernholz (2003), p. 1.

Delving into the vast and controversial field of inflation theories lies beyond the scope of this investigation[25]. The purpose of the following paragraphs is less to analyze than to describe the characteristics of high and hyperinflation economies in general and of the Argentine case of the 1980s in particular, and, in consulting economic and political data, to draw the most plausible conclusions about the relevant cause-and-effect-structures. In doing so, it will nevertheless become clear that the neo-classical concept of money (neutral) and of inflation (affecting only nominal magnitudes, and, apart from a fiscal distortion due to the inflation tax, leaving the real economy functioning as normal) is of little use for the explanation of high and hyperinflation. More adequate models of high inflation are necessarily less clear-cut as they try to account for the complexity of the matter. As will become apprehensible, high and hyperinflations must be regarded as "pathological processes" and "the products of socio-political persistence in negative sum-games"[26].

### 2.2.1 Rising Money Stock

As Milton Friedman famously noted, "inflation is always and everywhere a monetary phenomenon". Indeed, it is an uncontested and empirically well-documented fact that all persistent inflations are accompanied by a rising stock of nominal money[27].

While price level increases cannot occur without commensurate increases in the money stock, it is important to note that that the money stock growth is usually less than proportionate since the demand for real balances declines. It is identical to say that the velocity of money circulation rises, as people effectuate the same volume of transactions with reduced amounts of cash that are turned over more frequently in order to minimise losses of purchasing power of the money held[28]. Thus, in

---

[25] For a detailed argument over existing inflation theories, see Heymann/Leijonhufvud (1995).

[26] Leijonhufvud (1990), p. 2.

[27] See e.g. Végh (1995), p. 39f.

[28] This can be illustrated with the equation of exchange as expressed by Irving Fisher, $M*V = P*T$: given a constant volume of transactions (T), a rising money stock (M) translates into more than proportionately rising prices (P) if and when at the same time the cash balances held by the public decrease – or, expressed the other way round, the velocity of money circulation (V) increases: V is reciprocal to the cash balances held by the public (k): $V = 1/k$.

Argentina, M3 amounted only to little more than 10 percent of GDP in 1989 and to around 5 percent in 1990[29].

The charts of figure 4 depict the exorbitant nominal money stock growth in Argentina during 1989 and 1990. Note that due to the scale necessary to catch these increases, the already very high money growth of the previous years – Argentina experienced high inflation during the whole of the 1980s – gets out of sight in these diagrams. To meet this shortcoming, the logarithmic plots are added for each of the diagrams.

Figure 4: Base Money, Money Circulation, and Money Aggregates 1984-1990

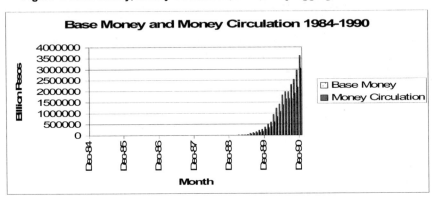

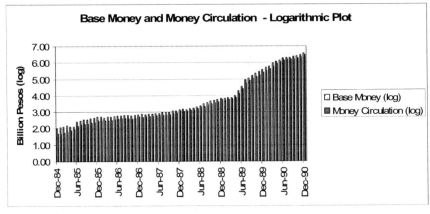

[29] See Kiguel (1999), p. 14.

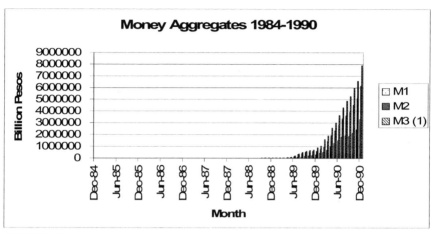

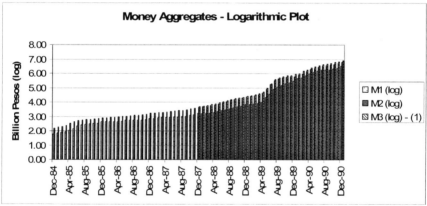

(1)     The Argentine aggregate M3 is calculated as M2 (notes and coins, checking deposits, saving deposits, time deposits) plus foreign currency deposits.

Source: Oficina de la CEPAL en Buenos Aires on the basis of official data.

### 2.2.2    Government Finance

Clearly, the rising money stock itself is not the ultimate cause of inflation. Typically, in high inflations, the government's financing requirements induce it to allow the money stock to rise at an inflationary rate. Rather than Milton Friedman's "monetary phenomenon", and as will become palpable further on, high inflations can better be described as "processes of unreliable interaction between the public and the private sector"[30].

All high inflation histories have in common the persistent failure of fiscal policies to operate within its means[31]. That said, it is not primarily the size of budget deficits that determines the inflationary outcome. Rather, it is the fact that the creation of money originates in the government's need for funds.

Given the undoubted relationship between monetary financing of budget deficits and inflation, does it also extend to full-blown hyperinflation? Kiguel (1989) shows that this is clearly the case. As soon as a government increases the size of its budget deficit to a level that exceeds the maximum inflation tax obtainable, an explosive path of inflation is taken[32].

Figure 5 shows the Argentine budget deficits during the 1980s. They reached maximum levels during the first half of the decade. As Heymann (2000) notes, the lower deficit levels towards the end of the decade do not properly reflect the seriousness of the fiscal situation: the more the economy approaches extreme conditions of very high and hyperinflation, the more deficit magnitudes are restricted by the abrupt fall in credit supply to the government and the decline in real money balances – which constitute the "tax base" for the inflation tax. Thus, the pressures on public finances during the late 80s were vastly higher than the figures suggest[33].

---

[30]   Leijonhufvud (1990), p. 2.

[31]   See Bernholz (2003), pp. 69 ff. Bernholz substantiates this by the empirical study of all 29 hyperinflations that occurred worldwide until 2003. All but four of the examined hyperinflations were connected with budget deficits of 20 and more percent of expenditures.

[32]   The decisive link is a perpetuated disequilibrium in the money market: money press financing of an increased deficit creates a temporary excess supply in the money market, thereby generating an increased rate of inflation. This reduces the demand for money, which further prevents the money market from clearing. Accelerating inflation which develops into hyperinflation is the result. This is independent of the assumption on the formation of expectations (adaptive or rational). See Kiguel (1989).

[33]   See Heymann (2000), p. 63.

## Figure 5: Budget Deficits 1980-1990

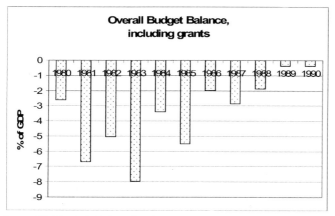

Source: Worldbank, 2003 World Development Indicators.

### 2.2.2.1 Inflationary Bias of Governments

What is the motivation behind a (democratic) government's decision to finance deficits via inflation? Public choice theory emphasises the so-called political business cycle, which describes the incentives of elected governments to choose and time their policies so as to maximise their chances of being re-elected. These chances are highest when the benefits of policy actions enjoy the highest possible popularity while the costs are distributed over the electorate as widely as possible, and thus felt as little and late as possible. Higher taxes to finance popularity-enhancing policies are counterproductive as they incur the costs of lost support from the taxed. Instead, higher borrowing is attractive as it does not hurt anyone immediately. The debt-financed additional spending, if timed well, stimulates the economy prior to the election, while the debt service will hurt later, after the election. Over time, however, the debt service consumes ever higher proportions of revenues, pushes market interest rates up and so crowds out investment. At some point, the perception that the government is an insecure debtor may even add significant risk premia to interest rates.

In such a situation – already highly indebted and struggling to gain voters' support –, the incentive for the government to choose money creation to help finance the deficit is very high. In the short run, it prevents higher interest rates and allows stimulating the economy, while the negative consequences of inflation occur only after the next election. Moreover, inflation has the additional "benefit" of reducing the debt stock in real terms. If the government chooses to fight inflation afterwards, it has to stop doing so in time and to produce new inflation in order to prepare for the next election. The consideration of the political business cycle thus leads to the assumption of an inherent inflationary bias of democratic governments[34]. This will all the more be the case in times of slow or negative growth (when higher taxation is even less of an option), or of wars or international tensions (which offer the excuse of an extraordinary situation)[35].

Figure 6 highlights the two years when presidential elections took place in Argentina: in 1983, after the defeat in the Falkland war and the collapse of the military regime, when Raúl Alfonsín of the so-called Radical Party won the presidency, and in 1989, when Carlos Menem of the Justicialists ("Peronists") took over in July amidst the first bout of hyperinflation. While the political business cycle argument will doubtlessly be demonstrable for several of Argentina's previous elections, the peculiarity of Argentina's situation in the 1980s seems to forbid explaining much of its inflationary performance in this way. Both elections were staged on the background of catastrophic economic (and, for 1983, political) situations, with an electorate plagued by high inflation and disillusioned since decades. The economic situation in neither year left much room for economic stimuli generated by expansionary monetary policies. Therefore, for the considered decade in Argentina, the political business cycle was certainly not of much relevance.

---

[34] Of course, autocratic governments are subject to similar incentives to secure their power. History provides very few examples of dictators that withstood these temptations due to their personal ideological belief or benevolence.

[35] See Bernholz (2003), p. 12.

Figure 6: Presidential Elections and Inflation

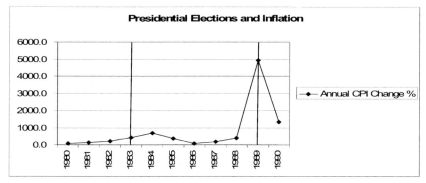

Source: Oficina de la CEPAL en Buenos Aires on the basis of official data, own arrangement.

However, Argentina doubtlessly constitutes a model case of another instance of governments' inflationary bias. This is related to its fiscal federalism, i.e. the distribution of tax revenues between the federal state and the provinces[36]. Argentina's inflation in the 1980s is at least partly to be regarded as an outcome of the fierce political struggles over the allocation of tax revenues between national and provincial jurisdictions. For instance, payments to the provinces under the distribution scheme were strategically delayed, to dilute their real value and change the real primary distribution. Thus, inflation served to mend the national budget ex-post, in effect softening aggregate budget constraints[37]. Clearly, inflation again fed back and gave incentives to the provinces to press for an automatisation of distribution mechanisms, thus rendering them even more inefficient and increasing budgetary pressures.

### 2.2.2.2 Debt Structure

Existing government liabilities in high inflation countries typically differ significantly in structure from those of stable economies: owing to their instable past, they have shorter maturities and higher rates that already include inflation

---

[36] This scheme, the so-called "coparticipación", will be discussed in more detail later.

[37] During the debates that preceded the new (and current) law for federal fiscal relations in 1988, the threat of inflating the economy as a last resort (in order not to have to further concede in distributional negotiations) was even pronounced expressly by the federal government. See Saiegh/Tommasi (1999), p. 197.

expectations. Foreign debt forms an important proportion of government debt when high yields have previously attracted speculative capital imports.

Often, the government at some point stops servicing foreign debt, or leaves its commitment to repayment vague. New lending from abroad is then near to impossible. With these financing restraints, governments are tempted to take recourse to indirect borrowing in the form of setting high reserve requirements on bank deposits. The result is a reduction in bank credit to the private sector – an indirect form of crowding out[38]. Under extreme pressure, the government may also fall back on delaying payments to suppliers or state employees. Whether and to which degree liabilities are repaid is at some point either arbitrary or determined by the pressure exerted by single creditors.

As the public perceives the financing restraints, the possibility of default enters their expectations and calculations, and increases interest premia. The increased interest burden in turn renders default more probable, and a run similar to a banking panic may occur, itself precipitating default.

Figure 7 shows the financing of the Argentine government's debt during the 1980s. Domestic debt played the paramount role in the first half of the decade, but ceased to offer much financing potential towards the end. The proportion of public debt financed from abroad shows a marked rise after the intermediate stabilisation attempt of 1985, but declines again over 1988-1990. The depiction of public foreign debt in absolute terms, as shown in Figure 8, confirms the finding that the Argentine government found itself increasingly indebted and struggling to find creditors at home and abroad during the final years of the 1980s.

---

[38] Moreover, with high reserve requirements, the government has to pay interest on reserves, in order not to cause large spreads between borrowing and lending rates of banks. See Heymann/Leijonhufvud (1995), p. 64.

**Figure 7: Government Financing 1980-1990**

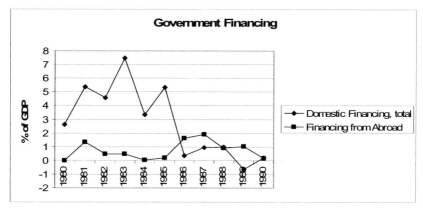

Source: Worldbank, 2003 World Development Indicators.

**Figure 8: Foreign Debt 1980-1990**

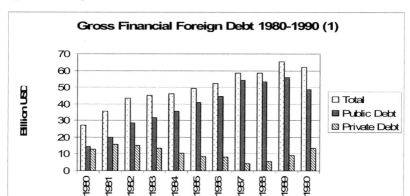

(1)  Debt Stock at the end of period.
Source: Oficina de la CEPAL en Buenos Aires on data of the BCRA and the Ministerio de Economía.

### 2.2.2.3 Are Budget Deficits a Cause or a Consequence of Inflation?

There is a case for asking whether the causation might not be reverse, so that budget deficits are caused by inflation. Indeed, the lag between receiving and spending public funds works to reduce their purchasing power by high inflation, with the consequence that the real budget deficit grows even when expenditures are kept constant (the so-called Olivera-Tanzi effect). Thus, high inflation complicates fiscal management and in effect feeds on itself[39].

The proof that budget deficits are not initially caused by inflation can be seen in the observation that in nearly all historical cases massive budget deficits preceded the occurrence of high inflation. Since these deficits generally cannot have been financed exclusively on capital markets, the financing of the budget deficits via the money printing press has to be regarded as the initial trigger[40].

Figure 9 confirms this reasoning for the Argentine case: massive budget deficits in the early 1980s preceded the most significant increases in yearly inflation rates of 1984/85 on the one hand, and of 1989 on the other.

**Figure 9: Budget Deficit and Inflation 1980-1990**

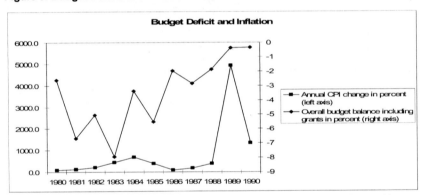

Sources: Worldbank, 2003 World Development Indicators and Oficina de la CEPAL en Buenos Aires on the basis of official data.

### 2.2.2.4 Erosion of Tax System

Whereas stable economies most of the time manage to bring their projected spending in line with their actual or potential taxing capacity, high inflation economies are characterised by a loss of control over their budgets.

Inadequacies of the tax system typically account for much of the budget deficits. The most important taxes, VAT and income tax, usually would offer much more financing potential if properly collected. Instead, governments often impose various

---

[39]  See Kiguel (1989), p. 156.
[40]  See Bernholz (2003), p. 72.

excise taxes at high rates that cause significant distortions and yield little compared with other sources of taxation.

Tax collection is erratic and inefficient, since the performance of the public sector in general, and also of the tax agencies, gets worse the more the economic disorder caused by high inflation radiates. Corruption and tax evasion get widespread, but even for honest taxpayers there are often legal loopholes and exemptions.

With high inflation, the time lag between tax accrual and collection reduces real tax revenues. The ever-present incentive for taxpayers to pay late is magnified by the additional inducement created by inflation, and real tax revenues dwindle further. Indexation of taxes would offer no solution since the time-lag problem is unavoidable.

The first chart of figure 10 shows that Argentine tax revenues covered highly variable proportions of GDP over the decade (between 8 and 14 percent). Tax revenues never exceeded 15 percent of GDP, which is a poor proportion compared with industrial countries with proportions nearer 50 percent, as well as with emerging economies' average levels (around 20 percent). The tax structure equally proves to have been very instable, as displayed in the second chart: taxes on income, profits, and capital gains form a minor part of tax income, whereas taxes on goods and services over most of the decade covered more than a third of total government revenue. Thus, Argentina's tax system on the whole failed to offer sufficient and stable government revenues. Not covered by official tax numbers, of course, is the increasing proportion of inflation tax that made up for deficient tax revenues.

**Figure 10: Tax Revenue and Tax Structure 1980-1990**

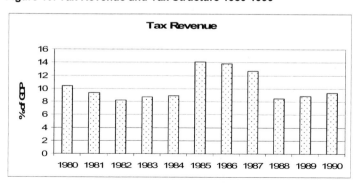

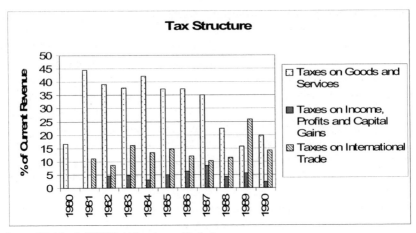

Source: Worldbank, 2003 World Development Indicators.

### 2.2.2.5 Lack of Structured Budgeting Process

Fiscal stability requires a rational and well-defined budgeting procedure where conflicts over the distribution of funds are dealt with in a simultaneous negotiation between all entitled groups, and where the result becomes legally binding for the whole of the fiscal year. Furthermore, it is important that there is no "shadow budget", but that all items of public activity are included in the official budget.

With high inflation, it becomes impossible to project budgets for a whole fiscal year. Planning horizons shorten, and renegotiations, often without due parliamentary legitimation, become more frequent. Negotiations with pressure groups are not conducted simultaneously, but sequentially, which renders an ultimate control of expenditures near to impossible. Then, there is neither potential nor incentive for claimants to negotiate compromises with each other, and each group tries to maximise its own stake. Government departments, provincial and local governments, public utilities, nationalised industries, and other fund claiming organisations thus all work in the same direction, i.e. towards a maximisation of the deficit. The threat to reduce public services, e.g. in hospitals or schools, works to push their claims through, with the effect that these groups de facto operate under "soft budgets"[41].

---

[41] The phenomenon of soft budgets also affects the private sector: with high inflation, money fails to be a reliable unit of account, and calculation and cost control become impossible. E.g., to

Often, extraordinary expenditures, e.g. for warfare, reparations, or foreign debt service, worsen the budget additionally. Furthermore, the government typically faces financing restrictions as government debt is not marketable in the required volumes and/or at reasonable interest rates. The result is not only allocation inefficiency and inequality, but also time-inconsistent and non predictable budgetary policies.

Under these circumstances – unable to contain expenditures, to raise sufficient funds by conventional taxation, and to borrow from the public – there is a strong incentive for governments to rely on money creation to finance budget deficits. At that point, a clear line between fiscal and monetary policies cannot be drawn any longer[42].

The Argentine public sector of the 1980s offers a textbook example of these characteristics. A widespread codex of behaviour among officials and functionaries, developed over decades at least, was characterised by nepotism and corruption, rulings by decree, and a disregard of any legal and judicial institutions meant to secure checks and balances[43]. The procedures around the official budget were shaped correspondingly. In addition to the pressures generated by high inflation, the financing of the Falkland war and the mounting foreign debt services put massive strain on the budget.

### 2.2.2.6 Inflation Tax

The government's proceeds from money creation, the so-called seigniorage, results from the real value of newly created base money as well as from the loss of purchasing power of the existing money stock. The latter element in effect acts like a tax levied upon holders of money. However, this "inflation tax" differs from other forms of taxation in an important aspect: it is not decided upon in the same formal way and by the same body as are regular taxes, but rather represents a kind of

---

find out whether a profit centre is profitable at all, big Brazilian firms even developed methods that used intern input price indices to calculate the amount of inputs the sales revenues of its outputs offered command over, i.e. that used physical rather than monetary indicators. See Heymann/Leijonhufvud (1995), p. 80.

[42] In the case of complete reliance on money creation for the financing of a budget deficit, the real value of the monetary increase must match the real budget deficit. For a formal foundation see Heymann/Leijonhufvud (1995), pp. 14ff.

[43] Any compendium of Argentina's history in the 20th century, like e.g. that of the Encyclopaedia Britannica, reads like a seemingly endless repetition of the same political behaviour patterns, interchangeable between civil and military governments.

"emergency" finance for a government unable to stick to a consistent fiscal policy and to withstand political pressures on the budget.

The inflation tax is easy to impose and collect, but carries high social costs compared with other forms of taxation. First, there is the amount of time and effort spent by individuals to economise on cash balances in order to reduce the "tax base". These efforts imply huge overall efficiency losses. Second, the incidence of the inflation tax is strongly regressive: lower income people's cash balances form a higher proportion of their wealth than those of the better-off, and their possibilities to evade or minimise taxation are less.

The general relationship between tax rates and tax revenues is generally described by the Laffer curve. Applied on the inflation tax, an economy can be located either on the "good" side of the Laffer curve (where higher inflation leads to higher seigniorage revenue) or on the "bad" side (where higher inflation reduces seigniorage revenue due to a reduced money demand). When seigniorage is raised in excess of the revenue-maximising inflation tax (i.e. the maximum set by the prevailing demand for money), inflation accelerates and, if not fought back, eventually moves towards hyperinflation[44].

For the Argentine case, Kiguel/Neumeyer show that for most of the 1980s, the economy stayed on the "good" side of the Laffer curve, i.e. increases in inflation yielded increases in seigniorage revenue. During the period of 1982/84, however, seigniorage reached levels (over 7 percent of GDP) that could not be sustained by a stable rate of inflation, and it can be argued that the economy was from that time on an explosive hyperinflationary path – a view that is supported by the fact that inflation doubled in 1983 and again in 1984. After the intermediate Austral stabilisation attempt, seigniorage reached excessive levels again in 1989 (around 9 percent of GDP), and hyperinflation took off[45].

Inflation reduces the real value of regular tax revenues. The inflation tax therefore must be higher than the real losses in other tax revenues to prevent total government revenues from decreasing. By increasing inflation, real tax revenues decline further, and the inflation tax revenues have to grow further – a vicious circle that results in accelerating inflation. Data on the inflation tax show that in the 1970s,

[44] See Kiguel (1989), p. 149. It is the inflation elasticity of the money demand and the size of the fiscal deficit in relation to the maximum seigniorage revenue that decide upon an economy's location on the Laffer curve.

[45] See Kiguel/Neumeyer (1995), p. 681.

a 4 to 5 percent monthly inflation rate yielded seigniorage of about 5 percent of Argentina's GDP, whereas in the late 1980s, a monthly inflation rate of 15 to 20 percent was necessary to produce the same yield[46].

Finally, an important theoretical consequence is that, if money is issued to cover public financing needs in real terms, monetary growth becomes itself dependent on the inflation rate, and the money stock is determined endogenously[47]. The fiscal deficit then remains as the only exogenous variable in the complex picture of high inflation.

Figure 11 shows the overall deficits of the Argentine non-financial public sector and the way these were financed for three periods of the 1980s. Seigniorage always played an important role in financing the deficits.

**Figure 11: Fiscal Deficits, Seigniorage, and Inflation**

|                              | 1979/80 | 1982/84 | 1986/87 |
|------------------------------|---------|---------|---------|
| Fiscal Deficit               | 7.0     | 14.6    | 5.9     |
| Net Borrowing                | 5.4     | 4.6     | 5.9     |
| Seigniorage                  | 5.2     | 7.8     | 3.7     |
| Inflation (annual average)   | 128.3   | 340.4   | 109.7   |

All figures in percent of GDP, except for the rate of inflation which is percent per year.
Fiscal deficit = domestic borrowing + central bank loans to the treasury.
Source: Kiguel/Neumeyer (1995), on data from World Bank, IFS, and DATAFIEL[48].

### 2.2.3    Monetary Regime

#### 2.2.3.1 Monetary Constitution

Clearly, the monetary constitution plays a key role in the explanation of inflation. Historical evidence yields the conclusion that economies with currencies based on a metallic (gold or silver) standard experienced little or no inflation, whereas paper money standards have been more prone to inflation. Within paper money standards, those with central banks independent of political authorities, or those bound by a regime of fixed exchange rates to stable currencies (that are themselves either on a metallic standard or managed by an independent central bank) are less inflation-biased[49]. Clearly, budget deficits can be financed via money creation only when the

---

[46]  See Heymann/Leijonhufvud (1995), p. 20.
[47]  See Cagan (1989a), p. 181.
[48]  See Kiguel/Neumeyer (1995), p. 673.
[49]  See Bernholz (1995b), p. 10.

monetary authority can (i.e. is not legally bound to keep a certain ratio between the domestic money base and foreign exchange reserves) and will (i.e. is not legally and de facto independent from the government) accommodate the government's needs[50]. The criteria "central bank independence" and "exchange rate regime" are not independent: a central bank stringently bound to maintain a fixed exchange rate necessarily has to have a high degree of independence of political authorities. Hence, at least for developing countries, it can be assumed that the type of exchange rate regime matters more for the inflationary outcome than mere central bank independence[51].

Before the 1991 Convertibility law, Argentina's central bank never enjoyed any notion of independence. As in most developing economies, Argentine civil as well as military governments kept ready access to central bank financing. Justification could always be constructed from the central bank's Keynesian-inspired charter[52]. Suiting central bank governors were appointed and at will replaced by the respective governments.

As to the exchange rate regime, there were basically two different regimes in Argentina during the 1980s. The famous "Tablita" period (lasting two years from January 1979 until January 1981) included a pre-announced path of a devaluing exchange rate, and was characterised by a high degree of international capital mobility, and market-determined interest rates. The ensuing period, from spring 1981 until the end of 1989, saw higher restrictions on capital flows and fixed exchange rates with discretionary, unannounced devaluations, and the development of parallel markets for foreign exchange.

Thus, over much of the decade, the central bank tried to use the exchange rate as a nominal anchor for disinflation, but was less than successful, because there

---

[50] However, inflation-averse monetary constitutions may well carry some long-term risks of inflation: as investors feel secure from inflation by the performance of a central bank that is either independent or bound by a fixed exchange rate, they are prepared to lend at lower yields, which in turn encourages governments to borrow more. Rising debt ratios at some point are likely to lower the hurdles that stand in the way of a government choosing to get hold of the central bank. Also, it can be shown that the monetarist hypothesis that a constant budget deficit exclusively financed by the issue of bonds is non-inflationary is at least partly invalid. See McCallum (1984).

[51] See Siklos (1995), p. 6.

[52] The Argentine central bank's charter stems from 1935, the Bank's founding year, and was designed (primarily by Raúl Prebisch) to put an end to the previous currency board, and – in the light of the experiences during the Great Depression – to implement a then completely new, anti-cyclical monetary policy.

were neither important efforts to tackle the problem of lax fiscal policy nor attempts to restrain the government's access to central bank financing. Rather, frequent changes in regulations regarding interest rates and foreign exchange markets led to more financial instability (which was only temporarily alleviated by the Austral plan and the accompanying liberalisation of interest rates around the middle of the decade). Widespread macroeconomic instability persisted over the whole of the decade, developing into the extremes of hyperinflation from 1989 onward[53].

### 2.2.3.2 Monetary Policy

Monetary policy in high inflation economies typically does not follow any pre-defined long-term rule or self-commitment. Rather, it is determined by actual economic conditions and political pressures, and it reacts to these pressures in a short-term discretionary manner. Decisions to accelerate, keep constant, or decelerate the growth of the money stock are made on the basis of currently pressing necessities without consideration of their effects in the long run[54]. That means, for the economic agent, that the uncertainty in predicting future price levels increases exponentially with distance from the present, and the more so, the more frequent and important monetary policy actions are.

The rapid change of governments and economic policy staff may underline this point for Argentina: between 1980 and 1990, Argentina saw 6 different presidents, 11 ministers of finance and economy, and 10 central bank governors, chosen out of military, Radical and then Peronist ranks[55].

The explanation of such conduct of monetary policy generally focuses on the time inconsistency problems associated with the reliance on the inflation tax. Governments in high inflation economies are supposed to maximise inflation tax revenue in the short run and not to commit themselves to a certain inflation limit. In other words, their time preference is strong enough as to increase seigniorage in the short run at the expense of higher inflation and lower seigniorage in the long

---

[53] See Kiguel/Neumeyer (1995), p. 674.

[54] This is called a „random walk monetary standard" by Heymann/Leijonhufvud (1995), pp. 50ff.

[55] For the period between 1945 and 1990, the respective numbers are: 19 different presidents, more than 40 ministers of economy and finance, and equally more than 40 central bank governors. See e.g. the central bank's homepage at www.bcra.gov.ar .

48

run[56]. Yet, as will be shown below, the interaction between the government's incentives and the expectations of private agents leads to an acceleration of inflation rates and a reduction of inflation tax revenues.

### 2.2.4    Inflation Expectations

The demand for real money balances is dependent on the expected rate of inflation: the higher inflation expectations, the lower the amount of money an individual wants to hold. Assumptions over the formation of the public's expectations therefore are central when trying to predict the reaction to price increases.

One way of forming expectations about the future is to look back and project the past development into the future. Such adaptive expectations (as described by Phillip Cagan in 1956[57]) are accurate only under the condition of a constant rate of inflation. With rising inflation rates there is a chronic lag of adaptive expectations behind actual inflation rates. Backward-looking expectations in a wider sense include more data than the inflation rate itself and may calculate the expected inflation rate as a stable function of past data.

Forward-looking expectations, in contrast, are based on anticipated future developments. Most influential is the hypothesis of rational expectations (as formulated in 1961 by John Muth[58]), according to which the unboundedly rational economic agent is able to predict the inflation rate on the basis of any available information, including statistical data and theoretical models as well as political assessments. For instance, when given financing needs of a government are expected to be financed by the inflation tax, a rational economic agent can estimate a rate of money creation and translate it into an expected inflation rate.

In high inflation episodes, neither the model of adaptive expectations nor the over-ambitious notion of perfect foresight fit well with the actual behaviour of the public. A more realistic approach to the formation of expectations is to acknowledge the fact that the conditions determining an economic outcome are far too many and too complex for any individual to be adequately reflected in her decision making. Economic agents cope with this complexity by developing certain "reasonable" rules

---

[56] Cukierman (1995) argues in the light of the German hyperinflation of 1923 that such behaviour is not necessarily irrational. See Cukierman (1995), pp. 137 ff.

[57] See Cagan (1956).

[58] See Muth (1961).

and simplification strategies[59]. Such reasonable rules are determined by the particular state of and experience with policy-making authorities: the public has gained experience in recognising the patterns that govern policy-decisions[60]. In forming expectations through pattern recognition in government behaviour, an individual relies on incomplete information and is well aware of the limits of her ability to predict future policy actions.

Therefore, even in a stable environment, different sets of observations, different internalised "models" and different interpretations of facts across individuals must to a certain degree lead to an incoherent "collective state of expectations". When past government action has been unsystematic, expectations and ensuing behaviour are in addition likely to get highly volatile. Then, in the interaction between policy makers and the public, no one can rely on the behaviour of the other, and the outcomes of actions get unpredictable[61].

### 2.2.5 Symptoms of High Inflation

Price instability affects every aspect of economic activity in the public as well as the private sector. It forces everybody to pay heed to it in even the commonest daily transactions. Indeed, the capacity of individuals to live with high inflation is sometimes astonishing. It grants that economic activity can go on for a long time – in an inefficient, resource-wasting and socially damaging way.

#### 2.2.5.1 Decreasing Demand for Real Money Stock

As previously pointed out, a decreasing stock of real money can be observed in all high inflations. The explanation is straightforward: economic agents try to rid themselves of money before it loses much of its purchasing power. At the same time, the economy as a whole is swamped by an increasing nominal money stock. As the demand for money decreases while its supply rises, prices rise more quickly

---

[59] "The modern economy has not evolved fully to exploit the cleverness that its inhabitants possessed all along. Rather it has evolved to a complexity beyond human understanding, because people with limited cognitive capabilities have devised ways of getting along without dealing with the full complexity of the system." Leijonhufvud (1990), p. 19.

[60] And, vice versa, political authorities have learnt how the public behaves. This set of mutual expectations on the part of the public and of policy-making authorities is caught by the concept of the "monetary regime". See Heymann/Leijonhufvud (1995), p. 39.

[61] Heymann/Leijonhufvud call this an "unreliable regime". Regimes can be reliable on the part of political authorities either through a gained reputation of consistent behaviour or through rules imposed on its behaviour. See Heymann/Leijonhufvud (1995), p. 43.

than the money supply. The real stock of money, defined as the nominal stock divided by the price level, falls.

The reduction of real money balances claims high costs in terms of time and transactions used to synchronise payments and receipts. The efforts undertaken are not only a matter of individual choice, but sometimes also require co-ordination between transactors, as e.g. between companies that agree on deals to temporarily shift unwanted surpluses of money when their respective cash flows are out of phase, or between firms and employees agreeing on a shortening of payment periods. Often, these efforts also include physical investments – one example is the speeded up installation of automatic teller machines[62]. All those efforts are necessary because money retains its property as a medium of exchange, although taxed exorbitantly.

The same volume of transactions is now performed with smaller amounts of real money. This is possible with three major developments observable during high inflations: the rise in money velocity, a return to barter trade, and increasing currency substitution.

### 2.2.5.2 Currency Substitution

In high inflations, the reverse of Gresham's law is working: good money drives out bad money, the latter quickly losing value (given flexible exchange rates between the two)[63]. The typical sequence in the course of accelerating inflation is that, first, foreign currency is used as a unit of account, then as a store of value, and finally as a means of payment. Data on the use of foreign currency circulating is scarcely available, as governments are interested in financing their deficits via the inflation tax, i.e. enforcing the use of the domestic and suppressing the use of foreign currency. Strict foreign exchange controls are often enacted, and circulating foreign currency made illegal.

Currency substitution not only offers people a currency with a lower "relative price" to meet their money demand. It can be shown that a high degree of currency substitution also reduces the rate of inflation of the original currency. This can be explained by the fact that the rate of inflation required to sustain hyperinflation, i.e.

---

[62] These investments allow to operate with lower money holdings permanently, which means that stabilisation will not bring back previous levels of money demand. This hysteresis effect lowers the base for the inflation tax in the long run. See Heymann/Leijonhufvud (1995), p. 87.

[63] This can also be called Thier's law. See Bernholz (1995a), pp. 98 ff.

to induce people to hold less money, is reduced during the process of financial adaptation, and especially dollarisation[64].

In Argentina, to compensate for the rapid decline in value, domestic currency was increasingly replaced by the US-Dollar, starting with Dollar denomination of longer-term financial assets and the use of Dollars on markets for real assets and durable consumer goods, to extend to ever shorter financial assets and more everyday products. One illustration of this is the development of foreign currency deposits, as shown in figure 12 (note that the first chart denotes foreign currency deposits as percentage of M3 which, as shown above, itself exploded towards the end of the decade). In 1991, 40 percent of deposits were denominated in Dollars[65].

Another dimension of currency substitution is the exodus of capital out of the inflationary country. By 1987, an estimated 45 billion US-Dollars were stored abroad by Argentine investors, a number which increased by much during the following years[66].

**Figure 12: Foreign Currency Deposits 1980-1990**

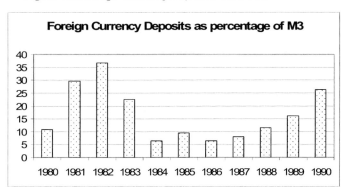

---

[64] See Sturzenegger (1994). He explains the lower levels of inflation during the second bout of Argentine hyperinflation in early 1990 with the rapid increase in currency substitution during and after the first bout in mid-1989.

[65] See Setzer (2001), p. 22.

[66] See Pastor/Wise (1999), p. 496.

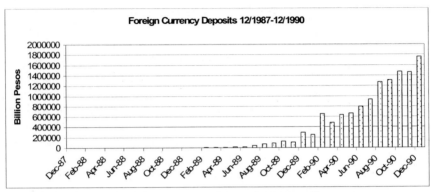

Source: Oficina de la CEPAL en Buenos Aires on the basis of official data[67].

### 2.2.5.3 Undervaluation as a Consequence of Currency Substitution

Most high inflations produce a real undervaluation of the domestic currency, i.e. the nominal exchange rate does not reflect the relation of the price levels of the domestic economy and the respective trading partner's[68]. In other words, the nominal exchange rate rises, i.e. devalues, faster than domestic prices (corrected by foreign prices). Where foreign exchange controls prevent the official exchange rate from rising, it is the black market (or parallel) exchange rate that moves towards an undervaluation.

According to Bernholz (2003), the reason becomes obvious when considering the individual calculation of a money holder: comparing the opportunity costs of holding domestic or foreign currency, the value of domestic money for future uses has to be discounted by more as it is subject to higher inflation rates than foreign money. Therefore it is valued less than the prevailing purchasing power parity would imply[69].

However, limits to the degree of undervaluation (and to currency substitution) are given by three facts: First, the undervaluation of the domestic currency works to encourage exports and discourage imports with the result of a higher supply and

---

[67]   See Heymann (2000), p. 174.

[68]   That is, the purchasing power parity is not granted: the nominal exchange rate ($e_n$), defined as the price for a unit of foreign currency expressed in domestic currency, exceeds the relation of the domestic ($P_{int}$) to the foreign price level ($P_{ext}$): $e_n > P_{int} / P_{ext}$.

[69]   For a formal model that derives undervaluation from the comparison of present values of holding domestic or foreign currency, see Bernholz (2003), pp. 90ff.

lower demand of foreign currency, which tends to counteract the undervaluation. Second, governments usually penalise the holding of foreign currency, i.e. the increased costs of holding it moderate the above calculation. Third, and with the same effect, the widespread use of domestic currency makes its holding comparatively more sensible, as it is easier to find trading partners accepting domestic currency.

Figures 13 and 14 depict the development of the Argentine currency's nominal and real exchange rates during the 1980s. Nominal as well as real exchange rates[70] show increases at the beginning of the decade and, more significant, in 1989, whereas the mid-1980s saw modest declines following the intermediate stabilisation of the Austral.

**Figure 13: Nominal Exchange Rates 1980-1990**

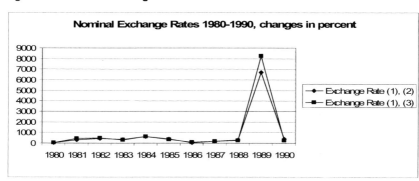

(1)  Averaged monthly rates.
(2)  These numbers refer to the average exchange rate in foreign trade, measured as simple average of the rate which is applied for import payments and an export exchange rate which is derived from a weighted average (on the basis of the export structure of 1993) of the effective exchange rate for primary export payments and of that for other export payments allowing for rights or tax incentives.
(3)  Between Oct. 15th, 1987, and May 19th, 1989, and since Dec. 20th, 1989, free market exchange rate. During other periods, parallel exchange rate.
Source: Oficina de la CEPAL en Buenos Aires on the basis of official data.

---

[70] The real exchange rate can be defined from different perspectives. One is to correct the nominal exchange rate by the relation between the price levels abroad and at home: $e_r = e_n * P_{ext} / P_{int}$, with $e_r$ being the real, $e_n$ the nominal exchange rate, and $P_{ext}$ and $P_{int}$ the exterior and interior price levels, respectively. The other is to focus on the relative prices of tradable and non-tradable goods: $e_r = e_n * P_t / P_{nt}$, with $P_t$ being the price of tradables and $P_{nt}$ the price of non-tradables. Of course, under the simplifying assumption that tradables' prices are set by the exterior, while non-tradables' prices reflect the domestic price level (and allowing for the snag that the domestic price index also includes tradables' prices), both aspects condense to the same content.

## Figure 14: Real Exchange Rates 1980-1990

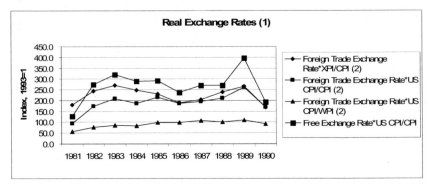

Real Exchange Rates (1)

(1)  Real exchange rates are defined as: nominal exchange rate * international price index / domestic price index. They have been calculated in different modes by using as international price indices alternatively: the price index of Argentine exports, here called XPI (expressed in US-Dollars), and the CPI of the United States of America, and as domestic price indices: the Argentine CPI and WPI.

(2)  The first of the indicators (Foreign Trade Exchange Rate*XPI/CPI) is calculated by using an average exchange rate for exports which is derived from a weighted average (on basis of the structure of 1993) of the effective exchange rate applied to primary export products and of that applied to other export products. The two following series are calculated by using an average exchange rate for foreign trade which is measured as a simple average of the effective exchange rate for exports as defined above and the effective exchange rate for imports.

Source: Oficina de la CEPAL en Buenos Aires on data of the INDEC and other sources.

### 2.2.5.4 Acceleration and Variability of Inflation

Beyond a certain level, inflations have the tendency to accelerate. Explanations are inherent in many of the points discussed above: for one thing, while the nominal money stock increases as the government tries to finance its budget deficit, the propensity to hold money declines, and prices rise even faster than the money stock. This mechanism is amplified by the Olivera-Tanzi effect according to which the real budget deficit grows due to the loss of purchasing power of government income alone. Moreover, currency substitution reduces the "tax base" on which inflation tax can be imposed so that the "tax rate" must rise to generate equal revenues.

The most disturbing factor for the real economy, however, is not acceleration itself, but the variability of inflation, which is empirically also shown to rise with inflation rates[71]. Thus, inflation gets less predictable the higher it becomes.

This unpredictability causes typical reactions with economic agents and severe distortions in the real sector. Considering how prices are set is illustrative in this

---

[71]  See Logue/Sweeney (1981), p. 500.

respect. With accelerating inflation, producers and traders realise that their usual calculation method does not serve them any longer. The mark-up method, by which producers add a profit margin to the production costs, leaves them with real losses as the input has become more expensive over the time of the production process. Traders cannot replenish their stocks at prices that are covered by the proceeds of their effectuated sales. Their reaction is a change in the calculation paradigm: selling prices are no longer based on the input costs de facto paid but on the input costs that are expected to prevail at the time of selling the product – usually calculated with the help of price indices. In other words, backward-looking price-setting behaviour is replaced by forward-looking behaviour[72].

As inflation not only accelerates but also gets more variable, this kind of calculation gets hazardous. Inflation variability aggravates the main problems inherent in using price indices through the effect that higher inflation variability causes the real value of indexed prices to get more variable as well[73]. Increasingly variable inflation leads to even more inadequate price settings than would be the case with merely rising inflation, and to highly variable real and relative prices.

Monthly statistics fail to capture most of intramonth price variability, and this is all the more the case for yearly data. Correspondingly, Blejer (1983) demonstrates for the period between 1977 and 1981 that individual commodity prices in Argentina fluctuated over a much wider range than the aggregated CPI, and that the captured disparities are much smaller on a yearly than on a monthly basis. Moreover, he found that the deviation of individual price rises from the monthly mean is due to few large single rises, and that this "skewness" increases with inflation[74].

### 2.2.5.5 Real Price and Wage Variability

With accelerating and variable inflation rates, real prices inevitably get desynchronised with respect to the inflation rate. This is largely due to the existence of "menu costs", i.e. the fact that prices cannot be changed instantly to reflect every change in inflation, although the intervals of price adjustments generally shorten with rising inflation rates. The reaction of price setters is, each time prices are

---

[72]  See Végh (1995), p. 36.

[73]  The situation of importers is somewhat better in that their, much more reliable, "index" is the exchange rate. With rising inflation, using the exchange rate as an index spreads gradually throughout the economy so that foreign exchange is the measure behind nearly all pricing decisions even if it is not (yet) used as a means of payment. See Bernholz (2003), p. 96.

[74]  See Blejer (1983), p. 480.

changed, to include into their prices the inflation expected until the next price change. Therefore, prices are set at higher levels than would correspond with the actual inflation rate, but in the course of rising inflation fall below that level – until the next price rise occurs.

The result is a seesaw pattern of real prices, with peaks at the time of price rises and subsequent steep declines until the next peak. Not surprisingly, this pattern also applies for the development of real wages. When inflation adjustment in wages is no longer settled in regular negotiations but gets subject to a price index, the deflections are supposed to get shorter and less extreme, but this is again counteracted by the increasing variability and acceleration of inflation. Apart from allocation inefficiencies caused by highly variable real product and factor prices, highly variable real prices and wages have a significant potential to disadvantage wage earners.

Figure 15 shows longer-term trend shifts in real prices and wages. Overall, Argentine real wages decreased steadily from 1984 until 1990. They fell between 1985 and 1990 alone by around 25 percent, thus continuing a trend that had begun in the mid-seventies[75]. The relation between industrial products and industrial wages, itself more variable over the decade, shows a marked rise in the two years up to 1989 and thus reflects a decline in wages in relation to prices of industrial products.

Of course, besides prices, the institutional determinants of nominal wages play the other role in real wage development. Here, it appears that massive government interventions since the days of the military regime in Argentina, covering anything between wage freezes and restrictions in trade union activity, probably contributed at least as much to the decline in real wages as inflation[76].

---

[75] See Waisgrais (2003), p. 14.

[76] For the institutional and economic determinants of wages see, e.g., Waisgrais (2003).

### Figure 15: Prices and Real Wages 1981-1990

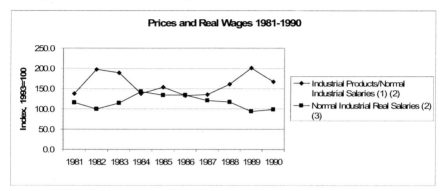

(1)    Industrial prices are measured by the national, non-agricultural WPI excluding typical Pampa products. Service prices are components of the CPI. Public and private services correspond to the international classifications CUCI and GCE (Grandes Categorías Económicas).

(2)    Normal salaries are defined as the sum of basic salaries (including extra hours) and bonuses and gratifications. They are unit values of the salaries paid during the reference period.

(3)    This refers to the average normal and permanent salaries, which are defined as the sum of basic salaries (including extra hours, bonuses and gratifications). They are unit values of the salaries paid during the reference period. Moreover, real salaries are defined as the amount of nominal salaries earned within a month, deflated by the average of the CPI of the current and the following month as an estimate of the value of the payment at month's end.

Source: Oficina de la CEPAL en Buenos Aires on data of the INDEC and other sources.

## 2.2.5.6 Distortion and Excess Variability of Relative Prices

The characteristics of inflation and price behaviour described above – acceleration and increasing variability of nominal and real prices – necessarily result also in distortions of relative prices, i.e. in prices of one class of goods as expressed in another class of goods. An increase in relative price variability is observable both across different products and across the same products at different locations. Different pricing schemes of various classes of goods add to these inherent distortions and may render them grotesque. Most conspicuous are dislocations between goods with fix (or "sticky") as opposed to flexible prices, or with regulated as opposed to unregulated prices. Also, large single movements in relative prices are often caused by "external" disturbances such as devaluations or discrete adjustments in public sector prices. Of course, these distortions reflect back on inflation and increase its variability.

A sufficiently stable structure of price relations within an economy forms the backbone of calculation and orientation of any economic behaviour. The rising instability in the gridwork of relative prices causes manifold violations of the "law of one price", with the effect that market forces no longer work to coordinate supply and demand. Markets become more fragmented and local prices more sensitive to specific shocks and idiosyncratic expectations. The system gets less well-coordinated both across space and over time. The limits are reached under the conditions of hyperinflation when agents cannot predict even the most immediate outcome of their economic actions and consequently reduce their exposure to business to a minimum.

Although relative price distortions are directly tangible for people living through high inflations, they are – as is the case with highly variable nominal and real prices – rarely adequately reflected in the statistics. While the more lasting components of relative price distortions are visible in month-to-month and longer-term data, the high intramonth (or even intraweek or intraday) variability of relative prices (the "noise" component) is not caught by monthly observations. Therefore, the positive relation between inflation rate and relative price variability seems to get weak at very high inflation rates.

The co-existence of nominal rigidities in some prices, arising from frictions in price setting ("menu costs"), and a high degree of flexibility in other prices are generally perceived as an important source of relative price distortions. Accordingly, sticky prices are to blame for much of these distortions as they fail to closely follow the inflation rate[77]. While the discrete and belated adjustment of nominal wages to inflation is the most important example, there are many other inter-sector and inter-firm price coordination tasks that include stickier and less sticky prices and that fail to produce efficient outcomes in high inflation[78].

A further typical distortion in high inflations is the distortion between goods and services supplied (or regulated) by the public sector on the one hand and privately supplied and priced goods and services on the other hand. Often, governments try as long as possible to keep prices for public goods low compared to overall inflation. Therefore, prices such as regulated rents for social housing, railway fares, and publicly supplied energy and water grow very cheap in relation, e.g., to food or clothing.

---

[77] However, empirical studies find that fix prices march more in parallel with the relevant indices than do flex prices. This reflects the observation that accelerating inflation leads to a higher than average number of fix prices being adjusted. Deviations of inflation from the trend therefore reflect these adjustments of fix prices, and not, as could be expected, the faster response of flexible prices. See Leijonhufvud (1990), p. 11.

[78] See Ball/Romer (1991).

Real estate and company shares also lose in relative value. This seems surprising since real assets are generally considered safe havens from inflation. But when rents are regulated, real estate loses its revenue potential and thus its value. The loss of value in company shares can be explained by the loss of information corporate reports provide: numbers become more meaningless the more the unit of account becomes unreliable. The evaluation of corporate performance becomes impossible, and stock markets cease to function properly[79]. As a consequence, stock prices lag behind general inflation because the dividends paid are lower in relation to the reported net profits than was the case before the inflation.

Another source of relative price distortions arises from different kinds of wage setting. Although wages generally lag behind inflation to a certain degree, this is less so for unskilled labour, whose wages are to a higher degree set by trade unions and/or possibly indexed. The higher skill and wages, the bigger gets the gap between wage development and inflation[80].

Examining relative prices of three broad product classes (food, non-food goods, and services), Blejer (1983) found for Argentina in the years 1977 to 1981 that the group of services showed a marked upward movement in its relative price. Furthermore, relative price variability within the food sector was much higher than within other sectors. Moreover, he showed that an opening of the economy (i.e. an increase in import-competition) worked to reduce relative price variability of domestic prices[81].

Figure 16 shows that Blejer's finding of services (here the denominator) growing relatively more expensive (here in relation to industrial products) applied also for the years 1983 to 1987, but shows the reverse development before and after, when prices of industrial products rose even faster than those of services. As for the different types of services, the relation of industrial products to public services shows less marked changes than the relation of industrial products to private services, implying a much closer linked development between industrial products and public services – in Argentina, the government obviously did not try to keep prices of public services artificially low. As the second chart of figure 16 shows, over

---

[79] See Heymann/Leijonhufvud (1995), p. 81.

[80] See Bernholz (2003), pp. 98 ff. He gives empirical and anecdotal evidence for the Austrian and German hyperinflations of 1922 and 1923 respectively.

[81] See Blejer (1983).

the decade, pampa products lost in relative value against industrial products – hurting the important Argentine agricultural sector.

**Figure 16: Relative Prices 1981-1990**

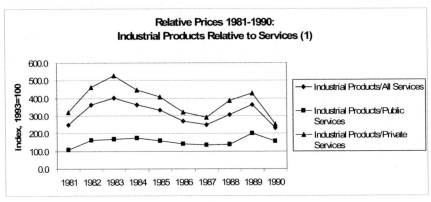

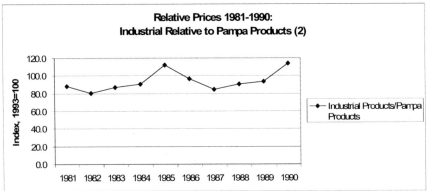

(1) Industrial prices are measured by the national, non-agricultural WPI excluding typical Pampa products. Service prices are components of the CPI. Public and private services correspond to the international classifications CUCI and GCE (Grandes Categorías Económicas).

(2) This measures the relation between two components of the WPI: the price index for industrial products as defined in the previous note and a compound of goods (primary, e.g. wheat, bovine livestock, and manufactured, e.g. beef, flour, vegetable oil) which are typical Pampa products or derived from such.

Source: Oficina de la CEPAL en Buenos Aires on data of the INDEC and other sources.

### 2.2.5.7 Contracting Strategies

As inflation rates and relative prices become highly variable in high inflations, their anticipation becomes a difficult task. Uncertainty increases with the length of planning horizons. There are different strategies to cope with this kind of uncertainty, each of them suitable for different kinds of transaction, and each of them observable in high inflation economies.

First, nominal contracts remain only if they refer to very short time horizons. This is the case in wholesale and retail markets for consumer goods, services, and intermediate products. Nominal contracting also remains in markets for short-run interest bearing assets, which are in strong demand from three sides: people try to move both out of money and out of long-term contracts, and speculative trades that exploit differences in inflationary expectations increase. But the higher and more erratic inflation, the shorter get the maturities of deposits people accept to hold, and in the extreme case of hyperinflation people refuse to keep deposits at all.

Second, longer-term contracts, for which re-negotiation is costly, such as property leases, longer-term customer-supplier relationships, and labour contracts, deal with uncertainty by including index clauses.

There are several problems with indexing: one is the question, which index, i.e. which basket of goods, to choose. Linking payments to one of the officially published price indices is attractive in several respects: they are available for all at the same time, they cannot be manipulated by the contracting parties, and bargaining costs are reduced. Furthermore, there is a certain stabilising effect when the practice of linking payments to the same index (usually the CPI) becomes widespread, because it imparts inertia on the inflation rate, which in turn limits the variability of the real value of payments. The main problem with indexing is that it is necessarily backward-looking and implies a reporting lag. This does not matter too much if the inflation rate is sufficiently steady, but causes serious misalignments between actual price movements and those reflected by the index in states of highly variable and accelerating inflations. Then, especially long indexed contracts generate highly variable real payments. The consequence is that, with highly erratic inflation, indexing will remain only up to a certain duration of contracts, and beyond that limit markets disappear[82].

The third strategy, dollarisation, offers a way out of the reporting lag, for the exchange rate is a price that is continuously measured and announced[83]. But

---

[82] Heymann/Leijonhufvud formulate the assumption that the duration of the longest remaining indexed contracts corresponds to the period during which the variance of the inflation rate remains within certain tolerance limits. See Heymann/Leijonhufvud (1995), p. 99.

[83] See Végh (1995), p. 62.

indexing to the exchange rate also has drawbacks because the real exchange rate in high inflations also becomes very volatile, and because it is not a domestic but a foreign basket of goods over which the exchange rate offers constant command. Moreover, governments usually try to forbid indexing to the exchange rate in order to keep currency substitution in check as long as possible. The same qualifications apply for the direct denomination of contracts in foreign currency.

Thus, different standards evolve for different kinds of transaction: dollarisation prevails in property markets and other long-lasting assets, wage contracts and property leases are indexed, while wholesale and retail markets as well as short-term financial markets continue to trade on a nominal basis. It is obvious that an economy operating on different transaction standards cannot function without friction, especially in markets that are affected by different standards – most conspicuously in the real estate sector[84]. Real incomes become volatile because the adjustment formulae in wage contracts do not properly reflect the changes in consumer goods prices. Since long-term financing of investments is not available, investors have to make use of several succeeding short-term loans at real interest rates that oscillate between positive and negative values. The use of certain kinds of indexation does not only imply costs but also significant risks (although intended to reduce risks) that reduce people's willingness to make binding long-term commitments[85]. Thus, financial management gains more resemblance with a daily gamble than with a productivity enhancing activity.

Which contracting strategies prevail depends on the magnitude of inflation, but also on a country's institutional characteristics and its experience with inflation. Formal indexation of financial contracts[86] or official wage adjustments based on

---

[84] This was the case also in Argentina: Property markets were in Dollars but mortgages were available neither in domestic currency nor in Dollars. Leases were indexed; exchange rate movements then changed the relative prices of houses and leases, causing excess supply in one market and excess demand in the other.

[85] A rather curious example is the Argentine "doctrina de imprevisibilidad" (unforeseeability doctrine), a law that allowed a party of an indexed contract to obtain a revision if the agreed escalator deviated by much of the actual price development. With high price volatility, however, the application of this law sometimes produced the opposite outcome, when the plaintiff was worse off with the revised contract because interim price swings undid the intended effects. See Heymann/Leijonhufvud (1995), p. 97.

[86] This was practised in Brazil in the 1980s and early 1990s, when even overnight credits with amounts higher than the equivalent of 3,000 US-Dollars were indexed. See Bernholz (2003), p. 94.

explicit indexing formulae may be chosen by some countries, while in other economies indexation remains less widespread.

The strategies prevailing in Argentina during the 1980s were the shortening of contracting periods rather than indexing, which remained a less important practice[87]. In the mid-1980s, with monthly inflation rates of 20 to 30 percent, wages were adjusted monthly, usually with reference to the CPI growth of the previous month, but without explicit indexation clauses[88]. Given highly variable monthly CPI growth rates in Argentina (in the late 1980s between 2 and 200 percent), indexing was of only little use, since the real value of payments from indexed contracts got highly variable.

### 2.2.5.8 Disappearance of Markets

Refraining from economic transaction is another strategy to deal with immense uncertainty. In high inflations, certain markets simply disappear, as there is no way to cope with uncertainty, especially in the longer term. Long-run positions will at most be held abroad. At the end of the 1980s, Argentine "longer-term" credit markets had completely vanished, so that the longest available credits had the duration of 14 days[89].

The intertemporal structure of markets shrinks: the higher the inflation rate, the shorter the remaining market terms. One aspect of this phenomenon, known throughout Latin America as "cortoplacismo", is the substitution of one long-term contract by two or more successive short-term contracts: economic agents prefer flexibility and forgo higher yields in return of a smaller degree of uncertainty. As a consequence, a reduction in short-term real interest rates and even the acceptance of persistent negative real rates can be observed[90]. Figure 17 depicts the development of nominal and real interest rates over the decade. Passive real interest rates were mostly negative, while in the years preceding the Austral stabilisation attempt, and again in 1989, even active real rates ranged far into the negative spectrum.

The shrinking volume and time dimension of the capital markets hurts the real economy. The intertemporal allocation of resources between the sectors of an

---

[87] See Heymann (2000), p. 85.

[88] See Heymann/Leijonhuvfud (1995), p. 98.

[89] See Bernholz (2003), p. 93.

[90] In this environment, low short-term interest rates should not be interpreted as the result of an underestimation of the inflation rate. See Heymann/Leijonhufvud (1995), p. 52.

economy is hindered and rendered inefficient by high and erratic inflation: in a decentralised market economy, financial institutions and capital markets work to coordinate consumption and saving of private households with production and investment of firms. Debt financed investment is rendered impossible when long-term financing is not available. Therefore, under high inflation, investment activity decreases, and the capital stock is doomed to get obsolete.

In the extreme, even retail markets are affected by "disappearance"[91]. This is illustrated drastically by the view of a sign that appeared in many shops during Argentine hyperinflation: "Closed for the lack of prices". Needless to say that at this point riots and anarchy are close and the state's survival is at stake.

**Figure 17: Nominal and Real Interest Rates 1980-1990**

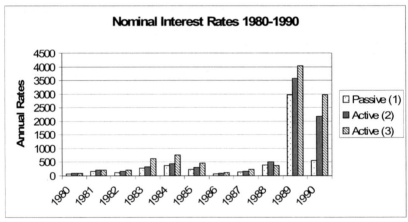

---

[91] Heymann/Leijonhufvud call this refusal of retailers to sell the „option to exit".

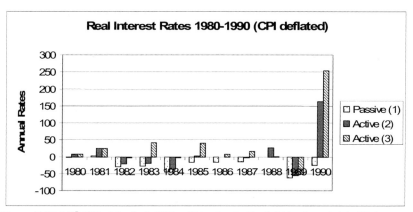

Real Interest Rates 1980-1990 (CPI deflated)

(1)     Until Oct. 15th, 1987, rate fixed by the BCRA on 30 days deposits. Since that date, witnessed rate (weighted average of
        the rates paid by banks on 7, 15, and 30 days deposits). For the first quarter of 1990, witnessed rate on deposits on
        savings accounts. Since April 1990, witnessed rate on time deposits, weighted by all maturities.
(2)     Until Oct. 15th, 1987, regulated rate. Since that date, rate applied by the Banco de la Nación Argentina on discount of
        documents for 30 days.
(3)     Active rate on inter-company operations for 7 days with BONEX guarantee. Average monthly rates.
Source: Oficina de la CEPAL en Buenos Aires, on data of the BCRA and other sources.[92]

### 2.2.5.9 Economic Performance

Assuming backward-looking expectations, additional money creation is able to
produce initial real effects in terms of higher output and employment, since agents –
even if free of money illusion – adapt their behaviour to the higher inflation rate only
with a lag. Permanent real effects can be obtained only at the cost of ever
accelerating inflation[93].

With the assumption of rational expectations, there is little or no Phillips curve
trade-off left between inflation and unemployment, since agents are able to perfectly
predict any systematic policy action. Only unsystematic policies (surprise inflation)
are able to deliver short-term effects, but are speedier adjusted to and incur high
costs in terms of increased volatility and uncertainty.

That said, although moderate inflation may be able to stimulate economic
performance temporarily, ongoing high rates of inflation repel that property[94]. This
can be explained with the observation that under high and accelerating inflation the
likelihood of unanticipated monetary policy stimuli gets very small, as individuals

---

[92] See Heymann (2000), p. 176.
[93] See Cagan (1989b), p. 203.
[94] See Bernholz (2003), p. 102.

become "immune" to the possibility of real effects from monetary policy[95]. High inflation destroys money's functions to such a degree that central economic institutions lose their effectiveness. There is no doubt that high inflation economies perform less well than they would under macroeconomic stability. Still, it has to be qualified in which ways they perform less well.

The causation chain between inflation and real growth generally focuses on relative prices and lost efficiency: rising inflation increases inflation variability, and hence uncertainty. Rising inflation variability increases relative price variability, which distorts signals for producers and consumers alike. Relative price variation creates additional uncertainty. The interpretation of shifts in prices or demand – the basis for decision making – becomes guesswork, as nominal factors become indiscernible from real ones. To the extent that such guesses are wrong, fluctuations in real economic activity and an overall efficiency loss occur.

While it is empirically proven that real growth variability increases with inflation, the effect of inflation on the long-run growth rate remains unclear. Does high and variable inflation only reduce the level of factor use or might it even induce the economy to take a long-term path of slower growth because the potential factor supply itself is reduced? As far as highly uncertain real returns increase the reluctance to invest (or to supply one's work force), both the physical and the human capital stock and thus potential long-term growth may indeed be reduced. Possible expectations of future capital losses and/or confiscations may deter investment or re-direct it into more labour-intensive, though less productive, sectors (such as services), both of which entails a long-term decline in income and productivity[96]. Put into the Phillips curve context, a fall in the factor supply may even lead to an inflation-unemployment trade-off sloping upwards in the long run, so that the same inflation rate now incorporates lower economic activity and higher long-term unemployment than before[97].

However, the relationship between inflation and long-run growth is difficult to prove, not least because it is difficult to separate the effects of high inflation on economic performance from other factors, such as other growth-inhibiting policies or external shocks, which usually are involved as well. Therefore, the microeconomic approach, i.e. the examination of the consequences of inflation for the behaviour of

---

[95]  See Siklos (1995), p. 24.
[96]  See Hopenhayn/Neumeyer (2003).
[97]  See Logue/Sweeney (1981), p. 500.

the public and private sector, feeds the analysis of the growth-inhibiting effects of high inflation.

The above considerations on the forming of expectations in mind, several ways of how high and variable inflation affects the economic performance become stringent. First, an incoherent collective state of expectations, reflected in differing real interest rates used in individual calculations of intertemporal resource allocation, leads to an inefficient allocation of capital in general. Second, the preference of short-term contracts and the ensuing disappearance of long-term finance markets make the financing of investment difficult if impossible, at least inefficient, with the result of worsening investment yields and reduced investment activity. Third, and perhaps more damaging and lasting than one is generally aware, a general "politicising" of the economy is observed, i.e. human resources are misdirected in a way which additionally reduces economic efficiency. In a highly inflationary and erratic environment, traditional skills in production, quality control, marketing, or distribution lose their relative value against qualities that enable an individual to better cope with the instable monetary environment[98]: the ability to predict monetary policy actions and to hedge against them becomes the most important human skill. The criteria for personal success change, and people such as financial experts, accountants, lawyers, and, above all, people with political connections get more valuable. Political interaction via pressure groups replaces the more productive ways of private co-operation[99].

Figure 18 shows the extreme volatility of Argentine GDP during the 1980s, with oscillations between -7.6 and +7.9 percent annual growth (both extremes reached in successive years), and a strong drift into the negative in the years up to 1989. Investment activity declined to a degree that did not suffice to maintain the existing capital stock, so that, as a consequence of high real interest rates, lacking demand, and increased importance of speculative financial activities, in fact a process of de-investment took place, boding ill for the country's long-term perspectives[100].

Unemployment grew over the decade from little more than two to 7.4 percent in 1990 (see Figure 19). The rate of underemployed persons was estimated to be at around the same proportion.

---

[98]  Indeed, banks and financial intermediaries have an incentive to expand their services and offer new money substitutes. The "physical" size of the banking sector tends to grow in high inflation.

[99]  See Heymann/Leijonhufvud (1995), p. 54.

[100]  See Wohlmann (1998), p. 119.

Argentina's dismal economic performance gets perhaps most palpable in comparison with the region's performance, as depicted in Figure 20: with the exception of the agricultural sector, hitherto the country's growth engine which managed to grow, albeit meagrely, over the decade, the economy shrank while the rest of Latin America grew.

**Figure 18: Inflation and GDP Growth 1980-1990**

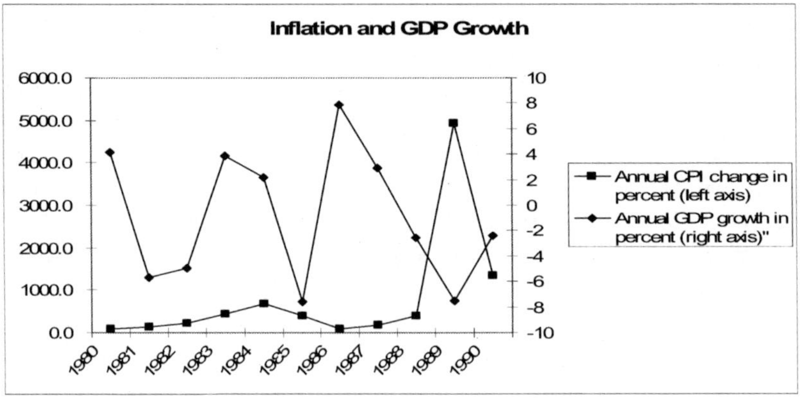

Sources: Worldbank, 2003 World Development Indicators and Oficina de la CEPAL en Buenos Aires on the basis of official data.

**Figure 19: Unemployment in Argentina 1980-1990**

Source: Worldbank, 2003 World Development Indicators.

### Figure 20: Output Growth in Regional Comparison 1980-1990

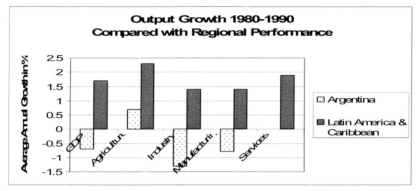

Source: Worldbank, 2003 World Development Indicators.

### 2.2.5.10    External Trade

The effects of high and erratic inflation on trade are mixed. As pointed out, the real exchange rate tends to move towards undervaluation as a result from high and erratic inflation. This should work to discourage imports and boost exports. In addition, both the decline in domestic demand caused by high inflation and the increased incentive to earn foreign currency affect export levels positively[101].

In Argentina, after the collapse of the Tablita in 1981, earlier attempts to reduce trade barriers reverted into an increase in protectionism, resulting in a complex import-discouraging system of tariffs, administrative controls, and special treatments. In the second half of the 1980s, following an agreement with the World Bank, tariffs were eased somewhat, their structure modified (with a maximum import tariff of 40%), and quantitative restrictions reduced[102] (moreover, various commercial agreements were signed with Brazil, which paved the way for the later signing of the MERCOSUR treaty[103]). This is visible in imports declining during the first half, and recovering somewhat in the second half of the 1980s, but ending up

---

[101] See Pastor/Wise (1999), p. 496.

[102] See Heymann (2000), p. 59.

[103] Between 1984 and 1989, 24 bilateral protocols were signed by Argentina and Brazil which regulated different areas of trade integration. In 1990, the existing bilateral agreements were systematised and intensified, and Paraguay and Uruguay joined the talks, which brought about the MERCOSUR founding treaty between the four members in early 1991. Chile and Bolivia have joined MERCOSUR as associated members.

much lower than in the beginning decade (see Figure 21). Exports as well as the overall trade balance improved significantly since 1987 which mirrors the limited recovery of the terms of trade during these years, after they had worsened massively during the first half of the 1980s (see figure 22).

**Figure 21: Foreign Trade 1980-1990**

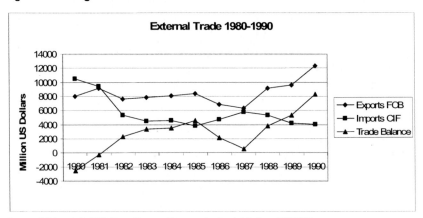

Source: Oficina de la CEPAL en Buenos Aires, on basis of data from MECON.

**Figure 22: Foreign Trade Prices (1986=100)**

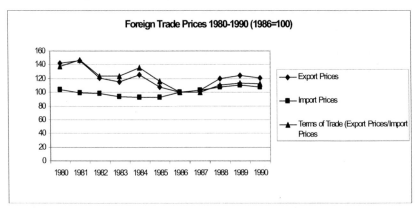

(1) Indices calculated on the basis of unit values expressed in US-Dollars.
(2) The indices correspond to the Paasche formula, i.e. they include not only the effects of price variations but also changes in the composition of trade flows.

Source: Oficina de la CEPAL en Buenos Aires, on basis of data from INDEC and other sources.

## 2.2.5.11    Distributional Effects of High Inflation

It has been previously stated that the incidence of the inflation tax is clearly regressive. Although people on average forcedly become financially more sophisticated in high inflation economies – at least they will be informed in detail about current monthly, weekly or even daily inflation rates, as well as about the development of different index components – the capability to minimise the exposition to the inflation tax differs significantly between the poor and the more well-to-do. Typically, the strategies to reduce real money balances for average households are restricted to building up inventories of consumer goods on paydays. Contrary to the poor, the better-off own things such as cars and freezers, or credit cards, which better enable them to avoid the holding of unwanted cash balances, or to realise more or less randomly occurring "bargains". Moreover, they have the possibility to place the rest of their received earnings either in short-term deposits or to transfer them into foreign currency, both options often being barred for lower income people by minimum size requirements. The striving to spend all money early in the payment period entails a reduction of precautionary balances and the risks associated with it. Then, unforeseen medical expenses, for example, may hit poor households badly and necessitate big cuts in consumption afterwards.

It has been pointed out that wage indexing tends to favour lower income groups as opposed to higher wage earners, whose contracts have to be renegotiated. This may be true for moderate inflations (where, however, indexing often is not practised), and would indeed incorporate a redistribution of income towards low wage earners in the long run[104]. However, as has been shown, with lasting and accelerating inflation, economic performance and employment is damaged in a way that claiming advantages for the working class from high inflation seems cynical, especially if one keeps in mind the uneven incidence of the inflation tax described above.

The distribution of wealth is affected by high inflation in a way that holders of nominal financial assets with fixed nominal returns lose much of their fortune, whereas debtors gain as the real value of their debt melts down quickly. The first group usually comprises private households who see their savings and life insurances vanish, whereas the second group is made up mostly of enterprises and the government. Owners of real capital – real estate and shares – also suffer losses

---

[104] This is sometimes used as an argument to regard anti-inflation policies as hurting the working class.

due to its reduced revenue potential, but to a far lesser degree than owners of nominal capital. As a consequence, inflation generally works to redistribute wealth in a way that hurts the middle class – with the ensuing potentially dangerous social and political consequences[105].

Figure 23 summarises the losses in real income for different Argentine population groups. Clearly, the poorest fifth of the population suffered most from high inflation, being left in 1989 with 25% percent of the real incomes they had disposed of in 1980. The top quintile's real incomes suffered least, ending up at 60% of their 1980 level.

**Figure 23: Real Incomes by Population Groups, 1980=100**

| Year | Poorest Quintile | Second Quintile | Middle Quintile | Fourth Quintile | Top Quintile | Total |
|------|------------------|-----------------|-----------------|-----------------|--------------|-------|
| 1980 | 100 | 100 | 100 | 100 | 100 | 100 |
| 1986 | 89 | 94 | 89 | 95 | 86 | 91 |
| 1989 | 25 | 37 | 40 | 48 | 60 | 49 |

Source: Página 12, cited after The Economist[106].

Considering the distribution of wages among the employed, the picture gets even more accentuated: while the poorest 30 percent lost 13 percent in their wage share, the richest ten percent gained 23 percent since the mid-seventies until 1991[107].

These numbers embody Argentina's striking development from one of the most "equal" Latin American countries to one of the most unequal: owing to its abundance in resources, its demographic structure (composed overwhelmingly by immigrated Europeans, and only few indigenous populations), as well as its Peronist past of pronounced social welfare, the Argentine society had been one of the most "equal" by Latin American standards until the mid-seventies. While the continuingly worsening distribution since that time is generally attributed mainly to structural changes, such as massive government interventions in wage negotiations (most

---

[105] See Bernholz (2003), pp. 107ff.
[106] See N.N. (1994), p. 14.
[107] See Waisgrais (2003), p. 7.

accentuated during the military regime, but also practised later in the eighties)[108], there is no doubt that high inflation contributed to this development.

Accordingly, the most common measure of income distribution, the Gini index, shows a rise in income inequality among Argentine households from 0.416 in 1980 to 0.437 in 1990[109]. In October 1989, more than 45% percent of people living in the Gran Buenos Aires area lived below the poverty line[110].

### 2.2.6    From High to Hyperinflation

As already noted, the demarcation line between high and hyperinflation is, by convention, drawn at the numerical limit of 50% monthly inflation. It has also been said that high inflations can persist for long while any economy, once caught in hyperinflation, is bound to collapse within short. The course of events that eventually triggers an inflationary economy's transition into hyperinflation is not easy to establish, and certainly cannot be generalised. But the above characterisations of high inflation economies deliver some central aspects.

The state of a high inflation economy can be described as excessively sensitive: time horizons over which people are prepared to commit themselves have shortened to a few days, and prices are changed with such frequency that inflationary impulses are spread very quickly. Uncertainty and nervousness concerning economic and political developments dominate everyday life. In such an idiosyncratic state, single unforeseen, often political, events are able to push the economy over the verge[111]. But the developments set in motion by high inflation may at some point well deliver the trigger on their own. E.g., once backward-looking indexing becomes unacceptable for wage earners and is replaced by forward-looking arrangements, one very important anchor that kept the economy off the shores of hyperinflation is given up, and one of the few remaining links between past and current prices is lost.

In Argentina, the double outbreak of hyperinflation in May to August 1989 and December 1989 to March 1990 was clearly connected with the collapse of two

---

[108] They included anything from state fixing of wages, minimum wage freezes, the suspension of trade union activities and the right to strike, to the abolition of collective bargaining. See Waisgrais (2003), p. 14.

[109] See Altimir/Beccaria (2000a), p. 432.

[110] See Heymann/Kosacoff (2000), pp. 32f.

[111] For instance, in the case of German hyperinflation, it was the assassination of Rathenau in 1922 that led to hyperinflation within short.

stabilisation attempts. "Plan Primavera" was given up after 8 months in early 1989. "Plan BB", introduced in July 1989, was even more short lived, and from mid-December hyperinflation was back again. In both cases, the inflation rate jumped from single-digit monthly figures to more than 50% within a few weeks.

While most of the setting in which both bouts of hyperinflation occurred is identical, there is one major difference. The degree of financial adaptation to hyperinflation, and especially the degree of dollarisation, increased during and after the first hyperinflation of mid-1989. The second bout of hyperinflation therefore met a better prepared public with more alternative monetary assets in place. It can be argued that this is the cause why monthly inflation reached 200 percent during the first, but "only" 100 percent during the second hyperinflation: the rate of inflation required to induce people to hold less money was reduced by the process of financial adaptation and/or dollarisation[112].

The depiction of hyperinflation differs from that of high inflation mainly in the degree of extremity. Plans have to be recalculated from day to day, even from hour to hour. The simplest transaction, like selling a product, becomes highly risky. These risks are reflected in ever higher mark-ups on production or restocking costs (with massive discounts offered for payment in foreign currency), or, on the limit, in the refusal to trade at all. Widespread shortages arise spontaneously, owing to the excessively delicate state of expectations of market participants.

Dollarisation gets ever more widespread and eventually dominates almost all markets – except retail markets for non-durable goods, which usually continue to be fed out of wages or government transfers paid in domestic currency. The exchange rate becomes the common reference for price setting, although being itself highly volatile[113]. Money demand falls drastically; in addition, unpredictable monetary policy injections, incoherent expectations and highly variable transaction volumes render money demand extremely volatile, which feeds back on goods and exchange

---

[112] See Sturzenegger (1994).

[113] Heymann/Leijonhufvud describe practices that emerged during Argentina's hyperinflation in inter-company relations. Mostly, goods were ordered without knowledge of the price, the latter being communicated only upon delivery. Another method was to determine the price as the equivalent of the Dollar price in domestic money at the moment when the contract was agreed upon; the buyer paid an amount calculated on the basis of the exchange rate prevailing at the moment of payment, and the seller recalculated the price using the exchange rate at the time of crediting the bill, so that, finally, the buyer issued a second cheque for the difference between the amount paid and the final price. See Heymann/Leijonhufvud (1995), p. 107.

markets. Nominal, real, and relative prices fluctuate widely all over the economy. Trade and consumer credit disappear completely, and so do the incentives to supply goods or effort to the markets. Real activity declines sharply, and unemployment rises. The operation of the state itself becomes impossible, as all sources of government finance peter out. Once caught in hyperinflation, there is no "soft" way back, and any stabilisation attempt has to work instantaneously and rigorously.

## 2.3 Options for Stabilisation in the beginning 1990s

### 2.3.1 Political Feasibility of Reforms

"Each case history [of high and hyperinflations] is a story of repeated attempts to cut the deficit. But in most cases it is as if a succession of failed attempts is necessary before a coalition can finally be formed to put into place a realistic stabilisation package. The commonly shared recognition that systematic taxation is collectively preferable to continued inflation does not by itself produce agreement on the concrete steps that could stabilise the public finances."[114]

The situation of an economy caught in hyperinflation offers no gradual way back to stability. The public has lost any confidence in the domestic money, inflation rates have reached exorbitant levels, and it does not matter any longer whether inflation expectations miss the actual developments by umpteen points since domestic money is nearly completely substituted by stable money even in cash transactions. The real stock of domestic money has fallen drastically, and inflation tax revenues dwindled to a negligible level. Other government revenues continue to fall as well due to the Tanzi effect and decreasing economic performance. At the same time, government expenditures have to rise to grant transfers to the increasing hoards of unemployed. The government is in danger of losing its authority.

In this situation, the economic conditions eventually make drastic reform efforts not only inevitable but also politically feasible. Since all other measures to revive the faltering economy now would immediately vaporise without effect, the proposal of a monetary reform will finally be able to gain majorities[115].

The case of Argentina, however, proved to be quite peculiar in this respect. Clearly, the second-to-last failed stabilisation attempt and the culmination of

---

[114] Heymann/Leijonhufvud (1995), p. 71.
[115] See Bernholz (2003), p. 163.

decades of monetary instability into hyperinflation dominated the presidential election campaigns of 1989 and led to a clear victory of Carlos Menem[116], who amidst food riots and hyperinflation took over the presidency five months early, in July of that year (when monthly inflation soared to 197 percent). However, in his campaign, he had publicly promised to pursue the purest of Peronism (which never had lost its popularity and had gained support among the working class the more high inflation had disadvantaged them), vowing to increase wages and to re-open bankrupt factories[117]. At the same time, he had sought the support of business and the middle class with his strategically vague promises to fight inflation[118]. However, Menem, soon after his election, removed the Peronist robe and turned to the free-market approach of his defeated competitor, adopting a rigid orthodox stabilisation plan with the currency board as its cornerstone.

### 2.3.2 Shape of Reforms Ending Hyperinflation

The measures necessary to end hyperinflation have to tackle its main causes and some of its detrimental effects. Crucial are a stop in money creation to finance budget deficits, the restoration of confidence in the national money, and the re-establishment of the real stock of national money. Given the difficulty of this task under the conditions of hyperinflation, and its extreme dependence upon the programme's credibility, it seems inevitable that the basic monetary and political institutions be exchanged and a new, credible, monetary and fiscal regime installed.

Still, any programme, credible and well-defined though it may be, cannot predetermine the stabilisation process in every respect but has to remain as flexible as to allow for adequate responses to unforeseen developments, e.g. with respect to the speed of adaptation of the public's inflation expectations. Thus, policymakers face a trade-off between strong commitments to gain credibility, on the one hand, and a certain necessary, but potentially trust-reducing, "room for manoeuvre", on the other. In addition, while there is a more or less standard menu of measures that constitute the necessary conditions for successful stabilisation, the set of actions that complements them remains to a large extent historically contingent, i.e., for each specific case a combination and sequence of steps has to be found that grants

---

[116] This was the first time in Argentina's history that a democratically elected president from one political party took over from a democratically elected president from another political party.

[117] See Jonas (2002), p. 8.

[118] See Pastor/Wise (1999), p. 479.

enough credibility as well as political and social acceptance[119]. Thus, there is no standard stabilisation programme with a built-in guarantee for success.

### 2.3.2.1 Monetary and Fiscal Reform

As mentioned, there are two key points of reforms that are necessary to end hyperinflations. First, an independent monetary authority has to be created, with a legally or constitutionally limited amount of credit allowed to be granted to the government. Second, the real stock of money has to be increased back to its normal level.

Achieving an increase of the real money stock via a fall in the price level at a constant nominal money stock would entail a severe recession and further employment losses. As this seems politically and socially unfeasible, the other road should to be taken: an adequate growth in the nominal money stock at constant, or very slowly rising, prices. Not surprisingly, putting the brake on prices forms the most difficult part: inflationary expectations have to be removed as far and quickly as possible, which can be achieved only when the reform is credible[120].

To gain credibility, in most cases a set of new institutions is necessary, including a new government overseeing the reforms, a new central bank under new leadership, and (possibly) a new currency unit. In other words, new policy, fiscal, and monetary regimes have to be installed and function as institutional safeguards of the reforms[121]. Moulding these institutional changes in laws or include them into the constitution enforces their credibility.

---

[119] See Heymann/Leijonhufvud (1995), p. 112.

[120] Végh argues that credibility is easier to obtain for hyperinflation stabilisation than when trying to stabilise lower, chronic, inflation economies. First, in hyperinflations, budget deficits and the government's need for seigniorage get more engraved in people's minds as the main motor of inflation than is the case during lasting, albeit high, inflations. Therefore, they are more easily convinced that a fiscal reform at the centre of a stabilisation programme is sufficient to halt inflation. Second, the sheer extremity of the situation and the obviousness that it cannot go on deliver an inherently higher degree of credibility to any stabilisation effort in hyperinflations – more than during chronic inflations where people have learned to live with the situation. See Végh (1995), pp. 62f.

[121] Bernholz (2003) stresses that these institutional safeguards can, from an historical perspective, not be unconditionally qualified as necessary ingredients of successful currency reforms, since there are rare cases of reforms that succeeded without these. Nevertheless, those reforms suffered from lower credibility. Accordingly, real interest rates remained relatively high after the reforms, which damaged economic recovery and resulted in a retarded defeat of inflation. See Bernholz (2003), pp. 166ff.

In addition to these institutional safeguards, some accompanying measures may be necessary to make the reform feasible or more acceptable in economic, political, or social terms. Although, over time, the recovering money demand will start to offset the loss of inflation tax, and real tax revenues will rise due to the Tanzi effect in reverse, the government will initially remain cash constrained. To bring down the interest burden, domestic and/or foreign debt may need reduction, e.g. via temporary moratoria on capital or interest payments (but with an eye on maintaining future creditworthiness), or via renegotiation of debts or reparations. If obtainable, a foreign bridging loan may cover interim balance of payments and budget deficits. The privatisation of public companies can relieve budgetary pressures and, if carried through sensibly, offer additional gains, such as enhanced industrial competition and effectiveness, as well as political support for the government through the demonstration of its commitment to more market-oriented policies. Finally, social acceptance of the reforms can be increased by partly redressing the uneven distribution effects of high inflation, notably by revaluing private long-term credits that lost their real value during inflation[122]. Existing exchange controls and protectionist obstacles should be gradually removed in order to restore confidence in the competitiveness of the (new) national currency.

Obviously, initial disinflation has to be consolidated into lasting stabilisation, which is why these mentioned one-shot measures are not sufficient to restore confidence but have to be followed by comprehensive fiscal reforms that restore viable public finances.

### 2.3.2.2 External Anchor: Fixing the Exchange Rate

The necessary monetary and fiscal reform can be strengthened by the adoption of a fixed exchange rate regime. A fixed exchange rate to a stable anchor currency may add to, or even replace, the creation of an independent central bank – in the latter case by introducing a currency board regime.

---

[122] The uneven distribution effects of disinflation itself may also need redressing. A possibility is to enforce schedules that depreciate all payments contracted before disinflation on the basis of high inflation expectations, and hence undo unwanted revaluations of real debts caused by sudden disinflation (this was done, e.g., during the Argentine "Austral" programme in 1985). In the wake of hyperinflation, however, longer-term contracts based on explicit inflation rates are virtually absent, so that these redistribution effects do not occur (this being one reason why the stabilisation costs are comparatively lower for hyperinflation than for moderate or chronic inflation economies). See Heymann/Leijonhufvud (1995), p. 123.

For a hyperinflation economy, adopting an external anchor is clearly superior to the alternative of an internal anchor, such as a monetary or inflation target. First, the high degree of dollarisation in a hyperinflation economy, where virtually all prices are indexed to, or quoted in, Dollars, means that stabilising the exchange rate is tantamount to stabilising the price level[123]. The exchange rate thus provides a much more direct and immediate link to prices than any monetary target, and as close a link as an inflation target. Second, given the higher transparency of an exchange rate target, and hence the higher potential immediate reputation costs of deviating from it, anchoring the national currency to a stable foreign currency will always be furnished with potentially more inherent credibility than a monetary growth, but also a direct inflation, target. Of course, this potential has to be exploited by institutionally safeguarding that the government cannot change the rate at its discretion, or create devaluation pressures by continuing to monetise budget deficits. In contrast, a simple self-commitment of the government to a certain monetary growth or inflation rate while floating (purely or managed) the exchange rate will comparatively lack confidence and thus prevent inflation expectations from declining quickly. The restoration of the real money stock will therefore be, at least temporarily, hindered by both ongoing inflation and the restricted rise in the nominal money stock which challenges the whole stabilisation effort.

This finding seems to be confirmed empirically: all of the most successful currency reforms following hyperinflations in history included fixed exchange rates to stable currencies or gold parities, whereas most of the least successful reforms did not[124].

Clearly, the adoption of a fixed exchange rate, like any tight monetary rule, entails renounced flexibility and hence potentially higher costs incurred in the case of shocks which cannot be encountered by the discretionary use of monetary policy instruments. These costs are, at least in the medium term (until the necessary reputation of the authorities has been built up and can step in to allow for an easing of the rules), unavoidable and form perhaps the worst long-term legacy of high and hyperinflation[125].

---

[123] See Végh (1995), p. 44.
[124] See Bernholz (2003), p. 187.
[125] See Heymann/Leijonhufvud (1995), p. 121.

### 2.3.3 Argentina's Choice

Argentina's decades-long history of high inflation (which was shared by most of the rest of Latin America during the 1970s and 1980s) represented an extreme legacy for the designers of reform in 1990. Whereas most of Argentina's neighbours sooner or later had managed to stabilise their economies (Chile in 1978, Bolivia in 1985, Mexico in 1987[126]), Argentina had only seen one failing reform after the other. Thus, whatever the shape of the announced reform, it would inescapably have to cope with a very low probability of success attached to it in the minds of the public. Thus, even defenders of exchange rate flexibility conceded that Argentina, with this legacy and the extreme credibility problem associated with it, had no other option left than resorting to a fully institutionalised mechanism of money issue[127].

The new government under Carlos Menem, having taken over in summer 1989 and, first of all, having to cope with the failure of another sloppy stabilisation attempt (Plan BB), rightly felt that the answer to the ensuing second bout of hyperinflation in 1990 needed to be final. Political survival now could only be brought about by seizing the most credible and lasting stabilisation option possible. Tying the own hands by strict monetary and fiscal rules seemed the only alternative left should the country be prevented from sinking completely into chaos[128].

In January, 1991, the man to accomplish this, Domingo Cavallo, was appointed as economics minister. The "father of Convertibility", as he was later dubbed, soon launched the CBA. It entered into force on April 1st, 1991, and established the ratio 10,000 Australes = 1 US-Dollar as the legally fixed exchange rate. Though the Banco Central de la República Argentina kept its name and formal status as a central bank, its executives were replaced and its powers massively restricted, in effect reducing its functions almost completely to those of a currency board: issuing domestic currency against foreign exchange. Money creation other than in exchange for existing Dollar reserves was ruled out by law. Finally, on January 1st, 1992, the Austral was replaced by a new currency unit, the Peso, at the ratio 10,000 Austral = 1 Peso, thereby establishing the simple and popular Peso-Dollar parity[129].

---

[126] See e.g. Végh (1995), p. 40.

[127] See Dornbusch/Goldfajn/Valdés (1995), p. 263.

[128] See e.g. Pastor/Wise (1999), p. 485.

[129] The legal and institutional configuration of the CBA will be described in detail in section 4.

Thus, although undertaken in various steps, the Argentine reform included all possible institutional cornerstones[130]. The crucial element of these was the choice of the strictest possible anchoring of the national currency, the adoption of the CBA.

Without anticipating the detailed analysis and interpretation of Argentina's economic performance following the stabilisation via currency board (see section 4), some central features characterising its success shall be mentioned here. Annual inflation rates decreased to 84 percent in 1991, to 17.5 percent in 1992, and to 7.4 percent in 1993, only to decline in the following years to less than one percent. The real stock of national money rose from its minimum in February 1990 of 15 percent of its "normal" level to 41 percent in mid-1992 and 44 percent in March 1993[131]. The still comparatively low level of the real money stock two years after the reforms, with inflation rates as low as the country had not experienced since more than a decade, reflects the fact that the high degree of currency substitution built up during the years of high and hyperinflation got reversed only to a limited degree. This is, on the one hand, probably due to an initial mistrust in the reforms, but is, on the other hand, also a consequence of the almost unrestricted acceptance of Dollars throughout the economy, as well as of the handy 1:1 exchange rate. The latter argument is strengthened by the fact that real interest rates were relatively low in the early 1990s, i.e. confidence in the reforms cannot have been as persistently low as to drive interest rates up[132].

The output costs of stabilisation itself seem to have been small. Positive output growth resumed in 1991, with real GDP growing by 10.6 percent in that year, and with continuing strong growth in the following years, averaging 5.8 percent between 1991 and 1998[133]. This corresponds with the often observed fact regarding the

---

[130] Of course, the fact that the institutional changes were not introduced at a stroke retarded the defeat of inflation in Argentina. This is the reason why Bernholz (2003) counts Argentina to the group of "less successful currency reforms": it missed the defined criterion for the group of "most successful reforms" – annual inflation below 25 percent in the year after the reforms – for the year 1991, but met it in 1992. See Bernholz (2003), p. 186.

[131] Bernholz (2003) defines the normal real stock of money as "its size in the year before the inflation began or when it had been very moderate", see Bernholz (2003), p. 75. It has to remain open exactly which level he defined as "normal" for the Argentine case.

[132] The active rate applied on discount of documents for 30 days was 22.4 percent in 1993, which results in a real rate of 15.4 percent for that year. See Heymann (2000), p. 176.

[133] See Heymann (2000), p. 103.

stabilisation of hyperinflations, namely that output costs are small relative to the costs that are incurred when stopping lower inflations[134].

In accordance with this finding, Argentina' unemployment rate did not rise in the immediate follow-up of stabilisation. Unemployment in the Gran Buenos Aires Area declined from 7.3 percent in 1990 to 5.8 percent in 1991, then rose slightly to a level still lower than during hyperinflation (6.7 percent in 1992), and kept on growing only in the following years. This retarded rise cannot be ascribed to stabilisation itself, but was mainly the effect of corresponding reforms, which included the opening of the economy as well as a massive privatisation programme that lay off the massive proportion of unproductive employment in the public sector, built up since the days of Perón.

---

[134] Végh demonstrates this with a simple model of a fully credible exchange rate-based stabilisation programme, and gives proof by examining historical cases. The reason for output costs being virtually zero in the case of a fully credible exchange rate-based stabilisation programme, in his model, is that, in a hyperinflation economy, everyone acts in a forward-looking manner, i.e. credibly changed conditions are immediately reflected in prices, with the effect that inflation is reduced abruptly at no real cost. See Végh (1995), pp. 43 ff. Ireland to some extent supplements this by stressing the role of fixed costs of price adjustments: high and hyperinflation stabilisation requires initial big changes of nominal prices – big enough to outweigh fixed costs of price adjustments. Hence, sticky prices pose no obstacle to immediate hyperinflation stabilisation – in contrast to low inflation stabilisation, where fixed costs prevent agents to immediately reflect small steps of disinflation in their prices, and so are responsible for real costs of disinflation. See Ireland (1997), as well as the comments delivered by Sargent (1997) and Blanchard (1997).

# 3 Stabilisation via Currency Board

The costs of following a sensible monetary rule are the price to pay
for the bad reputation that stems from a past of broken trust
and for the future economic development that regaining credibility
will eventually bring about.[135]

## 3.1 The Currency Board Idea

### 3.1.1 The Term

It is important to be aware that the term "currency board"[136] originally describes
the institution in the place (but not with all the tasks) of a central bank. A currency
board in this narrow sense is nothing more than a monetary authority that issues
money, keeps reserves, and on demand exchanges domestic currency against
reserves at a fixed rate. The naming originates from the early days of currency
boards when they were introduced as such institutions in British colonies in the 19th
century, mostly established without any formal legal protection, and mainly relying
on a long tradition of financial rectitude[137].

In the course of history and with the evolution of monetary theory, the institution
has lent its name to the monetary constitution of a country with a currency board. In
this wider sense, a currency board comprises the legal framework of the monetary
system as well as the body implementing it. The discussion of a currency board in
this sense extends to a discussion of a whole economic system[138]. To make this
perception more clear-cut, some authors use terms like "currency board system" or
"currency board arrangement" for this wider meaning of the term. This treatise uses
the term currency board in both senses, i.e. as the institution's as well as the
monetary constitution's name, according to the context of discussion.

---

[135] Zarazaga (1995b), p. 21.

[136] The correct German translation would be "Währungsausschuss", "Währungsrat", or
"Währungsamt", although the English term is used nearly exclusively even in German literature. For
Argentines, in contrast, the term "currency board" generally sounds unfamiliar; their currency board
was generally referred to as "la Convertibilidad" (from the name of the corresponding law "Ley de
Convertibilidad"), simply meaning "convertibility".

[137] See Hanke/Schuler (2000), p. 44.

[138] See Fuhrmann (1999), p. 86.

Also, some authors distinguish between currency boards which in all details follow the orthodox design (then called "currency boards") and currency boards that deviate from the orthodox concept in one or several respects, i.e. have somewhat modified rules (called "currency board-like systems", or "quasi-currency boards")[139]. Since most present and all "modern" (i.e. introduced in the second half of the 20th century) currency boards include at least some modifications as compared with the "pure" design[140], this distinction shall not be made here, i.e. the term currency board shall comprise both orthodox and modified currency boards. With the chosen terminology, this treatise sticks to the most widespread use in economic literature as well as political discussion.

### 3.1.2    The Concept

A currency board can be defined as a special case of a rules-based monetary system[141]. Like every rules-based system, it is designed to avoid losses incurred by discretionary decision-making, and to gain from enhanced credibility through rules-governed policies. A currency board's main feature is the nominal anchor in the form of a legally fixed exchange rate, which ties the domestic currency to a reserve currency[142]. This nominal anchor plays a pivotal role in the design not only of the monetary constitution, but also of the fiscal and structural disposition of a currency board country. With a fixed nominal anchor, a country undergoes severe self-restrictions in the use of policy tools.

The rule governing the system is very simple: the monetary authority (the currency board) is allowed to issue domestic currency only against reserves, at the

---

[139] See Hanke/Schuler (2000), p. 46, and Zarazaga (1995b), pp. 16-7.

[140] The only orthodox currency boards still in operation are those of the Falklands, the Cayman Islands, and Gibraltar. As Dolmas and Zarazaga state, today no independent country operates an orthodox currency board. See Dolmas/Zararaga (1995a), p. 1.

[141] Recommendable literature about currency boards in general: Baliño/Enoch (1997), Bennett (1994), Enoch/Gulde (1997), Enoch/Gulde (1998), Freytag (1998), Fuhrmann (1999), Fuhrmann/Richert (1995), Ghosh/Gulde/Wolf (1998), Gulde/Kähkönen/Keller (2000), Hanke (2000), Hanke/Schuler (2000), Humpage/McIntire (1995), O.V. (1997), Roubini (1998), Schuler (1992), Schuler (1998), Walters (1989), Williamson (1995), Zarazaga (1995a and c).

[142] The nominal anchor could also consist of two reserve currencies (as will be discussed for dual currency boards), or a basket of currencies, or even include a peg to a reserve currency with some variability (e.g. a pre-announced crawl), as Williamson (1995) states. These options have until now stayed purely theoretical, and the notion of a nominal anchor for a currency board has generally always implied a fixed peg to one reserve currency.

fixed exchange rate. These reserves may consist of a foreign currency or of other external reserve assets. The reserves requirement implies that the domestic monetary base (notes and coins in circulation) always is 100% backed by reserves. Increases in the monetary base can occur exclusively via corresponding increases in foreign reserves. Being subject to this rule, the monetary authority is deprived of some of the most important traditional central bank functions such as monetary regulation and lender of last resort activity. Furthermore, in tying money issue to existing reserves, deficit financing via the printing press is excluded, which is why fiscal policy in a currency board country is subject to hard budget constraints.

The main motivation for the adoption of a currency board is to produce price stability, especially in developing countries with long histories of inflation and devaluation, and in economies transforming from centrally planned to market economies, both of which typically face the need to adopt strong institutional constraints on their ability to inflate[143]. As the essence in the combat of inflation is credibility of policy measures, a currency board is designed to bring about a maximum of credibility of monetary policy. A stable currency will bring about lower interest rates: inflation as well as interest rates in a currency board country are supposed to approach the levels prevailing in the reserve currency country. Further effects of the choice of an exchange rate-based nominal anchor emanate from the requirement to earn reserves, hence to open up the economy and to strive for export-led growth. This in turn provides stimuli for fiscal, financial, and structural reforms[144].

Although a currency board is based on a very simple and transparent rule, a variety of different elements can govern its design. Indeed, pure currency boards in reality rarely existed; most countries have modified "orthodox" design elements in order to reflect local necessities or to gain a limited degree of flexibility. E.g., in many currency boards the minimum reserves are allowed to be less than 100% (thereby allowing for limited credit against monetary liabilities), whereas others prefer to keep backing at above 100% (in order to gain some flexibility and reserves for limited lender of last resort operations). While bringing about some flexibility in monetary policy, such modifications generally bear a risk to the currency board's

---

[143] This is the motivation for modern currency boards. The background of the introduction of colonial currency boards is different, as will be sketched later.

[144] See Fuhrmann/Richert (1995), p. 1039.

sustainability because they introduce discretionary power and therefore potentially reduce its credibility.

These considerations illustrate the central conflict inherent in the currency board idea which lies in the trade-off between credibility and flexibility of the system. This conflict regularly shapes discussions about costs and benefits of currency boards, in theory as well as in practice. A related source of dispute is the question of whether and when to view a currency board as a merely transitional or as a longer-term arrangement. Although possible exit options may be considered before setting up a currency board, their explicit pre-determination (via escape clauses) might again risk an undermining of its credibility from the beginning.

### 3.1.3    Currency Board vs. Other Fixed Exchange Rate Arrangements

A currency board is a special type of a fixed exchange rate arrangement. On the spectre of possible exchange rate regimes, which extends from the one extreme of freely floating exchange rates to the other extreme of definitely fixed exchange rates under a monetary union, the currency board is located between the less strict regime of fixed exchange rates (exchange rate pegged by commitment to an anchor currency, i.e. reversible at any time), and the stricter regime of official dollarisation (predominant or exclusive use of a foreign currency as legal tender)[145]. Hence, short to official dollarisation, a currency board is the most extreme option of exchange rate pegging a single country can choose[146].

Official dollarisation[147] is the closest relative to the currency board as it implies the same motivation and principle of importing the anchor's stability, and requires the same disciplined macroeconomic and structural policies. Accordingly, the strengths and weaknesses of dollarisation equal those of a currency board, with the main difference being the higher degree of irreversibility of the former. The gains of dollarisation in terms of transparency, credibility, monetary stabilisation, and

---

[145] See Mussa et al. (2000).

[146] Participation in a monetary union requires bi- or multilateral agreement.

[147] Unofficial dollarisation prevails when residents extensively use a foreign currency (in most cases the US-Dollar) alongside or instead of the domestic currency, and/or hold foreign currency notes or bank deposits to protect against high inflation in the domestic currency. Official dollarisation occurs when a government adopts a foreign currency as the predominant or exclusive legal tender.

impetus for fiscal discipline therefore are supposed to exceed those of a currency board[148].

Although a currency board also has much in common with a regime of conventionally fixed exchange rates, the distinction between the two (besides the wider discussion of fixed vs. floating exchange rate regimes, which shall not be extended here[149]) is directly relevant for the understanding of the motivation and the rationale of a currency board. As with the relation between dollarisation and currency board, the main advantage of a currency board over a system of purely fixed exchange rates is its higher implicit credibility[150]. This is mainly the effect of the high legal and procedural obstacles (often equalling the requirements for constitutional changes) in the way of modification or abolishment of the system, built-in to signal the high degree of self-commitment of the government[151]. With purely fixed exchange rates, in contrast, changing the exchange rate is a simple administrative matter, and expectations of such a change can by themselves bring about the expected change.

The legally fixed and publicised self-restriction in the use of monetary policy tools, mainly the exclusion of unbacked money issue, precludes fiscal policy relying on the monetisation of budget deficits, and thus requires sound fiscal policy. Time inconsistency and credibility problems of discretionary and/or commitment-bound policies, though not completely extinguishable by a currency board, are reduced as compared to a system of conventionally fixed exchange rates. The unwritten law of a currency board is, however, that the subordination of monetary and fiscal policy to the preservation of the fixed parity requires the acceptance of its costs, e.g. of prolonged periods of high interest rates, recession and deflation.

However, even constitutions can be changed, and credibility depends as much on rules and institutions as on attitudes. The simple self-commitment to a fixed exchange rate of one government may be as credible (or even more credible) as the

---

[148] The two main shortcomings of dollarisation as opposed to a currency board are that it requires the sacrifice of a country's own money, hence of a symbol of national sovereignty, as well as of any seigniorage income, as far as no bilateral agreement with the anchor country to share seigniorage income is sought. See Alesina/Barro (2001), p. 383, for some thoughts on possible compensation schemes between anchor and dollarised country.

[149] For a brief discussion of fixed vs. floating exchange rates see e.g. Hanke/Schuler (2000), pp. 67-8.

[150] See Alesina/Barro (2001), p. 382.

[151] See Eichengreen (1996), p. 238.

legal exchange rate fixed by another, not complying, government under a currency board scheme. Credibility of behaviour has to add to the credibility of rules. Thus, even for an established and stable currency board, a trade-off between rules and discretion similar to that of a conventional central bank may arise, e.g. in the question of the use of excess reserves[152].

### 3.1.4    Currency Board vs. Central Bank

Typically, a currency board operates in place of a central bank[153]. Like the latter, it is a government-owned body separate from the ministry of finance, and has the monopoly of issuing notes and coins. A currency board, however, does not have the high degree of discretionary power a typical central bank today has. The powers and functions of both institutions differ fundamentally. The stylised T-accounts of both institutions illustrate this.

In its orthodox form, a currency board issues base money (cash, i.e. notes and coins denominated in domestic currency) solely in return for the reserve currency at the fixed exchange rate. Its balance sheet comprises on the liability side the amount of base money issued, and the net worth, i.e. reserves exceeding the amount of issued money[154].

Sometimes, (unorthodox) currency boards also accept deposits of commercial banks or issue securities, both of which are subject to the same foreign reserve requirements as its notes and coins. In this case, the liabilities also comprise those deposits[155].

The asset side of a currency board consists solely of reserve currency holdings. These reserve holdings are directly related to the balance of payments position of the country, as reserves are acquired through current account surpluses and/or net capital inflows. Since money issue is tied one-to-one to the foreign reserves

---

[152] See Zarazaga (1995b), pp. 19-20

[153] A currency board can also operate as a parallel issuer alongside an existing central bank, although such cases have been rare and do not exist today. See Schuler (1998), p. 1.

[154] This difference (the net worth of a currency board) is usually maintained in a certain proportion in order to guard against the risk of a decrease in the market value of the assets. As the reserves of a currency board are legally required to be highly secure and liquid, this margin does not have to be high. In most cases, where the net worth exceeds 5 to 10 percent of the money issue, it has to be transferred to the government by law. See Williamson (1995), p. 3.

[155] The addition of deposits and securities does not significantly change the analysis if they are interchangeable for their holders and subject to the uniform foreign reserve requirement. See Hanke/Schuler (2000), pp. 7 and 43.

position, the monetary base varies with the variations in the balance of payments: a balance of payments surplus leads to an increase in the foreign reserves position and subsequently, other things equal, to an increase in the base money (and via the money multiplier, the money stock)[156]. Conversely, a shrinking money base is the consequence of a balance of payments deficit[157].

**Figure 24: Balance Sheet of a Currency Board**

| Assets | Liabilities |
|---|---|
| Liquid reserve currency assets | Notes and coins |
| | (Deposits of commercial banks) |
| | Net worth |

In the long run, monetary growth in the currency board country approximates the monetary growth rate of the reserve currency country, as can be illustrated with the simplifying notion that, for a currency board country to acquire reserves, the reserve currency country has to issue more money than its public wishes to hold. This effectuates decreasing interest rates and rising prices in the reserve currency country, which in turn creates arbitrage opportunities and leads to a capital account deficit in the reserve currency country. This deficit mirrors a capital account surplus in the currency board country, which causes its money supply to rise. This adjustment process is completely automatic and includes no discretionary action by the currency board.

The balance sheet of a typical central bank differs from a currency board's balance sheet in two main points. First, on the liability side, there are always notes and coins as well as deposits of commercial banks, the sum of both constituting the monetary base, M0. Again, the net worth of a central bank balances the difference between assets and liabilities.

On the assets side, a central bank holds liquid reserve currency assets, needed to manage the exchange rate, be it pegged or floating. Unlike a currency board, it is

---

[156] Hence, money supply under a currency board works in the same way as it does under a gold (or gold exchange) standard in which the central bank does not sterilise movements in reserves.

[157] Note that a currency board country does not have to maintain current account surpluses to expand the money stock. Net capital inflows may more than compensate for a current account deficit and allow for monetary expansion as well.

typically not required to hold a fixed ratio of foreign reserves to liabilities[158]. More important, besides those foreign reserves, a central bank also holds domestic assets. These domestic assets consist above all of government debt, but may also comprise commercial bank or even state industry debt. As in the case of foreign reserves, a central bank normally buys domestic assets against money, i.e. increases in the monetary base. It may in this way finance fiscal deficits through money creation. It may also buy domestic assets to prevent the monetary base from shrinking, e.g. when it has to sell foreign assets to support the exchange rate, i.e. it can sterilise unwanted contractionary effects on the monetary base[159].

**Figure 25: Balance Sheet of a Central Bank**

| Assets | Liabilities |
|---|---|
| Liquid reserve currency assets | Notes and coins |
| Domestic assets | Deposits of commercial banks |
| | Net worth |

As pointed out, a currency board has no discretion in monetary policy: it sells and buys foreign currency against domestic money according to the needs of the private sector, i.e. it acts completely passively. A central bank, in contrast, has the discretionary power to change the monetary base not only through foreign exchange transactions but also through the purchase or sale of domestic assets. It has also the power to change the exchange rate, to alter the foreign reserves ratio, or the regulations for commercial banks, powers that are inexistent for a currency board.

The discretionary power of a central bank includes lender of last resort activities to bail out banks in stress and so prevent, or mitigate, financial crises. Such lender of last resort activity is largely precluded for a currency board (or at least limited to a degree that is made possible by excess reserves earmarked for this purpose). This

---

[158] There may be binding minimum ratios, but a central bank may hold any ratio in excess of these.

[159] As Humpage/McIntire point out, this power to sterilise may be an advantage in the case of temporary balance of payments imbalances. If, however, the underlying causes of a balance of payments deficit are of structural and long-term nature, sterilisation can worsen capital outflows, nourish speculations of devaluation, and aggravate the situation. In such cases, the discretionary power of a central bank provides no advantage over the rule-bound currency board. See Humpage/McIntire (1995), p. 5.

limitation makes a sound banking system a significantly more vital interest under a currency board than under a central bank.

A currency board relies on a legally or even constitutionally fixed exchange rate. Central banks may operate under pegged or floating exchange rates, with pegged exchange rates typically not defined by law, and being subject to alterations at the will of the central bank or government.

A typical currency board does not regulate commercial banks. In most cases, it is the ministry of finance or a separate regulating office that passes banking regulations. Central banks, in contrast, often regulate commercial banks. The most basic form of regulation is the imposition of reserve requirements, according to which commercial banks are required to hold reserves in certain proportions of their liabilities at the central bank. Such reserve requirements are not imposed on banks under an orthodox currency board. Since the currency board does not guarantee the convertibility of bank deposits into notes and coins, commercial banks themselves are, in the absence of reserve requirements, responsible for holding enough notes and coins to be able to satisfy their depositors' conversion requests[160].

A currency board receives interest from its assets (reserves invested in highly liquid and secure foreign currency assets), but it does not pay interest on its liabilities (notes and coins issued). This interest income represents the currency board's gross profit (gross seigniorage). The deduction of the expenses of issuing notes and coins and of maintaining them in circulation generates the currency board's net profit (or net seigniorage)[161]. A central bank earns seigniorage from interest surpluses as well; they stem both from foreign and domestic assets. However, the most important source of seigniorage for a central bank may be inflation, caused by discretionary increases in the money supply[162]. As already pointed out, a currency board cannot create inflation, which is why this source of seigniorage is inexistent for an orthodox currency board.

Since a currency board is a very simple institution with very few and closely circumscribed functions, its activities are transparent and easy to monitor. A central bank, in contrast, has discretion in its activities and is by itself a market participant

---

[160] Put in the terms of monetary aggregates, under a currency board, M0 is backed 100% by foreign reserves, whereas broader measures of money supply, such as M1, M2, and M3, are not.

[161] See Hanke/Schuler (2000), pp. 61-2.

[162] For a concise definition of the so called "inflation tax" earned by a central bank see Roubini (1998), pp. 11-13.

and speculating institution, which is why its actions often are opaque or even sometimes need secrecy to be successful.

The rule-bound and transparent nature of a currency board makes it a politically sterile institution, whereas a central bank is, or may be, prone to political pressure, even if formally independent. The rules and transparency of a currency board give it a high degree of institutional credibility, which a central bank has not. The credibility of a central bank can at best be built up over years and decades through self-commitment and conduct, but there is no built-in credibility to begin with.

### 3.1.5    Excursus: Doctrinal History and the Currency Board Idea

A review of the main characteristics of the century-old debate over competing monetary theories and their opposing policy advices delivers valuable insights for the understanding of the ideological background of the currency board idea.

Much of the history of monetary theory reflects the struggle between the opposing mercantilist and classical camps. They lent their respective arguments to the views the Anti-Bullionist and Bullionist, later the Banking and Currency School adherents brought forward in the 19$^{th}$ century. Since then, depending on the economic problems prevailing at a time, the two camps have alternated in dominating the discussion. When unemployment was seen as the main problem, mercantilists with their prescription of cheap money to stimulate real activity tended to prevail, whereas classicals with their view of inflation as a purely monetary phenomenon were dominant in times when price stability was the main concern. Even today, mercantilist and classical views continue to compete for the more accurate explanation of the function of money and corresponding policy advices.

This paragraph will summarise the basic elements of this debate, focussing on the standpoints of mercantilists and classicals, and extending them to the famous English Banking-Currency controversy of the nineteenth century. While the debate continued and appeared in new editions in the twentieth century under Keynesian vs. monetarist flags, the early controversies already include the central aspects that are relevant for the understanding of the theoretical background of the currency board idea and of its supposed benefits as well as its drawbacks. It will become clear that the paradigm behind the currency board idea is directly derived from classical quantity views of money[163].

### 3.1.5.1 Doctrinal Positions: Mercantilist vs. Classical Views

The mercantilists' views take their origin in the pre-classical era of the 16th to 18th century[164]. Two outstanding proponents were John Stewart Law and Sir James Steuart. Their main argument was that a nation's wealth was constituted by its stock of precious metals. Countries without natural resources of precious metals (mainly gold) would have to accumulate their wealth through foreign trade. Accordingly, the mercantilist policy prescription included protectionist policies in order to achieve a permanent trade balance surplus matched by corresponding inflows of specie from abroad[165]. This prescription was based on an anti-quantity theory of money which held that (1) money stimulates trade, (2) price level and inflation are determined by real cost-push forces, (3) the interest rate is a purely monetary variable, determined solely by supply and demand of money and indicating the degree of scarcity of money, (4) cash not used for trade purposes is absorbed in idle hoards, (5) the money stock is endogenous, i.e. prices and real activity determine the amount and/or velocity of circulating money, so that the money stock passively adapts to the needs of trade, (6) overissue of money is impossible when money is backed by the nominal value of real property (land or commercial papers), and (7) discretion is superior to rules in the conduct of monetary policy.

Contrary to the mercantilists' proposition of wealth, classicals held that the wealth of a country consisted of its productive resources such as land, labour, and capital, as well as in the efficiency of their use. Both Adam Smith and David Ricardo stated that an optimal allocation of resources was best achieved via free trade rather than via mercantilist protectionism, thereby realising comparative advantages resulting from specialisation and division of labour. Classical monetary theory held that trade balance surpluses could not be permanent, as a country's additional specie would raise domestic prices, thus diminishing exports and stimulating imports until trade balance equilibrium would be restored (David Hume called this the "price-specie-flow-mechanism"). Similarly, according to the classical view,

---

[163] Indeed, the first proposal in the 20th century to install a "modern" currency board was made by John Maynard Keynes, then a Ricardian, who in 1918 designed a currency board with a sterling-backed rouble for war-ridden and inflation-plagued North Russia. See Hanke (2000), p. 52.

[164] For an overview over the mercantilist vs. classical debate, see Humphrey (1998).

[165] See Spahn (2001), pp. 63-8.

scarcity of money could not exist, since a country's trade could be driven with any quantity of money, on the ground that prices ultimately adjust proportionately to any change in the money stock.

Cost-push theories of inflation were rejected, as price increases were exclusively seen as resulting from increases in the money stock. Any rise of factor costs, e.g. of wages, would make labour-intensive goods more expensive, thereby reducing expenses for capital-intensive goods, which would lead to a cheapening of the latter. In the classical view, cost-pushes lead to a change in relative prices rather than to general inflation.

The mercantilist "money stimulates trade-doctrine" was shown by the classicals to be valid at best in the short run. Changes in the money stock in their view could initially affect output and employment because of the stickiness of prices (prices fail to adjust immediately due to imperfect information of price-setters) and because of distribution effects (additional money is initially concentrated in few hands and disperses only gradually). Eventually, however, prices would adjust fully to the new money stock and output would return to its initial level, so that, in the long run, money would be neutral.

Discretion in monetary policy was deemed to be destabilising: classicals doubted the knowledge and motivation of policy authorities. They advocated rules in order to stabilise real activity and to facilitate automatic adjustment mechanisms. One such rule was the gold standard: with a fixed currency price of gold and an assumed fairly steady gold price of goods, money prices of goods could be stabilised, and money could reliably function as unit of account and medium of exchange, rather than providing a source of financial crisis, as the mercantilist prescription would do in the classical view.

The mercantilist fear of deficient aggregate demand was, in classicals' eyes, unfounded. They argued that the act of production itself included the remuneration of factors, and thus the creation of the incomes necessary to buy the products off the markets. Factor incomes would either be spent or saved, with saving, via its translation into investment, eventually also leading to spending. In this way, each supply would create its own demand[166]. Permanent underemployment of resources could not occur in their view.

Classicals saw the interest rate as a real magnitude determined by productivity rather than as a merely monetary phenomenon. Accordingly, monetary control could

---

[166] This is Jean Baptiste Say's "law of markets".

not permanently influence the "natural" rate of interest. An increase of money supply could initially depress the loan rate of interest, but, as prices started rising, loan demand would also rise, which eventually would lead to higher interest rates again.

Finally, classicals argued that John Law's recommendation of a nominal backing of money through a linkage to the nominal value of real assets would render prices indeterminate, as random shocks raising prices of the assets would lead to monetary expansion, which itself could bid up asset prices again, and so on. Price stability in their view required a different principle of monetary limitation.

Figure 26 summarises the key points of discussion in the mercantilist vs. classical debate that constituted the base of the famous Banking-Currency controversy.

**Figure 26: Mercantilist vs. Classical Doctrines**

|  | **Mercantilists** | **Classicals** |
|---|---|---|
| Source of wealth | Precious metals | Productive resources |
| Prescription to achieve wealth | Protectionism in order to achieve permanent trade balance surpluses | Free trade in order to achieve optimal allocation of resources |
| Nature of money | Money stimulates trade | Money is neutral |
| Determinants of prices | Real cost-push forces | Stock of money |
| Nature of the interest rate | Purely monetary magnitude, influenced by changes in the supply of money | Real magnitude, not susceptible to monetary changes |
| Excessive money | Absorbed in idle hoards, not causing inflation | Causing prices to rise proportionately |
| Determination of the money stock | Endogenous (causality running from prices and economic activity to money: "reverse causality") | Exogenous (causality running from the exogenously set money stock to prices) |
| Overissue of money | Impossible ("real bills doctrine") | Possible, leading to price-level increases |
| Monetary policy prescription | Discretion | Rules |

### 3.1.5.2 The Bullionist and Banking-Currency Controversies

**The Early 19<sup>th</sup> Century Bullionist Controversy**

The Bullionist controversy emerged in the early 19<sup>th</sup> century focussing on the question of whether paper money should be convertible into gold on demand. This debate later led to the so-called Banking-Currency School controversy of the 1840s, which again laid the ground for a debate over the nature of money that in many ways is still continuing today.

In the United Kingdom of the 18<sup>th</sup> century, private banks issued banknotes which circulated as money[167]. These notes included a claim on gold bullion held by the bank. The conversion of paper money to gold was granted at any time since banks issued notes on the basis of gold reserves they actually held in their vaults.

At the end of the 18<sup>th</sup> century, a major bank run occurred in Britain following rumours of the landing of French troops on English soil. Customers hurried to their banks and demanded conversion of their notes into gold bullion. The British government subsequently averted a major banking crisis by allowing banks to suspend convertibility temporarily. Since convertibility was not restored immediately[168], banks continued issuing notes without respecting their convertibility into gold.

These events triggered an intellectual debate among lawyers, bankers, and statesmen over the question of whether convertibility into gold should be maintained or not. The "Bullionist" group demanded convertibility whereas the "Anti-Bullionists" argued for the maintenance of the prevailing status of suspension.

The Bullionists[169] argued with the temptation for banks to "overissue" notes without the duty to grant convertibility. This would lead to an excess supply of money, hence to a cheapening of money and to inflation. The Anti-Bullionists' argument was based on the mercantilist "real bills doctrine" which stated that banknotes were issued by banks against merchants' bills of exchange, i.e., according to the "needs of trade" [170]. Provided that the repayment of these bills was secure, there could be no excess issue of banknotes since they merely accommodated real transactions. Even if excess issue should happen, excessive

---

[167] For a detailed historical description and analysis of the Bullionist Controversy, see Laidler (1989), Davies (2002), pp. 293 ff, as well as Spahn (2001), pp. 69-83.

[168] Convertibility remained suspended from 1797 to 1821.

[169] Famous Bullionists were Henry Thornton, John Wheatley, and David Ricardo.

[170] Leading Anti-Bullionists were Richard Torrens, Bosanquet, and James Mill.

banknotes would eventually return to the banks in exchange for deposits or gold or in the repayment of loans, as the so-called "reflux principle" brought forward by the Anti-Bullionists held. Thus, inflation could never be the result of any excess issue[171].

History first seemed to support the Bullionists: the early 1800s saw a period of inflation, peaking in 1814. Anti-Bullionists saw in it the result of government purchases during the Napoleonic wars. The Bullionists argued for a resumption of convertibility, which was eventually restored in 1821. However, during 1815 to 1830, a prolonged period of deflation was recorded in the wake of the end of the Napoleonic wars. Thus, historical evidence was far from clearly supporting one of the views.

**The 1840s Banking-Currency Controversy**

The restoring of convertibility in 1821 had raised the question on whether the note issue of the convertible gold-standard currency required further regulation to prevent overissue. The predecessors of the Currency School, the Bullionists, had argued that such control was not necessary. Overissue would lead to domestic price increases, making British goods more expensive, which in turn would lead to increased conversion into gold in order to buy the relatively cheaper foreign goods. The ensuing drain on gold would force banks to restrict their issue, causing the money stock to contract and prices to fall to the initial level, and eventually give halt to the gold drain. Bullionists saw convertibility as its own guarantor.

However, history seemed to contradict this position: several monetary crises in the 1820s and 1830s had shown that the classical adjustment mechanism was far from self-correcting. Pure convertibility still had left banks with discretion in the trade-off between safety and profits since they faced no minimum reserve ratio. This had led to continued note issue in spite of concomitant gold outflows and to subsequent violent contractions sending monetary shocks throughout the economy[172].

The Currency School proponents[173] therefore concluded that banks' discretion in the note issue should be removed. Their proposal was to require a one-for-one change in issue with the change in gold reserves, and thereby to realise the "principle of metallic fluctuation" for a mixed (paper and coin) currency. Overissue,

---

[171] See Laidler (1989), p. 64.

[172] See Davies (2002), p. 312.

[173] They included Lord Overstone, James R. McCulloch, Thomas Joplin, Samuel M. Longfield, and former Anti-Bullionist Richard Torrens.

which via the balance of payments mechanism and the gold drain could threaten convertibility and create procyclical fluctuations, in their eyes could be prevented with this rule.

The debate seemed to be brought to an end by the Banking Act of 1844 which installed a fractional convertibility: for a fixed amount (equalling the amount of circulating money), one third of the value had to be covered by gold, whereas new issues of banknotes had to be 100% covered by gold[174]. The act also installed a monopoly of note issue, and split the Bank of England into a note-issuing Issue Department and a deposit-taking Banking Department[175]. The gold reserve requirement intended overexpansion to be corrected automatically, instantaneously and smoothly. It embodied the direct policy application of the classical price-specie-flow-mechanism.

The Currency School supported the act as it limited the amount of note issue, and thus in their opinion prevented inflation. Proponents of the Banking School[176] argued against it. Their arguments reflected those previously brought forward by the Anti-Bullionists[177].

In the aftermath of the 1844 Banking Act, convertibility had to be suspended three times[178], lending some credibility to the Banking School's arguments. However, gold parity to note issue was generally maintained until World War I.

### Findings with Hindsight

The Banking-Currency School debate and the ensuing historical experience in retrospect revealed several findings. First, the Currency School's prescription of a control of the volume of notes and coins failed insofar as it did not include the control of deposits, which formed a growing part of the circulating medium[179].

---

[174] The amount of 14 billion pounds, equalling two thirds of the estimated money in circulation, was regarded as the "hard core" of circulation that would probably never return to the banking system, and was not subject to the convertibility requirement. Apart from this unbacked amount, any note issue had to be fully backed by gold reserves. See Schuler (1992), pp. 10-1.

[175] See Spahn (2001), pp. 80-3.

[176] Famous Banking School adherents were Thomas Tooke, John Fullarton, and the young John Stuart Mill.

[177] A third, mostly neglected, group of participants in the debate was the Free Banking School, which favoured a system of free competition of banks including in the field of note issue, and which accordingly denied the need (and usefulness) of a central bank. See Schwartz (1989), pp. 44-46.

[178] In 1847, 1857, and 1866.

[179] See e.g. Spahn (2001), p. 84, and Schuler (1992), p. 11.

Therefore, since there was no reserve requirement for deposits, even after 1844, banks possessed significant room for discretionary control over deposits. Second, Currency School proponents refused to recognise the necessity of lender of last resort rescue in coping with financial panics. By the end of the nineteenth century it was widely accepted that liberal lending was the best way to deal with internal drains, which were caused by panic-led demand for gold and Bank of England notes[180].

On the other hand, the Banking School's real bills doctrine, which claimed that note issue tied to loan demand for productive purposes would prevent inflation, always suffered from not being able to close its open front: the sequence of rising production prices, correspondingly rising loan demand and note issue to finance the same level of real transactions was indefinite – inflation justified the monetary expansion necessary to sustain it. The real bills criterion failed to limit the quantity of money in existence[181].

### 3.1.5.3 The Currency Board and Classical Monetary Theory

The above outline of the century-old debate identifies the currency board idea as a clearly classical one[182]. With the currency board's main targets of disinflation and stabilisation, pursued via self-restriction in monetary (and, effectively, fiscal) policy, its location within the doctrinal spectre is evident. Although direct reference to the Currency School's ideas was rare in the official documents setting up early colonial currency boards, the historical analysis of the debates surrounding them leaves no doubt about their intellectual origins[183].

It is telling to review the fate of the currency board idea since its origins, as it goes in parallel with the history of economic thought, and with the development of political powers implementing it. Up to the 1950s, industrialised nations by and large kept to the gold standard, and imposed ideologically corresponding monetary constitutions, currency boards, on their colonies. Growing independence of colonial territories, the stress, and eventual abandonment of the Bretton Woods system, and

---

[180] The Bank of England accepted the doctrine of the lender of last resort in 1890, following the Baring Brothers crisis. See Schuler (1992), p. 12, and Spahn (2001), p. 86.

[181] See Schwartz (1989), p. 43.

[182] This is also made clear by Sir John Hicks: „On strict Ricardian principles, there should have been no need for central banks. A currency board, working on a rule, should have been enough." Hicks (1967), pp. 167-8.

[183] See Schuler (1992), pp. 8-12.

the surge of Keynesian thought, all played major roles in the decline of the currency board idea since the 1950s. The ensuing decades-long inflation and deficit spending experience of industrialised and developing countries alike triggered the surge of classical monetary theory and the primacy of price stability in the 1980s. Classical monetary theory has since largely set the tone in monetary policy in industrialised as well as developing countries. The financial experience of countries that had departed from currency boards without being able to install credible alternative monetary policies, however, proved to be dismal[184]. This experience, complemented by the breakdown of the Soviet bloc and the huge transformation task its economies faced, prepared the ground for a renaissance of the currency board idea in the 1990s, which, despite the near-catastrophic collapse of Argentina's currency board in early 2002, still seems to be lasting.

### 3.1.5.4 From Colonial to Present-Day Currency Boards

#### Rationale of Colonial Currency Boards

Currency boards were first established, and got most widespread, in British colonies in the 19th century. While a currency board had been proposed for the Province of Canada as soon as in 1841[185], the first currency board to be introduced was that of Mauritius, in 1849. The design of the currency boards was implicitly based on the ideas of the Currency School. According to one contemporary, currency boards were meant to "unite the 'advantages of cheapness and convenience which belongs to a paper currency' with the 'steadiness and uniformity of value, of a metallic currency, ... [thus, they] ought to be so regulated that the amount in circulation should vary according to the laws which govern the latter'."[186]

Before the establishment of currency boards, notes and coins of the imperial power were used in the colonies, where they served as a stable means of exchange and as a store of value. These were in most cases issued locally[187], by chartered

---

[184] Walters ascribes their degeneration to a large part to the abolishment of currency boards: "It is difficult to avoid the conclusion that the financial instability brought in train by the abrogation of the currency board system has played a considerable role in this process." Walters (1989), p. 110.

[185] See Schuler (1992), p. 14.

[186] Earl Grey, British Secretary of State for the Colonies, cited after Gunasekera (1962). See Baliño/Enoch (1997), p. 2.

[187] Walters assumes that Bank of England notes were issued exclusively in Britain, with the consequence that the risk of loss or destruction of notes in the colonies and the complications of

colonial or imperial banks, which were granted the right to issue Bank of England notes. However, their note issue was limited by legal restrictions in the maximum amount and in the denomination of notes. This caused frequent (and artificial) note shortages in some colonies. Economic theory and government policy of the time regarded those restrictions as necessary, and were opposed to unrestricted issue for fear of inflation. Regulated, monopolistic issue by a monetary authority, the currency board, seemed to provide the solution[188].

Hence, the main motivation for the establishment of currency boards was to give the colonies a monetary framework that provided stability of currency, and that took account of the colonies' monetary needs by easing trade-related money transfers between imperial power and colonies[189]. Moreover, with currency boards, the colonies were given a certain degree of independence by granting them their own, locally issued, currency, as well as the source of income from seigniorage, which was obtained by investing reserves in interest-bearing, secure, and sufficiently liquid assets.

Early currency boards differed from later currency boards in several respects. Initially, British currency boards redeemed their notes in gold or silver coins only. The West African currency board, introduced in 1913, was the first to redeem in pound sterling, and with this became the prototype for later (also non-British) currency boards, all of which adopted the sterling (or other currency) exchange standard[190]. Another difference between earlier and later currency boards refers to the type of assets allowed as reserves. Most early currency boards were allowed to invest in foreign, i.e. imperial or other non-colonial, government securities, but not in securities of their own colony. Later, currency boards were typically allowed to hold

---

replacing worn notes delivered a major argument for the establishment of currency boards. See Walters (1989), pp.109-10.

[188] See Schuler (1992), pp. 13-4.

[189] E.g., a money transfer from the colonial power (Britain) to the colony basically works as follows: the payer in Britain deposits reserve currency notes with the Bank of England, which again deposits them with the currency board in the colony. The currency board changes the notes into the local currency at the fixed parity and pays them out to the payee (or the payee's branch bank). This transaction causes the money supply in the colony to expand by the transferred amount. A payment from the colony to Britain works in reverse, causing the colonial money supply to shrink.

[190] See Schuler (1992), p. 18.

local securities up to a certain degree, which meant a deviation from the strict currency board design towards more central bank-like options[191].

### Currency Boards Since 1849

Shortly after the introduction of the first colonial currency board on Mauritius in 1849, the New Zealand currency board was established in 1850, followed in the late 19th and early 20th century by many Asian, African, and Middle Eastern currency boards[192]. Besides in almost all British colonies all over the world, currency boards also operated in Argentina (1902), the Philippines (1903), then a US colony, and Panama (1904). Later non-British currency boards include North Russia (1918)[193], Danzig (1923), Ireland (1928), Somalia (1950), Libya (1950), Sudan (1957), North Yemen (1964), and Swaziland (1974). In French colonies, systems similar to currency boards were put in place (the so-called "Instituts d'Emission"), notably in the still existing CFA-Zone, which consists of West and Central African countries in a currency union, with the CFA-franc linked to the French franc.

The currency board system reached its greatest extent in the 1950s. By then, currency boards operated in approximately 50 countries, most of them (former) British colonies, among them the economically important territories of Hong Kong and Singapore, as well as New Zealand. After the 1950s, the currency board system experienced a swift decline. By 1974, it had shrunk to 10 countries, again nearly all existing or former British colonies. The reason for this decline was that most territories with currency boards, after having gained independence, quickly sought to underline their independence by creating their own sovereign currency and installing central banks. This trend was also fed by the conviction, prevailing among economists and politicians at the time, that monetary arrangements with central banking better fit a country's economic, and especially development, needs and were superior to the currency board system, which then was perceived as rather antiquated[194]. In the period between 1974 and the 1990s, the only newly

---

[191] See Schuler (1992), pp. 35-6.

[192] Schuler (1992) gives a comprehensive study of the history of currency boards, also containing a complete list of currency boards (excluding currency boards established after 1990), pp. 107-12.

[193] Interestingly, this currency board was instigated by John Maynard Keynes, and installed by the British Treasury. See Williamson (1995), p. 5.

[194] At the time, currency boards were even regarded by some as manipulative colonialist or neo-imperialist monetary mechanisms. See Walters (1989), p. 111.

established currency board was that of Hong Kong, installed in 1983 and still operating today[195].

The 1990s, finally, saw a renaissance of the currency board idea. This revival was closely related to the acknowledged quality of currency boards (or, for that matter, any monetary regime based on an external anchor[196]) to bring about currency stability. Currency boards were no longer seen as monetary constitutions adequate for dependent economies, but were rather perceived as a means to provide stability for countries that suffered major structural and political breaks, as well as for developing countries with long records of political and economic instability. The breakdown of the Soviet Union and the emergence of a number of new market economies in Eastern Europe, as well as the independence of post-war Ex-Yugoslavian countries, yielded constellations in which the currency board idea gained new attraction.

Among the transforming countries of the former Soviet block, Estonia introduced its currency board in 1992 (backed by the German mark, now the Euro), Lithuania followed in 1994 (first backed by the US-Dollar, since 2002 by the Euro), and Bulgaria in 1997 (German mark, now Euro). Bosnia and Herzegovina introduced their new currency, linked to the German mark, now Euro, under a system resembling a currency board in 1998.

Among the inflation-plagued developing countries, Argentina was the sole to introduce its (latest[197]) currency board in 1991, with the objective to stop hyperinflation. This is the only recent case of a currency board that had to be abandoned under stress, in early 2002. Some other Latin American countries recently chose a similar, if stricter, path through outright dollarisation (as did Ecuador, in 1999, and El Salvador, in 2001).

Today, currency boards are operating on the Bermudas, the Cayman Islands, the Falkland Islands, in Gibraltar, on the Faroe Islands, in Brunei Darussalam, Djibouti, Estonia, Lithuania, Bulgaria, and Hong Kong. Systems resembling currency boards are operating in the Eastern Caribbean, the CFA-Zone, in Singapore, Latvia, and Bosnia-Herzegovina[198]. Recommendations to introduce currency boards have

---

[195] Hong Kong had given up its second currency board, which dated from 1945, in 1974.

[196] See Bordo/Jonung (2001), p. 266.

[197] In Argentina, currency boards had already been operating from 1902 to 1914, and from 1927 to 1929.

[198] See Hanke/Schuler (2000), pp. 41-2.

been made, during the 1990s, for countries such as Mexico (after the 1995 crisis), Peru, Brazil, and Russia.

## 3.2 The Specifics and Functioning of a Currency Board

### 3.2.1 Constitutional Elements of a Currency Board

#### 3.2.1.1 Anchor Currency

The choice of the anchor currency should be guided by several considerations. First, the anchor currency should be selected among stable currencies with deep and developed financial markets that offer a broad range of international financial instruments. The anchor currency therefore should be one of the few large international reserve currencies[199], which include the Dollar and the Euro (with the yen being a further, but recently questioned candidate). A long record of low inflation, high credibility, full convertibility, and low real interest rates are the qualities that make them likely to continue their good performance. With the choice of a stable anchor currency, the currency board country strives to import the stability of the chosen reserve currency.

Within this set of possible anchor currencies, the most important criteria relate to the question of which reserve currency is best able to shelter the currency board country from real shocks inside and outside the currency area. This is a crucial question, since the currency board country is deprived of monetary policy options to deal with such shocks and therefore has to minimise these risks as far as possible. The best choice of anchor currency is given when (1) as many countries as possible, whose enterprises compete with those of the currency board country, share the peg to the reserve currency, i.e. form a single currency area with the reserve currency, when (2) a high proportion of the external trade of the currency board country takes place with the reserve currency country, and when (3) the production patterns of the currency board country differ significantly from those of the reserve currency country. As Freytag (1998)[200] shows, within these three criteria, the requirement of a high proportion of bilateral trade with the reserve

---

[199] Few currency boards have chosen other than one of the international reserve currencies. This happened mostly for historical reasons, e.g. in the case of Brunei which is pegged to the Singapore Dollar. See Enoch/Gulde (1997), p. 4.

[200] See Freytag (1998), pp. 5-11.

currency country seems to be the least indispensable, i.e. if it is not met, the damage caused by real shocks is smaller than if another of the three is not met[201].

Expected future shifts in trade patterns should be taken into consideration as well when choosing an anchor currency[202]. While a basket of reserve currencies might best reflect the trade patterns of a country and might provide a better shelter against external shocks, its disadvantages in terms of minor transparency and higher obstacles to credibility as well as higher transaction and management costs make it rarely seem a preferable option for a currency board country[203].

Finally, the domestic acceptance of the reserve currency may also provide an argument for the choice of the anchor currency. An economy already penetrated by a parallel currency that is highly valued among market participants might decide to choose this currency as its anchor even if trade patterns would predict a different anchor currency. Such a constellation could again provide a case where the missing criterion of strong trade connections with the reserve currency country would not provide a sufficient argument against the choice of an anchor currency that otherwise meets the above criteria.

The implications of the choice of reserve currency for the reserve country are also worthwhile considering. If the reserve currency has already been in wide use in the currency board country, the demand for it will probably decrease with the successful introduction of the currency board since people now can safely change their reserves into domestic currency. At the same time, the demand of commercial banks might rise as a consequence of reserve requirements or intensified capital flows, so that the net effect may be unclear. However, most currency board countries are small in economic terms, while the typical reserve currency economies

---

[201] Suppose for this purpose a positive productivity shock in the reserve currency country with a subsequent appreciation of the reserve currency. Worst would be the effects for the currency board country if production patterns in the currency board country did not differ much from those in the reserve currency country, but the criteria of strong trade connections with the reserve currency country and a large currency area pegged to the reserve currency were given: a large part of external trade of the currency board country would suffer. If, however, the criterion of strong trade connections with the reserve currency country were missing, but the other two were given, the pressure of such an external shock would be significantly smaller (also smaller than under the third possible constellation, a large currency area missing) since only small parts of the currency board country's exports would be affected by the appreciation. See Freytag (1998), pp. 10-1.

[202] See Rose/van Wincoop (2001), p. 388.

[203] See Williamson (1995), p. 24.

are big and their currencies in global use, so that the initial monetary effect of a currency board on the reserve currency country usually will be small[204].

### 3.2.1.2 Fixed Exchange Rate

The determination of the exchange rate is an important as well as difficult issue. Doubtlessly, the "appropriate" exchange rate is ideally identical with the exchange rate determined by market forces[205]. However, an undervalued exchange rate (as compared to the appropriate exchange rate) potentially entails several advantages: (1) The amount of foreign exchange needed to provide full backing of the monetary base is reduced, and (2) a built-in "cushion" of undervaluation can be designed to compensate ex ante for an expected real exchange rate appreciation during the initial phase of the currency board, and so to protect the currency board from a preventable overvalued exchange rate from the beginning. (3) Finally, an undervalued exchange rate may facilitate exports (although the question of a competitive exchange rate is seldom an issue in a country adopting a currency board with the typically preceding accelerating inflation and devaluation cycles[206]. On the contrary, the consideration that too expensive imports might hamper a modernisation of the economy might again speak against an undervalued exchange rate[207]).

An appreciation of the real exchange rate in the early phase of a currency board is likely to occur because of four facts. (1) A certain degree of inflation inertia will persist during the first months after introduction of a currency board, produced by lags in the adaptation of expectations of market participants and by structural rigidities (e.g. backward-looking indexation clauses, or overlapping contracts)[208]. (2) Concomitant measures at the time of fixing the exchange rate, such as price liberalisations, may produce price effects and prevent inflation from immediately approaching the level prevailing in the reserve currency country. (3) Growth in the currency board country may be higher than in the reserve currency country, which

---

[204] See Hanke/Schuler (2000), p. 55.

[205] Where the market rate is not clearly detectable, e.g. because of restricted foreign exchange markets, a brief period of unrestricted floating of the domestic currency may precede the determination of the exchange rate in order to have an indication for the unrestricted market rate.

[206] See Bennett (1994), p. 190.

[207] See Hanke/Schuler (2000), p. 49.

[208] See Williamson (1995), p. 21.

causes demand for labour, goods, and services, and hence their prices, to rise. (4) Net inflows of capital may increase demand and create inflationary pressure[209].

However, there are drawbacks of the tempting option to fix the exchange rate at an undervalued level. The most important is that, by commencing the currency board with an over-depreciated exchange rate, the credibility of the arrangement might be reduced from the start. The choice of a parity significantly below the prevailing exchange rate therefore bears the risk of giving an impulse to domestic inflation, which by itself would re-establish the previous real exchange rate.

Full foreign exchange backing can be obtained not only through the choice of a depreciated exchange rate, but also through a variation in the definition of reserves used[210], as well as in the definition of currency board liabilities to be backed[211]. Hence, for a country lacking reserves, the choice of the exchange rate most likely involves a trade-off between a per se highly credible full covering of a broad set of domestic liabilities through a narrow set of reserves (with the concomitant, potentially credibility-reducing high degree of devaluation), and a less credible wider definition of reserves to back a narrower definition of liabilities (which necessitates a smaller devaluation)[212]. The decision of whether and to which degree excess reserves for limited lender of last resort operations should be held from the beginning is closely connected and basically faces the same credibility conflict[213]. One way to achieve the necessary foreign exchange backing may be to allow for international reserves being gradually built up, or even to borrow the missing reserves through a medium or long term foreign loan. With strong underlying policies, the commitment to build up full reserve cover over time may be credible enough to grant sustainability of the regime.

A country adopting a currency board has to bear in mind that each detail deviating from the orthodox architecture of the currency board bears a potential to diminish its credibility and to evoke speculative attacks, so that costs and benefits have to be carefully weighed. This is especially true for such an obvious and transparent issue as the degree of reserve backing. While some economists

---

[209] See Freytag (1998), pp. 4-5.

[210] Foreign exchange reserves can be specified net or gross, and can include or exclude long term debt.

[211] They may include solely currency in circulation or (in the case of an unorthodox currency board) also deposits at the currency board.

[212] See Enoch/Gulde (1998), p. 5.

[213] See Bennett (1994), p. 201.

completely reject the adoption of an (even only slightly) undervalued exchange rate[214], it is certainly prudent to say that the degree of initial overdepreciation in setting the parity should be tightly limited in order to achieve maximum credibility while allowing for a small margin of inflationary inertia, but addressing structural problems as far as possible directly, instead of indirectly via the exchange rate choice.

### 3.2.1.3 Full Convertibility

A currency's function as a medium of exchange depends on its convertibility. There are different degrees of convertibility: (1) Cash convertibility means the ability of a currency to exchange bank deposits for notes and cash on demand, (2) commodity convertibility is the ability of a currency to buy domestic goods and services, and (3) foreign exchange convertibility comprises the unrestricted ability of a currency to buy foreign goods and services, including foreign currencies.

A currency with all three types of convertibility has full convertibility. Most currencies of developed countries are fully convertible, while most developing countries have currencies with restricted convertibility. The most typical restrictions of foreign exchange convertibility refer to capital account transactions (the purchase of foreign financial assets), whereas current account transactions (the purchase of foreign goods and services) are generally less restricted. The arguments for capital controls originate in fears of capital flight or, on the contrary, of massive foreign investment (which increases domestic prices of nontraded goods and reduces the competitiveness of domestic exporters), and in the fear of moral hazard for domestic banks and industries that rely on a bail-out by the government through devaluation in the case of unsustainable capital burdens through foreign debt[215].

Full convertibility is a constitutional element of a currency board because it is the precondition for the creation of a complete substitutability between local and anchor currency, for the reduction of country and currency risk premia, and hence for the successful import of stability[216]. To underline its commitment to full convertibility, a currency board should keep its exchange window open for anyone, including the public, and not impose any minimum or maximum exchange amounts. It should demonstrate that it stands ready under all circumstances to exchange currency board notes into the reserve currency. The currency board should not

---

[214] See Hanke/Schuler (2000), p. 49.

[215] See Hanke/Schuler (2000), pp. 21-2.

[216] See Fuhrmann/Richert (1995), p. 1035.

charge commission fees for the exchange, and keep trading spreads at zero or minimal, in order to minimise barriers to capital movements and arbitrage, and to keep the link to the reserve currency as close as possible[217].

Note that unlimited convertibility does not mean that a currency board is responsible for the conversion of deposits denominated in local currency into currency board notes and coins, nor for their conversion into the reserve currency[218]. This is the responsibility of banks. The currency board itself is only concerned with the convertibility of the notes and coins it issues.

While in some cases an immediate establishment of full convertibility (including full capital account convertibility) may be possible, other cases may require a more gradualist approach. This may be necessary when the banking sector is very fragile, and when revealed illiquidities and insolvencies of banks under the rigid system of a currency board might trigger bank runs. The purchase of domestic currency might then be restricted to the use for current account transactions, and it might be required that foreign exchange earnings be kept in the country[219]. In such cases, the process of adjustment to monetary disequilibria has to work over trade volumes and current account effects, an adjustment that is less smooth and rapid than over capital flows. In the course of stabilisation and strengthening of the financial sector, ongoing liberalisation of capital transactions will be facilitated in order to allow for a closer adaptation to the lower reserve country interest rates and for a maximum degree of substitutability between local and anchor currency[220].

### 3.2.1.4 Conduct of Monetary Policy

In its purest form, a currency board not only refrains from those components of monetary policy that imply discretionary elements, such as open market and lender of last resort operations, but also from any form of regulation or supervision of the financial sector. An orthodox currency board leaves financial institutions completely on their own, relying on the disciplining effect of the knowledge that there is no lender of last resort[221]. The currency board's credibility is based on the commitment to a completely passive conduct, and on the limitation of its responsibility to the provision of a fully backed money base.

---

[217] See Hanke/Schuler (2000), pp. 58-9, as opposed to Enoch/Gulde (1997), pp. 21-3.
[218] See Caprio et al. (1996), p. 630.
[219] See Bennett (1994), p. 202.
[220] See Enoch/Gulde (1997), pp. 25-6.
[221] See Eichengreen (2001b), p. 269.

However, the central role of foreign reserves makes a currency board country particularly vulnerable to external shocks. As it is deprived of active policy instruments to cope with such shocks, it is widely undisputed that a currency board should enact prudential regulations, which above all aim at structural and systemic characteristics of the banking system in order to make it as robust as possible and to reduce the need for situational support[222]. Reserve requirements and capital adequacy rules[223] are among the most undisputed elements of financial sector regulation. Additional prudential regulations may concern interest rate and liquidity risks, aiming at mismatches in the maturity structure of banks' assets and liabilities[224]. Of course, a strong banking supervision, proper accounting standards, and stringent disclosure requirements are preconditions for the enforcement of such regulations[225].

That said, although conflicting with a currency board's basic principle of limited discretion and even more clearly deviating from the "orthodox" currency board design, a certain capacity to deliver lender of last resort support might nevertheless be prudential in order to retain the ability to avert incipient banking crises, and to contain their possibly contagious effects, especially under conditions of uncertainty or large external shocks. Such lender of last resort capacity can, as long as it is funded by excess reserves set aside for this purpose, and follows specified rules, strengthen confidence in the domestic banking system and as a consequence lower intermediation spreads, without exposing the system too much to the imminent problems of reduced credibility and moral hazard[226].

---

[222] For transparency, credibility, and organisational reasons, a division of the institution currency board is advisable: a currency department then solely undertakes the tasks of exchanging domestic against reserve currency and holding the reserves, whereas a banking department is responsible for the monetary policy issues. See Fuhrmann/Richert (1995), p. 1038.

[223] Capital adequacy ratios are recommended to be fixed well above the Basle standard of 8 percent, and probably even above the 12 percent discussed for banks in emerging markets, given the greater riskiness of banking in developing economies and the higher need for self-reliance in currency board countries. See Enoch/Gulde (1997), pp. 13-4.

[224] See Baliño/Enoch (1997), p. 21.

[225] Banking supervision should ideally be transferred to an independent agency. Where the currency board itself undertakes banking supervision, it should credibly demonstrate that currency board rules will not be circumvented in case of banking sector difficulties. See Enoch/Gulde (1998), p. 7.

[226] See Baliño/Enoch (1997), p. 20.

## Control of Private Money Creation

A completely exogenous money supply and inflation rate would imply the absence of private sector money creation, as would be the case with a reserve requirement for commercial banks at 100%[227]. However, the 100% reserve requirement does not extend to commercial banks, and private money creation works under a currency board as in any two-tier banking system. Reserve to deposit ratios of commercial banks (the fraction of deposits held as reserves) as well as the currency-deposit ratio of the public (the fraction of deposits the public desires to hold in currency) are the determinants of the money multiplier, i.e. of the degree to which changes in the money base (which, under a currency board, mirror foreign reserve changes) translate into money stock changes in the economy[228].

An orthodox currency board does not influence the money supply by imposing reserve ratios or by regulating commercial banks, but leaves its determination completely to market forces[229]. However, private money creation can be a source of instability: with a high money multiplier, capital inflows may translate into unacceptably high rises in domestic credit, capital outflows into sharp contractions of the money stock. Though the responsiveness of the money supply is a central principle in the currency board idea, a currency board may wish to dampen the expansionary as well as contractionary effects of foreign reserve movements by imposing minimum reserve requirements. Thus, on the macroeconomic level, reserve requirements can serve to control inflationary pressures, to reduce adaptation costs of the domestic economy, and so to enhance the currency board's sustainability. On the microeconomic level, they can help strengthen the financial sector by ensuring it holds sufficient reserves to meet liquidity demands of its customers, and by establishing additional liquidity buffers that may be needed to smooth out interest rate volatility or limit the risk of settlement failures. For a typical central bank, minimum reserve requirements are also an important instrument of discretionary control of the money supply: rises and reductions in the reserve requirements serve as brakes or accelerators for money growth. While this latter function sharply contrasts with the concept of a currency board, the setting of

---

[227] See Fuhrmann (1999), p. 95.

[228] See Walters (1989), pp. 111-2.

[229] For a detailed description of money supply under a currency board see e.g. Hanke/Schuler (2000), pp. 26-39, Humpage/Owen (1995), pp. 3-5, or Zarazaga (1995a), pp. 1-2.

minimum reserve requirements, with the aim to keep the money multiplier adequate and constant[230], is largely regarded as a prudential issue even for a currency board.

If, as pointed out above, a currency board accepts the need for a certain lender of last resort capacity, the interest earned on foreign reserves held by the currency board to back banks' (unremunerated) reserves can be used to build up excess reserves earmarked for this purpose. Moreover, a currency board may wish some degree of discretion by keeping the option to adjust reserve ratios on an ad hoc basis in case of liquidity crises[231]. Again, the conditions of such adjustment should be transparent and well-defined ex ante in order to maximise the currency board's credibility.

However, the requirement for banks to hold high and unremunerated reserves with the currency board reduces their profitability, and so may put the banking sector's soundness at risk. Liquidity requirements, while serving the same macro and microeconomic purposes, may offer an alternative, especially when there is a risk of systemic liquidity crises[232]. Allowed to hold the required fraction of liabilities as liquid reserves within the banking system, banks can earn interest on their reserves, which strengthens their profitability. Liquidity requirements can be fine-tuned in a way that some of the liquidity risk that otherwise would imply externalities can be internalised: higher liquidity requirements can be imposed on liabilities that have short maturities, are volatile, or are close substitutes for foreign assets. A further advantage over reserve requirements is that banks can be allowed to deposit their liquidity reserves abroad. Thus, they can be given broad responsibility for the management and use of their liquidity reserves, which is likely to contain moral hazard more than with reserve requirements, and therefore may limit the need for discretionary central bank intervention[233].

---

[230] A typical phenomenon during stabilisation or transformation processes is the increase of non-cash payments and a reduction of the currency-deposit ratio of the public. Higher reserve requirements for banks can prevent increases in the money multiplier with the potentially destabilising effects. See Fuhrmann/Richert (1995), p. 1038.

[231] See Baliño/Enoch (1997), p. 20.

[232] See Baliño/Enoch (1997), p. 23.

[233] In addition, systemic stability can be enhanced via the imposition of an autonomous deposit insurance fund with limited coverage, funded by the banks themselves. Moral hazard can be limited by making insurance premia dependent on the riskiness of each bank's portfolio. See Hanke/Schuler (2000), p. 66.

### Clearing and Day-to-Day Monetary Operations

As pointed out, the design of a pure currency board does not include any engagement in operations with the financial sector other than the exchange of foreign reserves against domestic currency. As this implies a complete loss of control over interest rates, a country with an orthodox currency board has to rely on a functioning financial sector that is able to provide for a proper and timely allocation of liquidity and a smooth adaptation to interest movements. In the absence of a strong and sophisticated financial sector, it may again be justifiable to deviate from the orthodox principle in the design of payment systems and monetary arrangements in a way that allows coping with the limitations imposed by the currency board while sticking to its commitment to refrain from discretionary action[234].

For example, allowing banks to hold their settlement accounts with the monetary authority and granting their unconditional convertibility at the official exchange rate facilitates a smooth handling of liquidity fluctuations. To facilitate the provision of fully backed liquidity for commercial banks, the currency board may use foreign exchange swaps, which facilitate short-term capital flows and promote interest rate arbitrage[235].

More conflicting with an orthodox currency board design are provisions of standing liquidity facilities (e.g. a Lombard window) or conventional open market operations. While they can be used to facilitate settlements, meet daily changing liquidity requirements, and promote the adaptation of domestic interest rates to changes in foreign interest rates, the implied room for discretion potentially can undermine a currency board's credibility. It is important that such facilities are not used to gain control over the level of interest rates, since this would interfere with the mechanism through which banks equilibrate the distribution of monetary assets and liabilities. Accordingly, such operations have to be limited in scope and clearly defined.

### Lender of Last Resort Function

As already pointed out, a pure currency board does not include any room for lender of last resort operations. In signalling that the maintenance of the fixed

---

[234] See Bennett (1994), p. 199-200.

[235] While this intention does basically not contradict a pure currency board's objective, there is some risk that swaps may be used to postpone necessary policy actions, hence that they offer some discretionary leeway. See Baliño/Enoch (1997), p. 20.

exchange rate is the overriding goal, the abstinence from intervention is an important determinant of the credibility of a currency board. It is thought to promote the soundness of the banking system by enforcing market discipline, limiting moral hazard, and inducing banks to limit their risk exposure.

It is, however, impossible to obtain a complete reduction of banks' risk to failure. This is especially true where the banking system is (still) weak or where it is exposed to adverse external shocks. The risk is that a financial crisis undermines the currency board's political backbone and finally leads to its collapse. Most currency boards, therefore, hold a limited "safety margin" of excess reserves, kept aside for interventions in accordance with the currency board rules in order to gain some flexibility[236].

Unlike with other features of a currency board, the trade-off between credibility and flexibility does not seem so obvious for the lender of last resort issue. As long as sufficient reserves are available, some flexibility can, on the one hand, strengthen confidence in the domestic banking sector, add credibility to the currency board, and enhance its sustainability. On the other hand, it may limit its transparency, which might work against its credibility again. It might signal investors that the stability of the domestic banking system is deemed a goal superior to the maintenance of the exchange rate, which might evoke capital flight[237]. The exposure to moral hazard, a problem inherent in any constellation where economic agents can expect to be bailed-out in case of liquidity problems, is a further danger. It cannot be completely excluded[238], as even under a credible currency board it can be rationally expected that in the case of a systemic crisis authorities will eventually rescue banks in order to limit the damage and to prevent a collapse of the currency board.

These challenges for a currency board's sustainability can be limited to the degree that the excess reserves held for this purpose are strictly confined, and rules for their use are transparent and clearly defined. Besides the general need for proper prudential regulations and supervisory arrangements designed to reduce the

---

[236] Given a sound financial sector, the foreign exchange set aside for lender of last resort support can also originate from a common pool of commercial bank funds. Other possibilities to ensure the availability of funds in case of need are mutual support agreements with monetary authorities of other countries, or lines of credit with foreign banks, guaranteed by the currency board on behalf of domestic banks. See Baliño/Enoch (1997), p. 23.

[237] See Eichengreen (1996), p. 239.

[238] See Dolmas/Zarazaga (1996), p. 2.

need of lender of last resort operations in the first place, even these operations should rather address systemic problems in the banking system than bail-out single insolvent banks[239].

Another possibility is to transfer the lender of last resort function to the government, or even leave it to world capital markets[240]. Again, as with the currency board itself engaging in limited lender of last resort activities, the government will be able to deliver such support only to the extent that it disposes of foreign reserves, ideally accumulated over time through profit transfers from the currency board, or granted from external creditors. The advantage of such a constellation may be that the strict separation of the lender of last resort function from the currency board may increase the credibility of the arrangement[241].

A further and potentially very important factor limiting the need of lender of last resort operations is a high proportion of branches of foreign-owned banks within the domestic banking sector[242]. Branches of foreign banks generally face an elastic supply of reserve currency from their parent. Moreover, branching generally encourages diversification within the banking sector and the development of interbank lending markets. Thus, an open and minimally regulated banking sector reduces the likelihood of banking crises and the need for lender of last resort assistance[243].

### 3.2.1.5 Conduct of Fiscal Policy

As pointed out, a pure currency board issues money solely on the base of foreign reserves, and does not hold domestic assets. This means that any form of government financing through the monetary authority is precluded. As any fixed exchange rate regime, a currency board has to rely on the support of fiscal policy. Given the main motivation of a currency board to stop inflation, beforehand typically created through extensive central bank financing of the government, this restriction

---

[239] See Bennett (1994), p. 201.

[240] See Dornbusch (2001), p. 239.

[241] See Humpage/McIntire (1995), pp. 8-9, and Hanke/Schuler (2000), p. 65.

[242] A currency board, by largely eliminating exchange rate risk, is supposed to generally encourage branch banking, especially with large, global banks headquartered in the reserve country.

[243] See Humpage/McIntire (1995), p. 8.

116

represents a cut that is elementary for the establishment of a currency board's credibility[244].

Before the adoption of a currency board, governments typically faced soft budget constraints, i.e. were able to obtain funding through fresh money printed by de facto dependent central banks. Now they have to do without the previously earned inflation tax to finance fiscal deficits and instead have to rely on "open" sources of tax income[245]. This means that they are forced to consolidate budgets via tax increases and/or spending cuts, or to attract funds from domestic or international borrowers[246]. When relying on domestic sources of finance, e.g. loans from commercial banks, governments have to keep their borrowing requirements sufficiently low so as not to crowd out banks' lending to the private sector. Thus, a credible currency board makes governments (supposed they regard the costs of default as prohibitive) face the need to keep public borrowing requirements at or near zero, i.e. it imposes hard budget constraints[247].

If, as in most countries, fiscal policy is not concentrated upon a single centralised authority, then municipal, provincial, and central fiscal authorities have to agree on a common consolidation policy, which risks to be exposed to political dispute. Currency boards therefore might work better in countries where the fisc is centralised, or at least effective co-ordination mechanisms among the different fiscal levels are in place[248].

Again, modern currency boards sometimes make modest compromises with respect to the budget constraint, and allow a certain proportion of backing assets to be held in government debt denominated in the reserve currency. Although the credibility of the fixed exchange rate depends on the assets used to back it being external, limited and sufficiently small proportions of government debt, denominated in terms of the reserve currency, may stay without harm to the currency board's credibility[249].

Another problem to solve is how both day-to-day liquidity management and longer-term management of government debt, typically previously done by the

---

[244] See Enoch/Gulde (1998), p. 6.

[245] See Roubini (1998), p. 14.

[246] However, a credible currency board is able to compensate for the loss of inflation tax by lower interest rates and reduced debt service costs. See Dornbusch (2001), p. 239.

[247] See Hanke/Schuler (2000), p. 13.

[248] See Eichengreen (2001b), p. 272.

[249] See Bennett (1994), p. 198.

monetary authority[250], should be organised under a currency board. It seems clear that the purest and most transparent solution is not to allow the currency board to hold government deposits, but to pass government accounts as well as their management to commercial banks. If a currency board chooses to keep government deposits, possibly because the domestic banking sector is not (yet) able to undertake the related tasks, it should do so only under the conditions that government deposits are fully backed by foreign reserve holdings, that there are no overdraft provisions, and that interest is paid only if covered by the currency board's own interest income on reserve assets[251].

The question of how to handle stocks of outstanding government debt is closely related. The most conformable solution for a currency board would be to balance public budgets before its introduction, or to sell government debt to the market and stop buying new debt[252]. Open market operations related to government debt, such as the issue and marketing of treasury bills, should be passed to the fiscal authorities[253]. It is then their responsibility to balance the maturity structure of government securities, and to keep the securities markets sufficiently liquid, a task that is all the more important when government securities are an important fraction of the banking system.

With monetary and exchange rate policy severely restricted under a currency board, the conduct of fiscal policy is crucial for the success and sustainability of a currency board. Fiscal policy in this context may take over some of the tasks normally ascribed to monetary and/or exchange rate management, as, for instance, the dampening of business cycles (though boosting cycles has to be subject to budgetary limits). During incipient debt crises, fiscal policy can help restore confidence by reducing structural deficits. Fiscal surpluses can reduce the country's dependence on foreign savings and build up its international reserves position[254].

---

[250] Typical central banks hold and manage government deposits and provide overdraft provisions. However, movements in government deposits are associated with reserve changes that compromise the currency board.

[251] See Enoch/Gulde (1997), pp. 14-6.

[252] Where the currency board itself is divided into a banking and a currency department, the government debt can also be booked to the banking department in order to let the currency department operate as a pure currency board.

[253] Where organisational problems (e.g. staff qualification) exist, the currency board can also take over these functions passively, i.e. on a strict "fee for service" basis for the government.

[254] See Baliño/Enoch (1997), p. 18.

### 3.2.1.6 Institutional Preconditions

The core of a currency board's credibility, as opposed to the credibility of a merely fixed exchange rate, is the legal and institutional anchoring of the arrangement, meant to erect high obstacles to any change. A maximum degree of credibility is obtained by including the currency board into the country's constitution, or by requiring a parliamentary supermajority to reverse the arrangement. On this basis, a currency board law defines the new monetary regime. This law can be very simple and short[255]. It has to define the exchange rate and the reserves, the structure as well as the activities (and their limitation) of the monetary authority. Especially, it has to settle the currency board's relation to the government[256]. Finally, it has to rule that a well-defined set of statistics is published regularly, in order to establish a maximum of transparency.

The legal fixing of the exchange rate with the self-commitment of the monetary authority to sell foreign exchange at the defined rate is an important, but not sufficient precondition for the credibility and sustainability of a currency board: laws and even constitutions can always be changed when the political impetus exists. Nevertheless, the design of the legal setting can play an integral role in determining the degree of credibility. Especially, credible rules defining the behaviour in situations of distress or of adverse external developments can add substantially to the credibility of a currency board[257].

Despite its simplicity, the setting up and enacting of the legal framework requires time and comprehensive information of the political decision makers, and, to be credible, broad and unequivocal support of a large political majority.

One of the biggest obstacles towards making a currency board credible is doubt about the soundness of the banking system. Therefore, along with the reduction of monetary policy functions of the currency board, especially its lender of last resort function, commercial banks have to be prepared for the new regime in order to

---

[255] Hanke and Schuler recommend a very detailed and rigid currency board design and give a corresponding model for a currency board law. See Hanke/Schuler (2000), pp. 58-64 and 73-6.

[256] E.g., to demonstrate the currency board's sterility against government influence, it can be incorporated and required to hold its reserves abroad (e.g. in the reserve country, or another "safe haven" country), or be required to include a majority of foreign board members.

[257] E.g., Hanke and Schuler propose a rule according to which prolonged periods of strong deflation or inflation in the reserve country, both in degree and duration exceeding clearly defined ranges, force the currency board to either revalue or choose a new reserve currency. See Hanke/Schuler (2000), pp. 63-4.

make them as sound as possible, and to enable them for interbank markets that now have to function without permanent central bank intervention. As pointed out above, comprehensive prudential regulations as well as banking and stock market supervision, accounting standards, disclosure requirements, bankruptcy laws, and the payments system belong to the most important issues to be revised and strengthened. Where there is no realistic prospect for banks to comply with the new standards, the supervisory authority should be prepared to close them down. Privatising state-owned banks and allowing foreign banks to open branches in the country increases competition and efficiency, and reduces the need for lender of last resort activity, since branches of foreign parents generally will be granted liquidity assistance from abroad[258].

Further institutional conditions, though not directly related with the establishment of the new monetary constitution, arise from the interdependencies between the monetary and the real sectors of the economy, and typically require broad structural reforms. Most important, with a fixed exchange rate, the adaptation to real shocks has to occur via changes in prices and wages rather than via changes in the exchange rate[259]. Sustainability of a currency board therefore requires goods and labour markets that are flexible enough to absorb the effects of, say, an outflow of reserves that causes the money stock to decrease, interest rates to rise, and output and employment to shrink, through price and wage decreases, in order to re-establish internal and external balance[260].

Besides a broad deregulation of prices and wages, trade liberalisation is necessary to strengthen market forces and optimise factor allocation. Since state-owned enterprises can no longer rely on the soft budget constraints they previously enjoyed, their privatisation not only brings about their market-oriented realignment, but also contributes to restore government budgets[261]. The promotion of capital and know-how imports is a prerequisite for the development of key industries in developing or transforming economies.

Generally, the rigid external anchor imposed by a currency board necessitates a streamlining of the real sector towards an internationally competitive and export-

---

[258] See Enoch/Gulde (1997), pp. 12-3.

[259] See e.g. Broda (2001), p. 377, who examines the empirical evidence for the potential of the exchange rate regime to buffer real shocks.

[260] See Gulde/Kähkönen/Keller (2000), pp. 5-6.

[261] See Hanke/Schuler (2000), p. 13.

oriented economy, hence an economic alignment that requires a broad social consensus[262].

## 3.2.2 Strengths and Weaknesses of a Currency Board

### 3.2.2.1 Strengths of a Currency Board

**Simplicity and Transparency**

One major advantage over a central bank is a currency board's simplicity and transparency. As the currency board's conduct is reduced by a simple rule to quasi-mechanical behaviour, its function and motivation are easy to understand even for the broad public. Given an adequate information policy, its behaviour is completely verifiable and predictable. The straightness of the arrangement is directly tangible for the whole population, especially when the reserve currency already is in broad use as a parallel currency before the currency board's introduction, since foreign exchange transactions are simplified and freed from restrictions that typically prevailed before. In addition, the currency board's simplicity is underlined by the reduced need for staff and bookkeeping within the currency board.

Even where a currency board deviates from an orthodox design, and engages in certain regulatory, open market, or lender of last resort activities (as described above), its operations are clearly defined and limited in scope, thus easy to monitor[263]. This eliminates uncertainty and creates a calculable monetary framework for economic activity.

**Credibility**

A currency board's main objective is the installation of credible disinflation policies. The credibility of stabilisation policies decides over their success and sustainability.

With inflation being to a great part the result of economic agents' inflation expectations, typically shaped by past experiences of lax fiscal policy, accommodative monetary policy, and failed stabilisation attempts, the adoption of a currency board, by almost instantaneously eliminating the scope for inflationary policies, can quickly restore policy credibility and provide clear signals for the revision of expectations. The main determinant of this kind of credibility is the

---

[262] See Fuhrmann/Richert (1995), pp. 1038-9.
[263] See Baliño/Enoch (1997), p. 6.

severe self-restriction of the government and the preparedness to surrender flexibility for the sake of credibility[264].

For countries lacking a well-established track record of price stability, less strict ways towards building up credibility, e.g. through the self-commitment of an autonomous central bank, are very time-consuming and often doomed to fall victim to speculative attacks[265].

### Currency Stability

Apart from official dollarisation, a currency board establishes the closest link of the domestic currency to an external anchor. It introduces a high degree of substitutability between anchor and domestic currency, or, put differently, it imports the reserve currency's stability.

The convergence of domestic towards reserve country inflation rates is the result of the built-in automatic monetary adjustment mechanism of a currency board: a higher price level in the currency board country leads to a balance of payments deficit, reserve outflows and a shrinking monetary base, which causes a rise in interest rates that exerts a correcting deflationary pressure, which again improves the balance of payments[266]. Inflation differentials between anchor and domestic currency widely disappear, or, where they persist to limited degrees, reflect real rather than purely monetary developments (e.g. higher growth rates in the currency board than in the reserve currency country).

In the same way, nominal wage growth approaches the respective wage growth rates in the reserve country, plus an allowance for productivity gains. Real wages in a currency board country therefore can increase quickly when productivity increases[267].

### Interest Rate Convergence

Along with currency stabilisation, one of the main benefits of a currency board is that it promotes the convergence of domestic interest rates to reserve currency

---

[264] See Eichengreen (1996), p. 239.

[265] The experience of the Mexican Peso crisis in 1995 is an example of how coherent policy measures, though initially able to produce good results, were not enough to constitute a lasting credible monetary policy reputation. See Humpage/Owen (1995), p. 2.

[266] This is the famous price-specie-flow-mechanism first described by David Hume.

[267] See Hanke/Schuler (2000), p. 38.

levels[268]. This is, like the convergence of inflation rates, a direct consequence of the automatic monetary adjustment mechanism, according to which a supposed flight into the reserve currency will cause the domestic monetary base to shrink and domestic interest rates to rise until a level is reached where holding local currency becomes again attractive. Remaining risk premia demanded for holding domestic currency reflect the state of confidence in the stability of the domestic currency's purchasing power. They are supposed to decrease with successful stabilisation[269].

Risk premia are composed of country and currency risk. Currency risk can be described as the probability of exchange rate realignment. It can be measured as the differential between interest rates granted in the currency board country for domestic as opposed to reserve currency deposits. Country risk, in contrast, reflects the political, legal, and/or economic risks prevailing in a country. It can be assessed comparing the interest rates of reserve currency deposits (or, as well, reserve currency money market rates) in the currency board country with those in the reserve country[270]. Currency and country risk cannot be completely separated: the higher the currency risk (i.e. the risk that the exchange rate is changed), the higher the perceived country risk, as economic and political conditions of the currency board country would be severely affected by a change in the exchange rate. Similarly, a higher country risk (e.g. because of rising banking sector problems, or following external shocks) will immediately spill over to a higher currency risk by adding pressure to the currency. Therefore, for instance, as long as there is an institutional possibility that the currency board could be changed, or that banks may get illiquid, a certain risk premium will always remain, even if a currency board is doing well[271].

Bank rates, particularly long-term lending rates, in the currency board country often remain significantly above respective rates in the reserve currency country. This is to be explained mainly with higher domestic credit risk, different lending policies, lacks in transparency, and possibly unsound banks. Over time however, in the course of stabilisation and institutional reforms, risk premia should decline substantially.

---

[268] See Dornbusch (2001), p. 240.

[269] See Fuhrmann (1999), p. 92.

[270] See Baliño/Enoch (1997), pp. 32-4.

[271] See Bennett (1994), p. 206.

Besides the beneficial effects of lower interest rates on domestic investment and public households, interest rates converging to international levels due to reduced exchange rate uncertainty and the perception of orderly monetary conditions help promote international trade and access to international capital markets, and so facilitate international integration that is a prerequisite for a currency board country's growth.

Compared to conventionally fixed pegs, these benefits seem to be clearer, because the adoption of a currency board implies that the government is generally more inclined to strengthen policies overall, which results not only in lower interest rates demanded by investors but also in smaller interest rate changes (and concomitant costs for the economy) necessary to adjust to changes in monetary conditions[272].

### Financial Intermediation

The credibility of a currency board is supposed to strengthen the financial sector and stimulate financial intermediation and remonetisation of the economy, measurable in increasing ratios of broad money to GDP, growth rates of credit to the private sector, and ratios of deposits to broad money.

This is mainly the result of three effects, the first resulting from the abstinence of the monetary authority to provide a financial safety net and from the concomitant reduction of moral hazard for banks that cannot any longer rely on being bailed out by the authorities via devaluation of the domestic currency. This works to induce them to more responsible risk taking in liquidity, currency, and maturity terms. The absence of a central liquidity provider also stimulates and intensifies interbank lending[273].

Second, a credible currency board leads to a lengthening of agents' horizons[274], and hence to a return of domestic and international long-term lending to domestic banks and firms, which previously had been discouraged by the prevailing currency risk. Financial and real sectors get more liquid, and currency risks resulting from domestic currency assets and foreign currency liabilities in banks' and firms' balance sheets are covered by the exchange rate commitment. Similarly, maturity mismatches arising from long-term investments that under the previous conditions

---

[272] See Baliño/Enoch (1997), p. 9.

[273] The question of whether a strong financial sector is an effect or a precondition of a credible currency board will be addressed below.

[274] See Dornbusch (2001), p. 240.

of distrust and exchange rate uncertainty had to be forcibly financed by short-term loans, are reduced when currency risk is eliminated[275].

Finally, ameliorating economic and financial conditions work to attract international banks to open up business in the currency board country, leading to enhanced competition, a more efficient financial sector, and real credit growth. In short, a currency board, by eliminating exchange rate uncertainty, is expected to encourage the development of a sophisticated financial sector that serves the needs of a growing and diversifying local economy striving to intensify its integration into the world economy.

### 3.2.2.2 Weaknesses of a Currency Board

Not surprisingly, the weaknesses of a currency board are the flip side of its strengths. Notably, the fixed parity can become an obstacle to adequately respond to large exchange rate misalignments. Similarly, the rigid backing rule makes the financial system vulnerable in case of crises. Operational simplicity in central banking rules out important and otherwise possibly beneficial central bank functions. Finally, by preventing the government from lending from the currency board, an immediate fiscal consolidation is required that may be difficult to realise.

#### Nominal Exchange Rate Rigidity and Exchange Rate Misalignments

One of the biggest threats arising for the sustainability of a currency board is the danger of a growing misalignment of the real exchange rate[276]. A post stabilisation boom, as often experienced after successful stabilisation, may lead to a positive growth rate differential between currency board and reserve currency country. As a consequence, price levels in the currency board country, although approaching reserve country levels, often remain well above reserve (or trading partner) country levels due to higher demand for goods and services, which leads to decreasing competitiveness[277]. Other factors contributing to inflation differentials over the reserve country level can be increased productivity due to the opening up of the economy[278], or high capital inflows due to the newly perceived macroeconomic

---

[275] See Eichengreen (2001b), p. 269-71.

[276] See Roubini (1998), p. 5-8.

[277] Especially prices of nontraded goods, being in inelastic supply, often rise faster than in the reserve currency country.

[278] This is true for the so-called productivity bias that results from differential productivity growth within an open economy. With fixed nominal exchange rates, realised productivity gains in

stability of the country. Also, an initial undervaluation of the exchange rate, while partly chosen to provide room for inflation inertia, may by itself contribute to initial inflation[279]. An appreciation of the real exchange rate (defined as the quotient of nominal exchange rate and price level) is the result.

While exchange rate misalignments are a problem for most exchange rate based stabilisation programmes, they are a more serious concern for currency boards as the option of adjustment of the nominal exchange rate, i.e. devaluation, is barred. The correction of a misalignment therefore has to occur via the adjustment process through the balance of payments: a deterioration of the balance of payments (in the current and/or the capital account), a shrinking monetary base, and price and wage deflation[280]. Where prices and wages are sticky, the adjustment effectuates prolonged periods of tight liquidity and high unemployment, which may challenge the sustainability of the currency board.

Nominal exchange rate rigidity also makes a currency board country more vulnerable to external shocks or to an instable reserve currency. E.g., with incongruent business cycles prevailing in the two countries, changes in monetary conditions in the reserve currency country may lead to situations where interest rates of the reserve currency country are too high or too low for the current economic situation in the currency board country. The currency board then, in effect, has procyclical effects: imported interest rates that are too low for a booming currency board country can aggravate already prevailing inflationary pressures, too high interest rates intensify a monetary and real contraction[281]. When the value of the reserve currency changes in relation to the currencies of other trading partners, similar costs are incurred: a weakening reserve currency then results in a depreciation of the currency board currency vis-à-vis its other trading partners and hence in an inflationary bias, and vice versa in the case of an appreciation of the reserve currency. As pointed out above, the design of a currency board, and especially the choice of the anchor currency, decides to a great extent over the exposedness to external shocks.

---

the tradable sector translate into wage increases, which are transmitted to the nontradable sector. If productivity growth in the nontradable sector is less, this leads to increasing prices for nontradables and to inflation, which, if productivity growth in the reserve country is less, exceeds inflation in the reserve country. See Hanke/Schuler (2000), pp. 38-9.

[279] See Williamson (1995), p. 22.
[280] See Enoch/Gulde (1998), p. 2.
[281] See Williamson (1995), pp. 24-5.

### Financial Fragility in the Absence of a Lender of Last Resort

Compared to conventionally fixed exchange rates, the financial system has the overall preconditions to be less fragile under a currency board: sufficient foreign reserves have to be maintained to ensure convertibility, and bank runs motivated by expectations of exchange rate realignments are discouraged. Although this reduces the probability of bank runs, their occurrence is still possible. If one does occur, a currency board is more vulnerable than a system with central banking, since it is largely deprived of instruments to deal with crises (namely of lender of last resort functions)[282]. Comparatively small disruptions in the financial sector can spread fast and even lead to a national financial panic when the knowledge about the absence of any lender of last resort assistance accelerates bank runs[283].

A currency board grants full convertibility for notes and coins, but not for deposits. Therefore, although banks may keep sufficient reserves to meet "normal" conversion demands, a bank run (i.e. a sudden increase in the currency-deposit ratio of the public) may make them unable to honour requests for deposit withdrawals. Selling liquid domestic assets may help single banks, but do nothing to solve systemic crises, as it leaves the overall reserves base unchanged. While increasing interest rates offer a short-term solution, over time they damage confidence in the sustainability of the currency board[284].

Improperly managed public debt is another source of instability. If large proportions of public debt are outstanding in the short term, this may lead to speculative attacks exposing the government to a debt crisis even if the levels of public indebtedness are sustainable. In turn, when government securities form an important part of banks' liquidity, such a debt crisis may also trigger a banking crisis.

As becomes evident, in the absence of a lender of last resort, a currency board's fragility in case of financial crises increases with high capital mobility, a weak (or weakly supervised) banking sector, the dominance of local banks without access to foreign funds, and weaknesses in the structure of public debt.

---

[282] See Roubini (1998), p. 2-3.

[283] See Zarazaga (1995b), pp. 17-8.

[284] Empirically, persisting and high interest rate differentials to reserve currency levels, especially for long-term deposits and loans, generally reflect prevailing expectations of banking crises or a collapse of the currency board. See Baliño/Enoch (1997), p. 15.

### Loss of Other Central Bank Functions

Besides being restricted in its function to deal with financial crises, a pure currency board also refrains from other central bank functions, such as day-to-day monetary management and the settlement of payments.

A currency board is designed to leave liquidity adjustment to capital flows and interest rate arbitrage within the financial sector. However, unless financial markets are highly developed, market imperfections, transaction costs, and credit risk account for high volatility and intermediation spreads, which penalise capital flows and hamper arbitrage. Consequently, though capital account transactions may be fully liberalised and interest rates may generally follow international movements, capital flows may be unable to fully arbitrage interest rates with sufficient speed. Ensuing short-term liquidity mismatches then negatively affect financial and exchange markets, subject the economy to unnecessary fluctuations, and possibly undermine the currency board's credibility. This is why most modern currency boards do engage in day-to-day monetary operations to smooth out adjustment to short-term liquidity imbalances.

Similarly, under a pure currency board, clearing and settlement services are provided by the private sector. Then, settlement failures are possible, especially when the currency board provides no lender of last resort assistance. Again, deviating from the orthodox design and allowing banks to settle in the books of the currency board reduces this risk[285].

### Constraints on Fiscal Policy

Currency boards are expected to promote, but cannot guarantee, fiscal discipline[286]. Central bank financing precluded, fiscal deficits can still be (typically to a much larger degree than before) financed via debt issue on domestic and international capital markets, or through payment arrears. While all fixed exchange rate arrangements require sound public finances, a currency board is especially vulnerable in the case of fiscal indiscipline[287].

With a currency board, substantial fiscal deficits, if financed by foreign capital, exert inflationary pressures on the economy, as the inflow of reserves increases the monetary base. Even if financed domestically, by crowding out private financing

---

[285] See Baliño/Enoch (1997), p. 17.
[286] See Roubini (1998), p. 15.
[287] See Williamson (1995), p. 16.

needs and driving them towards international markets, fiscal deficits have an inflationary impact and lead to an appreciation of the real exchange rate. They can thus compromise the currency board's sustainability, and even lead to its abandonment in case of a debt crisis. As a currency board does not engage in accommodating treasury bill markets, short-term fluctuations in treasury cash flows may occur and create additional stress for public finances[288].

In the worst case, where governments cease to accept their financial subordination to the monetary regime, there is a possibility that they might "raid" the currency board in one form or another, e.g. by demonetising the currency board currency and issuing an own parallel currency. Therefore, although a currency board is able to reinforce an existing political commitment to fiscal discipline, it is jeopardised when such commitment is fading[289].

### 3.2.3 Considerations for Adopting a Currency Board

#### 3.2.3.1 *When is a Currency Board an Appropriate Choice?*

As Fuhrmann (1999) notes, there is no theory that would predict under which circumstances and preconditions the introduction of a currency board is an optimal strategy[290]. In this context, most economists refer to a number of criteria that stem from the theory of optimal currency areas, supplemented by some arguments that take account of the special application of a currency board as a stabilisation vehicle.

(1) Only small and open economies benefit from an external nominal anchor. For an open economy (i.e. one with a high proportion of imports and exports to GDP), exchange rate uncertainty induces greater costs than for a closed economy, and fixing the exchange rate will to a greater extent imply a fixing of the price level. Since small economies tend to be more open, both criteria are intertwined[291]. Therefore, the argument holds, for small economies with the typical low degree of diversification, the best strategy is to choose fixed exchange rates in order to adapt to international price structures and maximise the advantages that arise from the

---

[288] See Baliño/Enoch (1997), p. 18.

[289] See Williamson (1995), pp. 28-9.

[290] See Fuhrmann (1999), p. 86.

[291] Note that the criterion of country size is to be understood in economic, not geographical terms. E.g., Hong Kong, though geographically tiny, has to be regarded as a large "country" whereas Argentina, though geographically big, is a comparatively small economy in terms of GDP.

international division of labour[292]. Consequently, only small economies should adopt a currency board. (2) When shocks tend to hit the pegging and the pegged-to country symmetrically, the real costs caused by the adjustment process with fixed exchange rates are minimised for the pegging country, whereas a higher probability for asymmetrical shocks would rather be an argument for flexible exchange rates[293]. (3) High factor, especially labour, mobility between the pegging and the pegged-to country is desirable for a country with fixed exchange rates as it facilitates the adjustment process and contributes to price level equilibration[294]. (4) If there are aspirations of a country to integrate into a common trade area (or to prepare to join a currency area), a currency board with its highly credible fixed exchange rate may ease such integration more than strategies with central banks and simply pegged exchange rates. (5) Lacking central banking experience of a country delivers a further argument for a currency board because of its simplicity of operation as well as the high degree of credibility of its strictly rule-bound activities. (6) Finally, for a country with a record of credibility-lacking monetary policy, of high and persistent inflation, of currency crises, and of high risk premia required by international investors, a currency board, with its high credibility and almost instant anti-inflationary impetus, can provide an effective cure[295].

An additional criterion in this context may be the existence of a "natural" anchor currency, i.e. of a major reserve currency that fulfils the requirements of a suitable anchor. At the margin, the lack of such a natural candidate to peg to may provide the decisive argument against a currency board[296].

The consideration of the suitability of a currency board for a country extends to an evaluation of the expected advantages and disadvantages of a currency board

---

[292] See Fuhrmann/Richert (1995), p. 1036.

[293] An additional consideration in this context refers to the assumption that a currency board (or a common currency) increases economic integration between the countries and so works to synchronise shocks and cycles, thereby increasing its advantageousness. See Alesina/Barro (2001), p. 383. A possible counterargument is that when countries get more integrated, they tend to become more specialised in production, with greater specialisation reducing the correlation of business cycles over time, thereby rendering a monetary union less attractive in the long run. Empirical evidence, however, points at specialisation occurring primarily as intra-industry specialisation, which tends to increase the symmetry of shock exposure within a monetary union. See Alexander/von Furstenberg (2000), p. 214.

[294] See Williamson (1995), p. 23.

[295] See Baliño/Enoch (1997), p. 6.

[296] See Williamson (1995), p. 24.

for the specific case. Some shortcomings in the starting position of a currency board country can certainly be addressed by precautionary measures, e.g. by allowing for a limited lender of last resort capacity, or by promoting the entrance of foreign banks into the financial sector in order to partly compensate for a still weak banking sector. Other risks are potentially harder to address such as the dangers related with substantial and lasting real appreciation that may translate into long-term risks difficult to assess in terms of growth, income, and employment.

Therefore, even if a country clearly appeared to be a candidate for a currency board, just adopting one would be far from automatically providing stability. The advantages of a currency board materialise only when supported by the described sustainable structural and macroeconomic, especially fiscal, policies. Indeed, adversaries of the currency board idea argue that stability can be achieved by the very disciplined policies without the need to establish a currency board in most countries, given a sufficient time horizon[297].

However, and this is an argument that even currency board opponents concede, a currency board can deliver stability quickly, and in this respect is superior to a central bank that has to build up its own credibility over an extended period. Put differently, for transformation economies without any track record of credibility, and for confidence-lacking high-inflation economies, the present value of a currency board's benefits is higher than that of a central bank's, with a central bank solution facing higher "sunk costs" and barriers to entry than a currency board[298]. All the more so for a hyperinflation country that is already looking back on several failed stabilisation attempts (such as Argentina was in the late 1980s): here the complete erosion of credibility can arguably provide an all-or-nothing situation where the adoption of a currency board seems to be the only chance to break the ever-accelerating cycle of inflation and depreciation[299].

In such a case, with the ills to cure so large, the potential remedy may justify very high costs even if the country is not in every respect an optimal candidate for a currency board. The challenge for such a country then will be to reap the currency board's short-term benefits without putting at risk the country's long-term position by not taking account of the currency board's potential dangers. Explicitly trying to re-direct trade flows in order to improve the anchor's long-term suitability, or else

---

[297] See e.g. Roubini (1998), p. 16.
[298] See Fuhrmann/Richert (1995), p. 1038.
[299] See e.g. Williamson (1995) p. 34, or Zarazaga (1995b), p. 22.

planning a timely exit after successful stabilisation, belong to the possible alternatives to confront these risks.

### 3.2.3.2 Implementation of a Currency Board

Although it is undisputable that the success of a currency board depends on strong supporting policies, the extent to which they are indispensable at the time of a currency board's introduction is subject to discussion. The statement that strong macroeconomic policies, a strong banking system, and flexible labour and goods markets are prerequisites for a sustainable currency board is unquestionable as such. On the other hand, it is exactly these qualities a country aspires to obtain via the adoption of a currency board[300]. There is some general evidence that a hard peg by itself is able to boost financial sector, fiscal, and labour market reform[301]. Therefore, earmarking these reforms as being indispensable preconditions to be fulfilled by a country that is only beginning to solve its severe problems of transformation or hyperinflation seems problematic at least.

A certain qualification can be made insofar as, among the prerequisites for a sustainable currency board, some are clearly indispensable for the start, whereas others that primarily aim at protection against potential shocks can be left for implementation (or improvement) when the currency board is already in place. The first, indispensable, category doubtlessly comprises a sufficient level of reserves to grant the conversion commitment, a sound fiscal policy stance, and a satisfactorily robust banking system. In contrast, efforts such as installing an efficient banking supervision or making labour laws more flexible can (but should rapidly) be made after the installation of the currency board[302].

Clearly, the risk is that, with the experience of a possible initial stabilisation boom following the currency board's introduction, politically queasy reforms, such as revising labour laws, are postponed or carried through half-heartedly. Neglecting these reforms can contribute to substantial exchange rate misalignments and to high real costs, including rising unemployment, which again can put the currency board under social and political pressure. The necessary political and social consensus for these reforms is easiest to obtain at the start of the currency board,

---

[300] See Eichengreen (2001b), p. 269.

[301] Eichengreen addresses this issue for the regime of official dollarisation. He finds that the case for dollarisation accelerating financial market and fiscal reform is strong, whereas its effect on labour market reform remains ambiguous. See Eichengreen (2001b).

[302] See Baliño/Enoch (1997), pp. 18-9.

when the pains of the previous regime are still felt and the preparedness to agree on hurting measures is biggest. This at least should provide the decisive argument for carrying out all, and especially the politically tricky, reforms as quickly as possible.

This leads to the consideration of two principal alternatives for the implementation of a currency board. The first is to introduce the new monetary regime in a kind of shock therapy, with the "shock" manifested in a sudden fixing of the exchange rate without a previous period of floating against the reserve currency. As pointed about above, the main problem is to find evidence for the "appropriate" exchange rate in terms of market conformity. The exchange rate therefore can only reflect an estimate that, if far from the imminent market rate, may not be accepted by the markets and induce potentially harmful capital movements. If the introduction of a currency board goes in parallel with a currency reform, the exchange rate of the new in relation to the old currency has to be set simultaneously, which implies similar problems[303].

The alternative to a shock therapy is a gradualist approach, which implies the announcement to introduce the currency board at a later date while allowing the currency to float freely against the reserve currency during the interim period. The advantage of this approach is that markets are expected to deliver an unequivocal notion of the appropriate exchange rate. For high inflation economies with a record of failed stabilisation policies, however, the problem will be to furnish the announcement with a maximum degree of credibility, in order not to evoke expectations of just another policy announcement that later will be abused for surprise inflation by the government. An announcement lacking credibility (because not immediately translated into visible action) would doom the preparation of the currency board's introduction and lead to capital flight and continuing devaluation of the domestic currency[304].

Further limitations to the gradualist approach arise from the problems of timing and sequencing of different reform elements. For instance, with the usually high proportion of administered prices in both transformation and high inflation economies, the revelation of the "appropriate" exchange rate is limited to the extent

---

[303] An overvaluation of the old currency in relation to the new one can create a monetary surplus that may challenge reserves and negatively influence distribution. A strategy of parallel currencies, with old and new currency floating against each other over a limited period, can moderate distribution conflicts. See Fuhrmann/Richert (1995), p. 1036.

[304] See Fuhrmann/Richert (1995), p. 1039.

that sovereign price fixing is not eliminated prior to the floating period. Price structures then are not yet adapted to the new regime, and the market equilibrium exchange rate does not equal the level that also would incorporate system conformity. Similar issues apply for fiscal reforms that require higher taxes and hence lead to a higher price level. Both price liberalisation and fiscal consolidation should ideally be in place before the floating period in order to reap its advantages in terms of an appropriate exchange rate. Both, however, require credibility, which may be challenged with a gradualist approach in high-inflation countries.

Therefore, gradualist approaches may be a more viable choice for transformation than for high inflation economies. As pointed out, the central advantage of a currency board is its immediate effectiveness, an advantage which for high inflation countries may only be obtainable by opting for some sort of shock therapy[305].

### 3.2.4 Duration and Termination of a Currency Board

Colonial currency boards functioned adequately over long periods. However, in terms of motivation, environment, and functioning conditions, they are not fully comparable to present-day currency boards. The long-term character of currency boards that survived from colonial times generally is not doubted even today. Currency boards introduced during the last two decades of the 20th century offer a mixed picture. Hong Kong's currency board is generally viewed as a permanent arrangement, as, for many, was also Argentina's, whereas Estonia and Lithuania seem to provide examples of currency boards implicitly designed to govern a limited period of transition, in order to prepare their economies for an eventual membership in the European Monetary Union.

This paragraph tries to qualify under which conditions a currency board can be viewed as a transitional or a permanent arrangement, and addresses the related question of when and how to exit from a currency board.

#### 3.2.4.1 Currency Board: Permanent or Transitional Arrangement?

Currency boards can be viewed and implemented as permanent arrangements when a currency board allows realising trade and other benefits for a country that belongs to a common currency area. Likewise, when a country experiences persistent high inflation and real appreciation of its currency, and/or is systematically

---

[305] See Fuhrmann (1999), p. 94.

exposed to speculative attacks, a currency board can, and should, be designed and presented as a long-term arrangement.

In contrast, a currency board can be perceived as a transitional arrangement when a country experiences a transformation process from one economic regime to another, e.g. from socialist to market economy. Similarly, when a country faces a political regime change intending to stop deficiencies such as hyperinflation, money press funding of fiscal deficits, political promiscuity[306], or when a country faces other major institutional changes (e.g. the installation of a newly independent monetary authority that is still lacking a record of credibility), a currency board can be designed and perceived as an interim arrangement. In such cases, a currency board is expected to promote credibility and stability until a switch to a different monetary or exchange rate regime becomes feasible[307].

Depending on the initial motivation for the installation of a currency board, therefore, the decision for, and timing of, an exit has to be chosen according to different criteria. If the currency board was introduced primarily as a transitional arrangement intended to give time and stability during the building-up of institutional conditions for a functioning central bank, or for the joining of a monetary union, then the degree to which those functions are brought into effect decides about the timing of an exit. The abandonment of the currency board then is a desired development.

Currency boards introduced to gain monetary credibility are different from the above insofar as the time for an exit is determined by the degree of credibility assumed to prevail after the termination of the currency board. Strong policies over a prolonged period of time are required to build up credibility. This implies also to endure potential exchange rate misalignments, which carry substantial risk for the sustainability of a currency board. Especially in cases where a currency is overvalued, the currency board is prone to speculative attacks as well as to internal political pressures, which, if turning extreme, can not only make the currency board appear unsustainable, but also render the choice of the best time for an eventually unavoidable exit difficult. The optimal exit point then would have to be gauged according to the achieved building-up of credibility over time on the one hand, and to internal and external pressures on the other hand, and would have to be viewed as an optimisation and the result of a trade-off.

---

[306] See Williamson (1995), p. 34.
[307] See Baliño/Enoch (1997), p. 24.

### 3.2.4.2 Exit Options

Typically, in the initial phase after the successful installation of a currency board, the public usually perceives that it would be irrational for the authorities to abandon the arrangement early. Over time, however, the weaknesses owed to the inflexibility of the arrangement become more visible and hurting, possibly evoking doubts about the sustainability of the currency board[308].

If at the same time the justification of the currency board as a vehicle to promote credibility is losing weight because confidence in the government has grown and institutional conditions have improved, this may deliver an argument for a gradual relaxation of the rules ("growing-out of the currency board") and an eventual exit from the currency board[309]. This would then be viewed as the natural and desired development of a transitional process during which credibility is built up, institutions are installed, and financial markets are developed. If, in addition, external conditions are favourable, a country is able to abandon the currency board out of a position of strength, i.e. to realise a so-called soft exit[310].

If, in contrast, the weaknesses of the currency board are felt, while the currency board's expected achievements do not materialise, possibly because institutional, structural, and fiscal reforms have been delayed or ineffective, and confidence in the government is declining, the risk that the currency board eventually has to be abandoned under stress is substantial. Unfavourable external developments, such

---

[308] As Zarazaga points out, maybe the biggest risk to a currency board's sustainability can be circumscribed by the time inconsistency problem, inherent in all kinds of policy rules. Since currency boards, especially in the long run, are almost certainly subject to pressure some time (be it caused by external shocks or by internal developments, such as price and wage deflation, or rising unemployment), it becomes at some point attractive for policymakers to abandon the chosen policy rule, arguing that the present situation is different from the original and therefore justifies a deviation. The perceived time inconsistency of monetary policy rules, here of the currency board rule, reduces credibility and hence the effectiveness of the very policy rule. See Zarazaga (1995b).

[309] See Williamson (1995), p. 35.

[310] A textbook example for a gradual exit is Ireland, which in the 60s and 70s gradually relaxed the currency board rules that, since 1927, had tied the Irish pound to the pound sterling. Other examples for an exit out of a position of strength, though not gradual, are given by Singapore and Malaysia in 1973. See Baliño/Enoch (1997), pp. 26-7.

as an appreciating anchor currency or a sharp decline in capital inflows, may add to the stress and force the country to opt for a hard exit[311].

The theoretical options to exit from the fixed exchange rate comprise its replacement by a different (depreciated or appreciated) fixed exchange rate, by a fixed exchange rate pegged to a different anchor, or by a (freely or managed) floating exchange rate. While the move to a float inevitably comprises a complete exit from the currency board and a change to some form of central banking, changes resulting in a modified fixed exchange rate regime can be compatible both with the introduction of a central banking system or with a continuation of the currency board under a modified rule (also treated as "exit" for this purpose).

As will be argued, any possible termination or modification of a currency board should be based on rules defined ex ante, i.e. on escape clauses built in at the time of its implementation.

### Built-in Escape Clauses

Considering possible exits from a currency board, the only means to avoid the perception of a breach of policy commitment is the provision of ex ante built-in escape clauses. Although the discussion of rules versus discretion in monetary policy seems to reveal that contingent rules (i.e. rules with some flexibility) are superior to non-contingent rules[312], this cannot unconditionally apply to currency boards since their essence is that they fully rely on rules to build up credibility (instead of on a reputation of credible behaviour)[313].

Escape clauses that offer room for genuine discretion of the currency board (i.e. that leave possible actions or escape cases vaguely or not defined) are doubtlessly harmful to its credibility and introduce the stability risks associated with simple

---

[311] All of Argentina's three currency boards (1902-14, 1927-29, 1991-2002) had to be given up under stress, with external shocks triggering the exits of 1914 and 1929. See Baliño/Enoch (1997), p. 26.

[312] See Zarazaga (1995b), p. 20.

[313] The case of the gold standard may illustrate this. Although the gold standard appears to have been a non-contingent rule, in reality it had implicit escape clauses: the temporary suspensions of convertibility of the pound Sterling into gold during wars and financial crises can be viewed as applications of an inherent escape clause. However, the use of such discretionary leeway did no harm to the Bank of England as it could rely on an excellent reputation. See Zarazaga (1995a), p. 3.

pegged exchange rates[314]. Such escape clauses can at best be envisaged for very extreme (and clearly discernible) situations such as national emergency.

Escape clauses, however, that clearly pre-define actions and the constellations under which they are allowed, are different from the above, in that they do not open discretionary leeway. Whether even such well-defined built-in escape clauses undermine a currency board's credibility from the beginning, or, on the contrary, entail an increase in credibility in reducing uncertainty about a currency board's behaviour remains disputed.

The main argument against such escape clauses relates to the criteria that are meant to trigger pre-defined actions (e.g. inflation or exchange rate limits exceeded by the reserve currency). Such trigger points, when approached, bear the potential to cause capital flows that render the escape case more probable than would otherwise be the case[315]. Thus, as opponents of escape clauses argue, the mere existence of (even well-defined) escape clauses can by itself trigger speculative capital flows and lead to a termination of the currency board, which possibly might have survived without escape clause[316].

Advocates of escape clauses retort that it is uncertainty that feeds speculation. If uncertainty is removed in the sense that the behaviour of the currency board is rule-bound not only within but also beyond pre-defined ranges (e.g. of reserve currency appreciation/depreciation or inflation/deflation), there is no room left for speculation. The development of the reserve currency then is the only thing that remains uncertain, and speculative capital flows remain limited, as they do not attack the currency board's commitment[317]. Apart from that, the effect of speculative capital flows on the development of the reserve currency (usually a major international reserve currency) will be small at best, so that self-fulfilling prophecies are unlikely to arise from any escape clause included in the currency board law of a usually small economy.

---

[314] See Fuhrmann (1999), p. 103.

[315] Consider, for instance, an escape clause that allows the currency board to devalue as soon as the reserve currency exceeds a pre-defined appreciation threshold against another major currency. Any appreciation bringing the reserve currency near the trigger point would render the escape case more likely, which from a certain point would lead speculators to sell currency board currency and buy reserve currency, thereby increasing the likelihood of the escape case.

[316] See Baliño/Enoch (1997), p. 28.

[317] See Hanke/Schuler (2000), p. 64.

Therefore, in order not to put achieved credibility at risk when the currency board faces extreme situations, and with a view to the credibility of potential future monetary regimes, it is certainly better to stick to well-defined rules, known in advance to the public, to govern an exit from the existing currency board rule, than to behave in improvised ways[318].

### Depreciation

For a currency under pressure through inflation and real appreciation, with no alleviation to be expected in the medium term, an early exit from the currency board may limit the degree of overvaluation and of the connected real losses. However, an exit followed by substantial depreciation is certain to undermine the credibility of policymakers unless it can be clearly justified by major external shocks.

The main problem with depreciation is that, if anticipated or announced, it induces capital flight, as the public tries to convert domestic assets into the reserve currency and to transfer them abroad. The resulting domestic interest rate increases can cause banks to break down, and the perceived risk can by itself cause bank runs and exacerbate the situation.

Alleviating, if politically questionable, measures can consist in temporarily suspending convertibility of deposits, or in a forced conversion of all deposits into the reserve currency at the pre-depreciation exchange rate. These measures however are likely to further damage policymakers' credibility.

A pre-announced downward crawling peg may provide a possible solution. It may limit the credibility loss caused by breaking the exchange rate rule, although it does not provide an insurance against losing control of the situation in terms of a devaluation-inflation-spiral.

### Appreciation

An exit followed by a substantial appreciation does not carry penalties similar to those of an exit followed by depreciation. The change of law carries no adverse effects, as the central objective of the law, the maintenance of the currency's value, is not violated. The legal hurdles imposed by the currency board are meant to

---

[318] During the 1995 tequila crisis and thereafter, the different performance of Mexico (which returned to floating and discretion) and Argentina (which stuck to the currency board law and confined crisis management to the pre-defined options) can be viewed as offering a backing for this finding. See Zarazaga (1995b), pp. 20-22.

prevent surprise devaluations, and as such can be overcome without damage in the case of appreciation.

A soft exit with the goal of appreciation of the domestic currency will probably become public well before the respective legal change. This will attract capital inflows, which potentially can undermine the appreciation strategy, as foreign reserves may cease to provide full backing of the expanded monetary base at the intended new exchange rate. In any event, an appreciation increases the value of the currency board's liabilities in relation to its assets, which causes losses for the currency board.

Again, a controlled and gradual upward crawl of the currency can be introduced to mitigate these problems by gradually allowing domestic interest rates to decrease and to keep capital inflows at bay[319].

### Switch to a Floating Exchange Rate

The switch to a floating exchange rate regime is most appropriate when the domestic currency is undervalued, especially when the pressure to appreciate is not too big. The switch to a float can be taken in steps, so as to allow the exchange rate to float initially within a band that can be widened gradually or be defined as a crawling band.

In cases of strong depreciation pressure, however, the switch to a float is unequally more dangerous, as it bears the risk of loss of the nominal anchor and of accelerating devaluation and inflation.

### Switch in the Peg

Another exit option consists in the change of the anchor currency. In changing to a reserve currency that is expected to depreciate vis-à-vis the main trading partners' currencies, a currency board can realise (provided these expectations materialise) a desired real effective depreciation of its currency (and vice versa for the case of a desired real effective appreciation)[320]. Destabilising capital flows can largely be prevented when the switch occurs at the relevant market cross exchange rates at the time of its implementation. However, the structure of domestic interest

---

[319] See Baliño/Enoch (1997), p. 25.

[320] See the proposal of a dual currency board, described in the next paragraph, where peg switches are intended ex ante to occur automatically as soon as a cross exchange rate defined by the currency board is reached. The pre-determination of peg switches makes them seem like a special kind of built-in escape clause, under avoidance of possibly destabilising effects.

rates will change with the new anchor currency, which is likely to bear some real costs, and possibly have an adverse impact on capital flows. These costs have to be weighed against the expected future benefits in terms of avoided real exchange rate misalignments. The reliance on mere expectations of nominal exchange rate movements, however, makes this strategy quite risky.

### 3.2.5    Dual Currency Boards: An Extended Proposal for Currency Stability

One interesting extension to the currency board idea deserves special attention: the proposal of so-called dual currency boards, brought forward by S.E. Oppers[321]. It shall be briefly sketched here in order to show how some of the drawbacks of the currency board idea can – so far only in theory – be avoided.

The idea is derived from the ancient experience with the gold and silver-based bimetallic monetary system, which dominated monetary constitutions from the Renaissance until the 19th century (when it was replaced by the gold standard). Under bimetallism, gold and silver competed for dominance with the effect that, according to Gresham's Law, "bad money" drove out "good money" and so prevailed as the circulating medium. While the system of competing specie was sometimes condemned as fundamentally unstable, the quality of the system to bring about quick and automatic changes in the peg constitutes the main advantage for the dual currency board.

The idea underlying the dual currency board idea is to extend the promise of convertibility to a second reserve currency, with the convertibility guarantee always subject to the availability of the respective currency in the reserves of the currency board. If one of the reserve currencies is not available, convertibility of the domestic currency into the other reserve currency is guaranteed. A shortage of the currency board of one of the reserve currencies is not to be seen as weakening the currency board's credibility, but, on the contrary, reflects the stabilising mechanism of the dual currency board as will be described with the following example.

Assume a country's currency is convertible by law into either one Dollar or one Euro. The rates of 1 unit of domestic currency per 1 Dollar or 1 Euro are the official "currency board rates". Total reserves can consist of one or both of the reserve currencies and always provide full coverage for domestic notes in circulation, valued at the currency board rates. At all times, conversion into one of the reserve currencies is guaranteed at the currency board rates. The currency board's activities

---

[321] See Oppers (2000).

include nothing that exceeds "orthodox" currency board activities: it only buys and sells both reserve currencies at the defined currency board rates upon demand and thus behaves completely passive. This frame yields a mechanism that Oppers illustrates with the help of the empirical development of the Dollar and Euro exchange rates during 1999 and 2000.

In January 1999, the market exchange rate of the Euro was 1.17 US-Dollars. With the defined currency board rates of 1 Euro = 1 Dollar = 1 unit of domestic currency, the Euro is undervalued in the domestic monetary system, which is why the currency board cannot hold or retain any Euros: they would quickly be bought by arbitrageurs at the currency board rate and profitably sold at the market rate. The reserves of the currency board therefore solely consist of Dollars, thus making the convertibility guarantee operational with respect to the Dollar only. The domestic currency is effectively pegged to the Dollar.

The Dollar's appreciation during 1999 stays without effect as long as the Dollar-Euro parity is not reached. However, when the market exchange rate of 1 Euro declines to below 1 Dollar (as happened in early 2000), it gets profitable for arbitrageurs to buy Dollars from the currency board, sell them in the exchange market at the market rate against Euros and sell those Euros to the currency board against domestic currency, so realising a riskless profit. As long as arbitrage processes are taking place, the deviation of the market exchange rate from parity will remain small as the currency board continues to sell Dollars. During this process, the mechanism enhances exchange rate stability in the region of the defined parity.

When Dollar reserves are sold, however, and the reserves of the currency board solely consist of Euros, the change of anchor currency has taken place and the domestic currency is effectively pegged to the Euro. It is important to stress that this switch in the peg is purely the effect of the dual convertibility guarantee and of rationally acting currency traders. It happens completely automatically and without intervention of any authority. Also, the currency board does not incur any loss as a result of the switch, since its reserves are always valued in domestic currency at the currency board rates[322].

---

[322] It can be argued that the currency board forgoes capital gains by leaving arbitrage opportunities to private traders, but there is no reason why the currency board should not realise those gains itself as soon as the respective cross exchange rate is crossed.

The beneficial effect of this switch is that the domestic currency is always pegged to the relatively more depreciated currency – in the same way as Gresham's law predicts that "cheap" reserves drive out "expensive" reserves. The crucial relation is the one between the Dollar-Euro market exchange rate, on the one hand, and their currency board rate, on the other. This relation indicates which of the reserve currencies is "relatively more depreciated" in the currency board country and, therefore, which is the effective peg.

This mechanism invalidates one of the main arguments against currency boards. The much-feared real overvaluation of the domestic currency as a result of an appreciating reserve currency, with its detrimental effects on the real economy, is avoided by making sure that the domestic currency is always pegged to the relatively more depreciated of two reserve currencies[323]. With respect to the criteria for the choice of reserve currency, this advantage of the dual currency board over the traditional form becomes prominent: with ever more diversified trade patterns, the choice of more than one reserve currency can better mirror existing trade patterns. If, as in the above example, foreign trade of the currency board country is split approximately evenly between the Euro area and the United States, the choice of the Euro and the Dollar as reserve currencies provides a better insurance against imported appreciation and loss of international competitiveness than would be the case with a single reserve currency.

Possible concerns about inflationary impacts of always pegging to the relatively more depreciated currency can be largely neglected, as long as the choice of reserve currencies has been made out of a set of stable currencies. It has to be borne in mind that the description of a currency as the "relatively more depreciated" one does not mean that it is constantly depreciating. On the contrary, if the cross rate implicit in the peg is near the point where it reflects something like long-term purchasing power parity, and if both reserve countries follow similar anti-inflationary

---

[323] As Oppers notes, the idea can theoretically also be extended to three or more reserve currencies, as well as to a basket of reserve currencies. While, in this way, existing trade patterns could be reflected even better and the real exchange rate could be kept more stable, the lack of transparency and rising transaction costs (as well as more likely re-weightings over time) render such options less desirable.

policies, the reserve currency cross rate will oscillate around the currency board cross rate, and the opposite effects tend to cancel out over time[324].

The effects of a dual currency board on interest rates are governed by the fact that a switch of peg also effectuates a switch of interest rate connectivity. As Oppers shows, the relatively more depreciated (hence the reserve) currency will always have a higher interest rate than the relatively less depreciated currency. This is the result of the implicit structure of the convertibility guarantee (which, in fact, incorporates "call options" for the reserve currency[325]). Nevertheless, a dual currency board country's interest rates need not be higher than they would be with a "simple" currency board regime, as the risk premium on the domestic currency should be lower with a dual currency board, reflecting the relatively lower risk of real overvaluation and ensuing credibility loss.

As becomes clear, the choice of the currency board cross rate is central because it decides over the probable timing and frequency of peg switches. It should optimally be set at an "equilibrium" rate, at which neither of the reserve currencies is significantly over- or undervalued vis-à-vis the other and, implicitly, vis-à-vis the domestic currency. Additional considerations could lead to the decision to define the currency board rate at a level at which the domestic currency would probably be pegged most of the time to one of the two reserve currencies. In this way, a switch in peg could still avoid the worst degrees of overvaluation, while, apart from that, the domestic economy could stay with the (preferred) peg throughout acceptable movements in valuation[326]. Equally, the currency board rates could be realigned at any time, e.g. by adapting one of the conversion rates to long-term real exchange rate developments, in order to correct relations which have initially been set at unfavourable levels.

As mentioned above, ongoing arbitrage processes during the switch in peg enhance exchange rate stability in the region of the currency board cross rate[327].

---

[324] Oppers has substantiated this assumption with empirical evidence for a hypothetical dual currency board with the Dollar and the Euro as reserve currencies in the period from 1979 to 2000. See pp. 8 and 20.

[325] See Oppers (2000), p. 9.

[326] Such a strategy could be envisaged for "dollarised" countries, i.e. where the economy is already significantly penetrated by one of the reserve currencies. See Oppers (2000), pp. 9-10.

[327] This is brought about not only by the arbitrage processes themselves (a directly stabilising effect) but also by the anticipation of rational investors who expect them when the market cross rate

While the global exchange rate stabilising influence of one single dual currency board should not be overestimated, the possibility of various countries establishing dual currency boards reveals further potentials: in pooling their reserves, co-ordinated dual currency boards (setting currency board rates at identical or slightly different implicit cross rates) could contribute significantly to global currency stability[328].

Thus, the dual currency board idea provides an appealing way to avoid one of the most important weaknesses of an orthodox currency board. Significant and lasting real overvaluation of the domestic currency and the connected economic costs can be largely prevented through a simple and transparent extension of the currency board rule, the addition of an alternative reserve currency. In addition to the beneficial effects on the local economy, obtained by completely market-conform and non-interventionist mechanisms, a dual currency board exerts a stabilising effect on exchange rates, which even could be maximised when several countries adopted and co-ordinated the system. Against the argument that the system could be considered more complicated and hence less credible than a traditional currency board stands the historical experience with bimetallism which shows that its functioning can be well understood by the public and provide stability over long periods.

---

approaches the currency board rate, and behave accordingly (indirect effect). See Oppers (2000), pp. 10-1.

[328] Again, there is an encouraging historical parallel with bimetallism. See Oppers (2000), p. 12.

# 4 The Argentine Currency Board Arrangement

Argentina has a story to tell the world: a story which is about the importance of fiscal discipline, of structural change, and of monetary policy rigorously maintained.[329]

## 4.1 Features and Implementation of the Argentine CBA

### 4.1.1 The Legal Fixing

#### 4.1.1.1 The Convertibility Law

On March 27th, 1991, Argentina's legislative announced the Convertibility law, to be enforced on April 1st, 1991.

This very short and concise law decrees a fixed exchange rate between the domestic currency, then the Austral, and the US-Dollar (10,000 Australes to equal one US-Dollar) and ties the emission of the former to the amount of available central bank reserves: article 4 states that free gold and foreign exchange reserves held by the BCRA be equal to 100% of the monetary base. Article 6 defines the monetary base as money in circulation plus demand deposits held by financial institutions with the BCRA. While the BCRA is committed to sell foreign exchange at the defined parity (art. 2), it is not required to buy them at the fixed exchange rate (art. 3). The whole of existing inflation adaptation mechanisms, namely all kinds of indexation, whether legally or privately contracted, are declared invalid and enforced to end before April 1st, 1991[330]. Article 12 states that the "post April 1st" Austral is to be regarded as a new currency, and that it can be given a new denomination and numerical expression at a later point of time. This provision was implemented nine months later, when 10,000 Australes were replaced by one Peso on January 1st, 1992.

---

[329] The IMF Managing Director Michel Camdessus during a press conference held at the IMF Annual Meetings on October 1st, 1998. See IMF Independent Evaluation Office (2004), p.12.

[330] See República Argentina (1991), Articles 7 to 10. Outstanding payments covering periods before April 1st, including periodical payments, are allowed to be inflation adapted up to a maximum of 12 percent annually – until April 1st, date from which all contracts, new and existing ones, are legislated to exist and continue as nominal contracts.

### 4.1.1.2 The New Central Bank Law

As a supplement to, and substantiation of, the Convertibility law, the central bank law ("carta orgánica") was modified in September 1992 to define some important details of the Argentine CBA.

Besides obliging the BCRA to "develop a monetary and financial policy directed to safeguard the functions of money as store of value, unit of account, and means of payment", the central bank law states that it "will not be subject to orders, indications, or instructions from the national executive power"[331], i.e. it decrees the BCRA's formal independence. The law provides for a standing central bank president and directory, appointed for the duration of 6 years by the national executive (i.e. the Argentine president) with consent of the Senate. This article intends to grant steady central bank governance and make the removal of the central bank president difficult[332].

Among the operations allowed for the BCRA are the exclusive issue of notes and coins, limited short-term rediscount and repurchase operations with financial institutions, the trade on bond, foreign exchange, and international credit markets, as well as the (interest free) acceptance of domestic and foreign currency deposits. The law expressly forbids, inter alia, the granting or guaranteeing of credit to the national government as well as to private banks, provinces, or municipalities. However, the BCRA is allowed to buy negotiable titles issued by the treasury, valued at market prices, which are allowed to form part of the reserves backing of the monetary base, within two limits: their nominal value to grow by not more than 10% annually, and never to constitute more than a third of the reserves[333]. Profits are to be used to build up a reserve fund up to a limit of 50 percent of the bank's capital, before they are to be transferred to the government[334]. Besides, the BCRA is entitled to perform its traditional (remuneration free) task as the government's

---

[331] República Argentina (1992), art. 3, own translation.

[332] See República Argentina (1992), article 7. It did not prevent, however, the later removal of central bank president Pedro Pou in the midst of crisis in April 2001 (over alleged money laundering charges, but obviously amid disagreements with the government).

[333] See República Argentina (1992), articles 17 to 20, 30, and 33. Article 60 further confines the allowed proportion of government bonds to 20% of the reserves base during the first 6 years, i.e. the term of the first central bank directory. In addition, it states that after that period, the limit of 33% may be reached only transitorily (up to 90 days), and only in cases of liquidity needs within the financial system, or of losses in the market value of the respective titles.

[334] See República Argentina (1992), article 38.

sole financial agent to manage the whole of its banking and financing operations[335]. As an instrument to control monetary aggregates and the functioning of financial markets, the BCRA is entitled to impose reserve requirements upon financial institutions. Finally, regulations to publish monetary and financial statistics and to exercise the full range of banking supervision tasks complete this law.

### 4.1.2 Assessment of the Argentine CBA's Configuration

#### 4.1.2.1 Orthodox and Non-Orthodox Elements

The above laws clearly show that Argentina's CBA cannot be qualified as an orthodox currency board. The existing Argentine central bank continues to carry out most of its previous activities as a monetary authority. The conversion function (which exhaustingly characterises an orthodox currency board) here constitutes only one function among many other, typical central bank, functions (the discount window, trading on financial markets, acceptance of deposits, imposition of reserve requirements, banking supervision, acting as a financial agent for the government).

Several particular features stand out in differentiating the Argentine CBA from the orthodox concept. First, the provision that up to a third of the reserves backing of the monetary base may be constituted by domestic government bonds represents a substantial deviation from the ideal and, if exploited, a potentially jeopardising element to the currency board's credibility. Second, the potential asymmetry in exchange rates for central bank purchases and sales allows de facto for a revaluation of the domestic currency[336] (which is however in accord with the stability oriented spirit of the law). Third, the acceptance of bank deposits also represents a deviation from the orthodox idea, but again that does not hurt since these deposits form part of the monetary base and are backed as such. Fourth, the BCRA regulates the banking and financial system via reserve requirements and money market operations, which incorporates the power to control the overall money supply. Here, as is the case with the "less than hundred percent" backing of the money base, considerable room is left for discretion.

Still, the very fundamental features of the legal frame sketched above absorb much of these potential credibility shortcomings. These are, first and most important, the legal provision of the central bank's independence. Second, the fixing of the nominal exchange rate by law, which implies that any change in the nominal

---

[335] See República Argentina (1992), articles 21 to 26.
[336] See Baliño/Enoch (1997), p. 4.

exchange rate would require the full legislative procedure and approval by Congress, i.e. would face significant hurdles. Third, the backing rule, which, although deviating from the 100 percent ideal, by itself signifies a strong commitment to the maintenance of the fixed parity. Fourth, the provisions to restrict the central bank's financing of budget deficits, which incorporate a drastic break with habits practised over decades. Fifth, the sudden prohibition of any indexation, meant to minimise inflation inertia. Sixth, the liberalisation of foreign exchange markets[337]. Finally, the stop of interest payments on the financial sector's required reserves, which previously always had been a source of quasi-fiscal deficits (as they were not compensated by corresponding interest earnings) and, in effect, subsidised credits to the private sector[338].

In sum, the legal conception of the Argentine CBA provided a drastic change in the conditions for monetary and fiscal policy. It erected in Argentina hitherto unseen rigid rules that implied a near-to-maximum of "tying hands". At the same time, it allowed for limited flexibility within those rules to keep a near-to-minimum space for "free hands". As it turned out during the following decade, the discretionary space the CBA left for monetary policy was used in an overtly responsible manner[339], so that it proved to be highly beneficial in contributing to a credible monetary constitution that eliminated inflation and generated beneficial conditions for investment, growth, and structural reform. Yet, as indicated before, the monetary constitution is only one, albeit central, element of a broader policy package to be embedded in.

### 4.1.2.2 The Choice of the Anchor and the Rate

It is often held that Argentina did wrong in choosing the US-Dollar as the anchor currency. Its trade pattern at the time of doing so gives this opinion every justification: the biggest share in Argentina's trade of 1990 was with the EU, where roughly 30 percent of its exports went (imports from the EU: 26%). The second destination of Argentina's exports were MERCOSUR countries (15%, imports 21.5%)[340], while the US occupied only the third place with an export share of barely

---

[337] In fact, foreign exchange controls had already been abolished in late 1989.

[338] See Kiguel (1999), pp. 8-9

[339] See Heymann (2000), p. 51.

[340] The treaty that established the MERCOSUR (Mercado Común del Sur), to be launched in January 1995, was signed on the very day the Convertibility law was announced, on March 27th, 1991.

14 percent (imports 21.5%). Therefore, to judge from existing trade patterns, there was no such thing as an immediate "natural candidate" among the world's potential anchor currencies. The anchor with most justification in this respect would have been the Deutsche Mark (to which most European currencies were pegged), and later the Euro. Nor can the argument be brought forward that the choice of anchor currency would have anticipated future shifts in trade patterns in favour of the US: exports to the United States subsequently declined, to hover around 10 percent and less over years. The only argument in favour of the US-Dollar that could be derived from the trade structure was that Brazil, the single most important trading partner, itself at the time had pegged its currency to the Dollar.

Yet, the argument which by far overrode any reflection on trade patterns was that of the existing pervasive dollarisation of the Argentine economy. As depicted in section 2, the US-Dollar had taken over nearly all of the domestic currency's functions, and left only the most basic consumer transactions to the Austral. The express recognition of the US-Dollar as a legal tender in a sense mainly ratified what was reality, shaped by years and decades of high and hyperinflation. Hence, in capitalising on the profound trust and familiarity that economic agents brought forth towards the US-Dollar, the choice of the US-Dollar as anchor made complete sense. It certainly helped overcome the massive handicap of initial lack of confidence which any plan would have had to deal with in the light of the precarious past.

The exact rate of exchange, besides providing an even and handy relation, was slightly higher than the free market exchange rate at the moment of the Convertibility law's enactment[341]. This had the advantage to allow for some initial inflationary inertia. At that rate, the BCRA's foreign exchange reserves of 6.2 billion US-Dollars[342] comfortably backed the monetary base which amounted to 4.9 billion in April and averaged 5.75 billion over the year 1991[343].

### 4.1.2.3 Suboptimal Currency Area

As pointed out, the urgent stabilisation necessity was the main motivation for the choice of the CBA, and the high degree of prevailing dollarisation the reason for

---

[341] See Canavese (2001), p. 7f.

[342] For the year 1991. See IMF Independent Evaluation Office (2004), p. 10.

[343] Source: Oficina de la CEPAL en Buenos Aires. These reserves were the result of a comfortable external trade surplus accumulated during 1990, when imports had been extremely low. See Heymann (2000), p. 50.

the choice of the anchor currency. Though these choices may enjoy every justification with respect to Argentina's peculiar situation of the time, this does not absolve from considering their medium term viability. Going through the checklist of the criteria for optimal currency areas, or hard pegs, delivers some important qualifications as to the economic medium-term appropriateness of the CBA.

On the positive side, Argentina's record of chronically credibility-lacking monetary policy, of high inflation and recurring currency crises, spoke strongly in favour of the choice of a CBA. If aspirations to move eventually towards official dollarisation played a role in the choice of the monetary and exchange rate regime, this was a strong argument for the CBA as well.

However, Argentina's real characteristics clearly did not support a hard peg to the US-Dollar. First, while Argentina was, in terms of economic size, a small country, it did not qualify as an open one. Its share of trade in output was, with around 16 percent of GDP[344], small. As a consequence, the adjustment to external shocks required a correspondingly higher change in the real exchange rate. Consequently, the real costs Argentina would have to incur in adjusting to shocks could be expected to be substantially higher with the Dollar-peg than with flexible exchange rates. Second, Argentina and the US were quite diverse in their economic and trade structures, and linked by comparatively little, especially intra-industry[345], trade. Thus, the two countries' business cycles were anything but closely correlated, and the probability of shocks hitting them asymmetrically was high[346]. In addition, Argentina's exports consisted mainly of homogeneous primary products, and as such were especially exposed to frequent global shocks.

The choice of the Argentine CBA in 1991 doubtlessly included economic and political time preference, understandable in the light of the desperate situation of the

---

[344] See IMF Independent Evaluation Office (2004), p. 15.

[345] The share of intra-industry trade in total trade between two countries can be viewed as an indicator of their economic integration, as it reflects the degree of similarity between their productive structures.

[346] In the light of both the geographical distance between Argentina and the dominant position of Mexico in the US' trade relations with Latin America, as well as the limited initial trade links between Argentina and the US, there was also little reason to expect, in the medium to longer term, substantially rising economic integration, and thus growing synchronisation of shocks and business cycles. Nor can factor mobility between the two countries be described as high, or growing, despite some cyclical emigration of Argentine manpower and, even more, capital, to the US, and some FDI of US companies, predominantly in the financial sector, in Argentina; the biggest chunks of FDI in the Argentine industrial sector originated from European countries.

country. With the hard exchange rate peg, but real characteristics that did not support it, the policy challenge for Argentina was now, on the one hand, to support the peg (via a firm commitment to it, via responsible fiscal policies, via a strengthening of the financial sector), and, on the other hand, to compensate for the loss of exchange rate flexibility by enabling the economy to adequately adjust to shocks, and thus to reduce the costs caused by the adverse real characteristics (via an increase in the flexibility of its markets, especially labour markets, and institutions)[347]. The following paragraphs will give a chronological documentation of both the relevant policy actions and the development of the CBA, in order to prepare the ground for the evaluation and assessment in section 5.

## 4.2    The Stabilisation Track during the 1990s

### 4.2.1    The Early 1990s' Economic Reforms

Partly preceding, but mostly paralleling and succeeding the monetary and currency reform, institutional reforms in many other areas complemented the "Ley de Convertibilidad" to make the Argentine economy fit into the new monetary frame it imposed[348]. The whole of economic reform that encompassed the CBA was generally referred to as "Plan Convertibilidad". It was supported by the IMF with a Stand-by Arrangement approved in 1991 and extended in 1992.

#### 4.2.1.1 Further Reforms Shaping the Monetary Frame

As soon as in 1989, banks had been legally obliged to repay deposits in the currency in which they were constituted. Also in 1989, faced with the impossibility to roll over its domestic currency debt, and in the light of the Austral's diminishing relevance and the rising Dollar demand, the government had taken several important measures to prepare the ground for the CBA. These included, first, the complete abolishment of exchange controls. Second, all Austral-denominated bonds and term deposits in the banking system had been converted by decree on January 1st, 1990, into 10-year US-Dollar denominated government bonds (the so-called BONEX) at LIBOR[349], with the intention to eliminate the large quasi-fiscal deficits of the central bank that arose from exorbitant Austral interest rates to be paid as

---

[347] See Andrade/Falcão Silva/Trautwein (2005), p. 67.

[348] For an examination of the interdependence between macroeconomic policy and structural reform, see also Begg (2002).

[349] See IMF Independent Evaluation Office (2004), p. 79.

remuneration for reserve requirements. Moreover, the government had empowered the central bank to accumulate foreign exchange reserves resulting from a large trade surplus due to extremely low imports[350].

### 4.2.1.2 Brady Restructuring

The initial step towards a more sustainable fiscal stance was to tackle the still unresolved debt crisis that had been dragging on since the early 1980s. Like many other emerging economies at the time, Argentina, in 1992, undertook a restructuring of its public debt with international commercial banks under the Brady Plan. Within that scheme, creditor banks swapped government bonds against bonds with longer maturities (up to 30 years) which incorporated discounts in interest or principal, these bonds being worth in total about 25 billion US-Dollars[351]. The principal and interest of the new bonds were securitised by US Treasury bonds, themselves financed by the international financial organisations. The Brady Plan included the commitment of debtor countries to implement far-ranging reforms towards market liberalisation (which, however, in Argentina, as in many other debtor countries, were being adopted independently from the Brady Plan)[352]. Its successful completion was seen as a precondition for Argentina to regain access to voluntary financing on international capital markets.

### 4.2.1.3 Tax Reforms

Other urgent fiscal measures included a general tax overhaul which had to tackle inefficient and highly distortionary taxes, myriads of exemptions and loopholes, as well as widespread tax evasion, and had to do without the previous main source of income, the inflation tax.

The "Ley de Emergencia Económica", legislated by the new government in late 1989, started public finance reforms. One of the first measures was, in 1990, to broaden the tax base for the most important tax source, the VAT, to include most goods and, especially, services, which had previously been exempt. In 1992, the base was broadened again to capture financial, insurance, and freight services. The VAT rate (after having been initially reduced from 15 to 13 percent in 1989) was

---

[350] See Heymann (2000), p. 50.

[351] See Heymann (2000), p. 54.

[352] For a short description and critical assessment of the Brady Plan see, e.g., Vásquez (1996).

increased several times, to 18 percent in steps until mid-1991, and (as an adjustment measure following the Tequila Crisis) to 21 percent in March 1995.

Taxes on profits and capital were modified as well. First, the tax rate on capital gains was reduced, and the tax levied on corporate net assets eliminated. Then, in 1991, a new tax on private person's assets was introduced. In 1992, the tax on corporate profits was increased from 20 to 30 percent, and to 35 percent in 1998, when it was, following the concept of a "renta mundial", also applied on profits generated abroad. With the same tax reform in 1998, corporate loans got taxed (in order to make financing by proper resources more attractive). The tax on corporate net assets was re-installed (to be settled with the profit tax).

Penalties for tax evasion were increased, and the collection system underwent a concentration process, as a result of which national taxes, as well as customs, were to be collected by a single agency, that disposed of an increased number of staff and innovated technical equipment and procedures. Tax compliance did improve somewhat, but not overwhelmingly: compliance of the nationally collected VAT, for instance, estimated at 34 percent in 1989, rose to 55 percent in 1994[353].

### 4.2.1.4 Federal Fiscal Relations

The relation between national and provincial public finances has since decades been a source of political and fiscal hardship[354]. Starting from a constitutionally very limited fiscal power of the federal government[355], the "Ley de Coparticipación

---

[353] Neighbouring countries have much higher compliance rates: 80 and 70 percent respectively in Chile and Uruguay. See Saiegh/Tommasi (1999), p. 182.

[354] The Federal Republic of Argentina consists of 23 provinces and the autonomous district of the city of Buenos Aires. The federal government is responsible for the collection of most taxes which are then allocated between the federal government and the provinces. The allocation scheme is referred to as "Coparticipación Federal de Impuestos" (or "coparticipación" in short). It was introduced in 1935 and has since been repeatedly modified, to evolve into a highly complex system which, as is undoubted, is highly inefficient as well as extremely rigid. For an excellent analysis of coparticipación see Saiegh/Tommasi (1999). They identify a myriad of perverse incentives and inefficiencies in what has been dubbed the "Coparticipation Labyrinth".

[355] Originally, the national government's sovereignty only included the imposition of customs duties and, in exceptional cases, temporary direct contributions. Taxes like the VAT, therefore, formally were imposed by provincial jurisdictions and administered by the national government on behalf of the provinces. With the constitutional reform of 1994, the national government received the right to impose indirect taxes in concurring legislation with the provinces. The 1994 constitution also ordained that the coparticipación be newly defined by law until the end of 1996 – prescription

Federal de Impuestos", in its current form of 1988, regulates the sources and transfer of revenue and obligations between the federal and provincial governments. Since 1988, it has been prolonged and modified several times following repeated negotiations. According to this law, taxes subject to "coparticipación", including VAT, taxes on profit, and special sales taxes, are attributed different distribution coefficients, with the effect that the federal government is assigned 57 percent of their total, and 42 percent go to the provinces (one percent being set aside "to finance unforeseen crises in the provinces")[356]. In 1991, agreements between the federal government and each of the provinces were negotiated to manage mutual debt relations, which concerned the control of hydrocarbon extraction and provincial bank's debt with the national government.

In 1992, the responsibility for many services in health care, education, and social security was transferred to the provinces, to be financed by funds delivered by corresponding shifts in revenue participation.

Also, the use of so-called "precoparticipaciones" was intensified. This construct means that parts of the shared tax revenues are deducted before the sharing mechanisms take hold, and used for other purposes. An important case of "precoparticipación" was agreed in 1992, when the federal government received the right to withhold 15 percent of the shared funds pool for the financing of social security deficits.

Special provincial duties such as stamp taxes, taxes on sales and on energy for industrial use were reduced, while the federal government cut back non-wage labour costs, both in the attempt to lower production costs[357].

In an attempt to reduce the scope of discretionary action by the federal government, the latter guaranteed a fixed minimum sum of the shared funds pool to be transferred to the provinces within the primary distribution (the fixed sum corresponds to roughly 90 percent of the pool)[358]. The introduction of these guaranteed fixed sum transfers to the provinces increased the coparticipation scheme's rigidity and hence its inefficiency; while the guaranteed minimum posed

---

that has not been implemented to date. See Article 75 and sixth "disposición transitoria" of the 1994 Constitution.

[356] See Saiegh/Tommasi (1999), p. 176.

[357] See Heymann (2000), pp. 70f.

[358] "Primary distribution" refers to the distribution between the federal government and the provinces as a group, whereas the "secondary distribution" defines the allocation of these funds among the provinces.

no problem in the context of expanding tax revenues (expectation, of course, it was based upon), it had to be fatal during recessions.

While other fiscal reforms following the CBA's introduction can be qualified as generally improving the fiscal stance, no such judgement can be made for Argentina's federal fiscal relations. The modifications taken in the early 90s did not do anything to improve fiscal health as they did not tackle the many shortcomings of the system which can be subsumed under a few key words such as "common pool" and "moral hazard" problems, "perverse incentives", and "multiple inefficiencies".

To illustrate this, suffice some of the most conspicuous traits: under the coparticipación scheme, provinces have incentives to overexploit the common pool of nationally collected taxes, to reduce their own provincial taxing efforts, and to rely on being bailed out by the national government. Moreover, they are induced to behave procyclically (as, e.g., in the case when, in a restrictive fiscal effort of the national government, the latter raises taxes: as a consequence, provincial tax allocations and thus their incentives to expand spending increase, and national policies in effect are being counteracted). For the federal government, non-shared taxes acquire greater weight relative to shared taxes (because they don't have to be shared), even if they are less efficient. National fiscal corrections are biased towards spending cuts (or even tariffs on trade) rather than tax rises (which often have to be shared). Provincial governments have little incentive to make efforts to increase tax compliance. They do have incentives to oppose the decentralisation of (and the responsibility for) taxes from the national government to the provinces. Within the highly complex and politicised system of coparticipation, most provincial governmental energy is directed towards lobbying for selfish redistribution[359].

### 4.2.1.5 Privatisation and Deregulation

The "Ley de Reforma del Estado" was one of the first acts of the Menem government in the second half of 1989. It intended to substantially reduce the scope of the public sector and set off a massive programme to sell inefficient and subsidised state industries or grant concessions to the private sector[360]. At the time of the enactment of the CBA, the majority of interests in two major state enterprises, ENTEL (telecommunications) and Aerolíneas Argentinas (airways), had already

---

[359] See Saiegh/Tommasi (1999).

[360] The privatisation debate focuses on the non-financial sector. The financial sector was initially not included in the privatisation programme. Privatisations of, mainly provincial, banks were, to the overwhelming part, undertaken after 1995, as a response to the Tequila crisis.

been sold. In the following years, a broad variety of state owned enterprises and assets were privatised, including road, train, and harbour concessions, postal services, hotels, banks, insurances, public utilities such as water and electricity, and steel and petrochemical firms. Apart from the big sales named above, further important sales concerned YPF (petrochemicals; between 1991 and 1993), EDENOR, and EDESUR (electricity; between 1992 and 1993)[361]. According to estimations, in 1997, a quarter of sales and two thirds of profits of Argentina's top hundred companies were realised by firms privatised since 1990[362].

The privatisation programme followed various objectives. First, there was the fiscal motivation. Besides the direct revenue effect from sales and the cancellation of debt, state transfers and subsidies to the respective industries were reduced or eliminated[363]. Second, privatisations intended to secure investment and the efficient proliferation of public goods and services via contractual obligations. Third, their signalling function as a visible, strong commitment to the general political direction was an important motive as well. It has been argued that the fiscal and the political motivation dominated the first generation of privatisations, when buyers were offered highly advantageous terms under the budgetary pressure to generate immediate revenues[364], and that more emphasis was given to microeconomic aspects only in later years[365].

Between 1990 and 1998, revenues of privatisations amounted to approximately 24 billion US-Dollars, whereof 90 percent were realised during 1990 to 1993, which reflects the enormous initial speed the privatisation programme was brought forward with. In 1991 and 1992, the proceeds from privatisation equalled around 1 percent of GDP (or 10 percent of tax receipts). From the fiscal point of view, therefore, the privatisation programme has to be viewed as very successful.

---

[361] For a detailed account of privatised entities see Heymann (2000), pp. 145 ff.

[362] See Heymann (2000), p. 58.

[363] Of around 400 state-owned enterprises, which together accounted for seven percent of GDP, the thirteen largest recorded combined losses of four billion US-Dollars in 1989, which also illustrates the extremely low productivity in the public sector. See Pastor/Wise (1999), p. 487.

[364] Purchase prices were often agreed to be partially paid in government bonds, taken at face value, at a time when they were worth only a fraction of that in the markets. So, nominally high prices actually incorporated sales at sometimes far below realistic values. See Heymann (2000), p. 55.

[365] For a microeconomic analysis of the privatisation process, see Galiani et al. (2003).

From the microeconomic perspective, however, the design of the privatisation programme and its regulatory framework deserves mixed credentials at best. In most areas, the quality of public services improved after their privatisation, starting of course from a generally dismal level. Following their privatisation, the respective industries generally showed remarkable dynamics and even outpaced GDP growth during much of the 1990s, benefiting not only from economic growth but also from significant unsatisfied demand prior to privatisation. Investment activity increased significantly as a result of privatisation (by as much as 350 percent between 1990 and 1998 in the privatised industries, as estimated by Galiani et al.[366]). The development of utility tariffs was heterogeneous (e.g., electricity prices decreased somewhat, while gas and telecommunications got substantially more expensive). Overall, however, it can be said that the strong efficiency gains recorded in the privatised industries did not translate into correspondingly lower prices. Moreover, a general bias in the development of tariffs was an increasing differentiation according to consumed quantities, which tended to favour big, industrial customers at the expense of households, and thus incorporated a substantial cross-subsidy from final consumers to the producing sector[367].

The most salient effect of the privatisation programme, however, was its contribution to rising unemployment. Staff reductions, or changes in its composition with respect to age and skills, were the consequence of most privatisations. Estimations suggest that total employment in the privatised industries was reduced by around 40 percent[368], while productivity in the privatised industries rose by an estimated 46 percent on average. The rising productivity, however, was also the result of production increases[369].

Generally, most contracts with privatised utilities were deficient in some way or another. Many of them had to be renegotiated subsequently. Also, in several

---

[366] See Galiani et al. (2003), p. 40.

[367] See Heymann (2000), p. 58. However, Ennis/Pinto (2002) find that the privatisation process produced only limited changes in inequality, as to judge from changes in relative prices, changes in access, as well as qualitative and quantitative changes in employment. See Ennis/Pinto (2002), p. 46.

[368] See Galiani et al. (2003), p. 18. They also point out that this number is likely to underestimate the true employment effect of privatisation, as staff was already reduced in the immediate pre-privatisation period in many instances.

[369] A further, often omitted, side effect of especially the water and sewerage sector's privatisation is its positive impact on sanitary conditions: the privatisation of water provision is estimated to have reduced child mortality rates by 5 percent. See Galiani et al. (2003), p. 31.

158

instances, private contractors failed to fulfil their contractual obligations in terms of committed investment, which often stayed without sanction. It has been argued that the implementation of the public utilities' regulation was very problematic both in terms of selection of the best offer in the auction and of consumer protection[370].

### 4.2.1.6 Financial Sector Reform

As pointed out, the CBA reduced the central bank's lender of last resort-capacities to a minimum. The fiscal constraint meant that the central bank could not further bear the losses of the banking sector, as had been done throughout the 1980s via implicit deposit insurance and repeated bail-outs[371]. This entailed the necessity of a strong private financial sector and a consequently reduced probability of crises that would require such stand-by. Banking regulations aimed at ensuring the safety of individual banks and of the banking system, and at increasing competition between banks.

Beginning in September 1991, capital requirements, previously inexistent, were implemented at an initial rate of 3 percent of assets, to be gradually increased to reach 11.5 percent in January 1995, thus surmounting the Basle standards recommended for industrial countries. At the same time, reserve requirements were set at very high levels to reach 43 percent on average on checking and savings deposits and 3 percent on time deposits[372]. Rules for risk diversification and the provision of loan-loss reserves were toughened. The existing voluntary deposit insurance scheme was abolished, partly in order to reduce moral hazard, but also because it was inefficient and suffered from low participation[373].

As the new monetary and banking regime implied a significant change in the risk-sharing rules governing depositors' relations with their banks, the former were in fact obliged to monitor the latter themselves. To enable depositors to do so, the central bank started, in 1993, a policy of larger information disclosure, forcing banks to publish detailed accounts and statements on asset quality on a monthly basis[374].

---

[370] See Artana/Navajas/Urbiztondo (1998), p. 46.

[371] Total losses to the central bank arising from such bail-outs amounted to 14.6 billion US-Dollars throughout the 1980s. See Schumacher (2000), p. 260.

[372] See Pou (2000), p. 14.

[373] It has been argued that its small volume, as well as the fear that a bank's decision to subscribe could carry a negative signal about its situation, reduced incentives to participate. See Heymann (2000), p. 52.

[374] See Schumacher (2000), p. 260.

Further regulations aimed at creating a free market environment in the financial sector and at promoting competition. Restrictions on the entry of foreign banks and on the opening of new branches of domestic banks were removed, and the domestic financial sector's restructuring and streamlining via mergers and acquisitions was facilitated[375].

### 4.2.1.7 Social Security Reform

Due to demographic changes, but also to the low proportion of workers paying social security contributions[376], the public pay-as-you-go pension system experienced increasing financial pressures. The relation of contributors to beneficiaries had fallen from five in the 1950s to two in the early 80s, and went on to decrease to 1.3 in the mid-1990s. During the 1980s, pensions had been partly financed by employers' and employees' contributions[377], and partly by direct transfers from the treasury and from energy and telecommunication sales effectuated by state industries. As the latter source was eliminated with the privatisation process, parts of VAT and profit tax were assigned to that purpose. However, in the early 90s, the government failed to meet its pension obligations and was massively sued, whereupon it decreed the partial payment of pensions in special 10-year government bonds[378]. Besides the financial difficulties, the public pension system was also criticised for unequal treatment of different groups of contributors, as well as for lack of transparency and reliability.

The congressional discussions of a major reform to introduce a capitalisation scheme started in 1992; after its legal enactment in 1993, the new system was to start in mid-1994. It was, as a result of political resistance resulting in a compromise, designed as a mixed system where the state kept a role in the provisioning of pensions. Active employees could choose the new capitalisation scheme and transfer their contributions to a pension fund, or remain in the old public pension system, which, however, was to be gradually phased out. At the same time,

---

[375] See Kiguel (1999), p. 12.

[376] In 1995, less than half of the total employed paid contributions to the national pensions system. This was for the biggest part due to the high proportion of informal employment, but also to the existence of some provincial pension schemes.

[377] Employers' contribution was 7.5 percent of the salary in 1984, and was gradually increased up to 16 percent in 1991.

[378] These were the so-called „BOCONes", issued on basis of the "consolidation law" of August 1991, and denominated optionally in Australes, later Pesos, or in Dollars.

rules for access to the public pension system were tightened[379], the minimum pension age increased in steps from 62 (57) to reach 65 (60) years for men (women) until 2001, and social security payroll taxes were reduced.

The reform was designed to gain younger employees for the capitalisation scheme, and in this respect was quite successful. However, the expectation that a system where individual contributions accumulated to deliver one's individual pension would increase the number of contributors did not materialise: in 1996, only half of those who had opted for the capitalisation system did actually pay contributions. So, the reform did not succeed in raising the proportion of formal employment and in improving the contributions situation[380].

A beneficial side-effect of the social security reform was the boost it gave to the development of local capital markets, as pension funds started to advertise for contributions and to seek diversified investment opportunities.

The fiscal cost of the transition to the new social security system consisted of an immediate transfer of funds from the public sector to the pension funds (mirroring the contributions employees changing to the new system had already paid into the old system), of smaller contribution revenues due to the reduced payroll taxes, and, in addition, of the takeover of the obligations of some of the bankrupt provincial systems by the federal government[381]. On the positive side stood a long-term reduction of public pension obligations, the calculation of the latter being subject to considerable uncertainty[382]. Within the first half of the 1990s, national expenditures for social provision rose by two points to six percent of GDP, constituting a peak since the 70s and by far the biggest chunk within total social expenditures[383]. The fiscal imbalance created by the social security reform has been estimated to worsen

---

[379] E.g., the minimum number of contribution years was increased to 20, the number of years upon which final pension levels are computed raised from 3 to 10, and requirements for invalidity pensions were tightened.

[380] See Heymann (2000), pp. 71ff.

[381] See IMF Independent Evaluation Office (2004), p. 34.

[382] In 1997, transfers from the public system to the pension funds equalled 1.1 percent of GDP, thus constituting most of the federal budget deficit. At the same time, most of these transfers were invested in Argentine government bonds.

[383] See Heymann (2000), pp. 76f.

gradually, with an annual overall federal fiscal revenue gap of 2.7 percent of GDP on average since 1994[384].

It can be argued that the social security reform, with the pertinent increase in fiscal deficits, simply made explicit the debt already implicit in the existing system, which markets were willing to finance. In the general perception of markets and the public, however, the visible immediate fiscal burden from the transition was taken at face value and not, as was hoped by politicians, discounted by the expected long-term relief[385]. Accordingly, capital markets did not price in the expected long-term relief for the social security system, and so added to the costs of the reform[386]. Although the pension reform was generally appreciated as one of the most important reforms in the 1990s, its pertinent budgetary implications proved to develop into a major source of diverging assessments of Argentina's fiscal situation.

### 4.2.1.8 Labour Market Reforms

Labour market issues initially did not stand at the centre of the Convertibility Plan's agenda – they gained more importance only in 1993/94, after an unexpected rise in unemployment figures. The labour market reforms of the early 90s treated the issues of temporary contracts and the related social security costs, of dismissal regulations, and of non-wage labour costs in general, the latter being comparatively high in Argentina[387].

In late 1991, without altering traditional employment relations, new temporary contracting variants with reduced non-wage burdens for employers (in terms of obstacles to dismissal, payment of indemnities, or social security contributions) were introduced and promoted[388]. These new variants were much debated (as to their effectiveness in creating jobs, but also their social impacts in terms of higher

---

[384] See IMF Independent Evaluation Office (2004), p. 34. For 2001, the revenue gap in the social security system has been estimated at as much as 3.8 percent of GDP.

[385] Opinion expressed by Roque Fernández in an interview conducted by the author in Buenos Aires in November 2004.

[386] "However, the evidence suggests that in emerging markets one cannot assume that the financing of the transition cost is guaranteed simply because the actuarial balance has improved with reform." Artana/López Murphy/Navajas (2003), p. 84.

[387] For the beginning 90s, Argentina's total non-wage labour costs in relation to gross salaries fared worst in regional comparison, with 64 percent (Peru: 61, Brazil: 58, Mexico: 47, Chile: 45). See Altimir/Beccaria (2000b), p. 351.

[388] These included, e.g., programmes for previously unemployed persons, for start-up enterprises, and for the training of young employees.

risks for employees). They gained significant acceptance only in the second half of the decade[389].

Also in 1991, an unemployment insurance scheme (previously inexistent) was introduced, financed by a payroll tax to be paid by employers. However, it failed to procure significant coverage among the unemployed (seldom above six percent of the total of unemployed) as the formal requirements to be eligible for compensation payments in case of unemployment were quite strict[390]. Further measures taken in this context were a tightening of indemnity claims following working accidents or diseases, and a move towards more flexible working time and vacation regulations[391].

In 1993, a rebate on social security contributions, varying between 30 and 80 percent according to region, was decreed, to benefit the manufacturing, primary, construction, tourism, and R&D sectors. After some interim reductions, the original rebates were reinstalled in 1996 and extended to all economic activities[392].

Moreover, various cash transfer programmes for the unemployed (on paper requiring participation in community or other projects) were initiated between 1993 and 1996, but they failed to gain significance[393]. In 1995, the probation period was lengthened (from three to six months) and several of the respective regulations were relaxed[394].

### 4.2.1.9 Trade Liberalisation

Comprehensive trade liberalisation was an indispensable prerequisite for the CBA, but for the relatively closed and still scarcely diversified economy which

---

[389] Their limited success has been attributed to the stipulated restrictions in their use, especially the requirement for union consent. See Marshall (2004), p. 17.

[390] Previous dismissal from a formal sector job without just cause and a minimum contribution period of one year are among the eligibility criteria. Employees in construction, agriculture, household services, and public administration are not eligible. If eligible, the unemployed receive a payment linked to their latest wage, with a threshold of three quarters of, and a ceiling of 1.5 times, the current minimum wage, for a period of four to twelve months. See Marshall (2004), p. 27.

[391] See Heymann (2000), pp. 79ff.

[392] See Marshall (2004), p. 13.

[393] "They were repeatedly used spuriously to benefit the political clientele, and often announced to avoid the emergence of conflict, or at electoral times, but then not implemented or rapidly discontinued." Marshall (2004), p. 42.

[394] For probation periods, the requirement to pre-announce dismissal was lifted, and they were exempted from the payment of pension contributions.

Argentina was at the beginning of the nineties there was no easy and quick way to get there. After all, with the exchange rate fixed, active trade and tax policies remained as the central instruments to influence the terms of trade and to strengthen the exporting and import competing industries. Both devices were relatively extensively used in the 1990s. The overall progress made towards trade liberalisation was substantial, above all in the reduction of import tariffs, which was, for the largest part, implemented unilaterally.

The new government had begun in late 1989 to intensify the trade liberalisation attempts that originated in the second half of the 1980s. The maximum import tariff was reduced from 40 to 30 percent (the average rate being 17 percent), and administrative controls were reduced. As an enormous simplification of the highly complex regime built up during the 1980s, in April 1991, imports were classified in four categories and charged according to the degree of value added (from primary goods and machinery with zero tariff to high value durable consumer goods, such as electronics, charged with 35 percent). It was later modified to decrease the dispersion between the categories, but not to reduce tariff levels. Quantitative restrictions were eliminated, with the notable exception of the automobile sector which continued to receive special treatment[395].

In 1992, the maximum overall tariff was reduced to 22 percent, and import categories again modified. A variety of anti-dumping measures, introduced in 1993 (concerning textiles, ironware, paper, and chemicals), and preferential treatments of industrial and agrarian inputs were enacted as a response to strongly rising imports, in order to support import-competing industries.

These unilateral measures were taken in addition to broader liberalisation agreements that had been already settled in the late eighties, multilaterally on the one hand within the Uruguay round, and bilaterally with Brazil on the other hand. Out of the latter initiative, the creation of the MERCOSUR customs union developed, which added an important dimension to Argentina's trade liberalisation strategy[396]. In April 1991, Argentina, Brazil, Paraguay, and Uruguay signed the founding treaty, according to which intra zone trade barriers were to be reduced gradually. In 1994, the structure of a common external tariff (however with extensive

---

[395] Here, import quotas were auctioned, with the successful bidders being allowed to import cars and car parts at a preferential tariff of two percent, in quantities that equalled their planned car exports. Individuals purchasing imported cars from these suppliers, however, were charged a tariff of 22 percent.

[396] See Sanguinetti/Pantano/Posadas (2002), pp. 3ff.

lists of exceptions for each country, and with several industries enjoying special treatment, as e.g. ironware, sugar, and automobiles) was agreed upon, and MERCOSUR entered into force in January 1995.

On the export side, nearly all charges on sales abroad were removed. From 1991 onwards, an export surcharge of 6 percent was left only for some oleaginous products. In 1991, an export subsidising scheme according to which exporters of "non-traditional products" received reimbursements on their VAT-payments was re-established (after having been abolished for fiscal reasons the year before). Such reimbursements were increased in 1992 (they ranged from two to 20 percent), after the real exchange rate's appreciation following inertial domestic inflation had encumbered exporters' situation[397]. The weighted average of these reimbursements rose from 3.3 to 6.3 percent of total export value. After the implementation of MERCOSUR, these measures were kept for extra zone, but progressively reduced for intra zone exports.

Argentina's tariff structures were continuously modified, and kept a considerable degree of complexity, but overall tariff levels decreased steadily. By April 1995, the average import tariff was half of what it had been in October 1989[398], and dispersion between tariffs was reduced. In 1997, import tariffs on extra zone trade averaged 14 percent, with a standard deviation of 7 percent[399]. Thus, the trade policies within the Convertibility Plan brought a substantial change with respect to import diversification and volumes, as well as to competitive pressures exerted on domestic production. Imports as a proportion of GDP rose from 6 to around 20 percent until 1997, with the largest increases in the chemical and mechanical engineering sectors. Imports from Brazil multiplied by a factor nine between 1990 and 1997, while Brazil's importance as an export destination grew from 11 to 31 percent of total exports within the same period[400].

### 4.2.2 The Early 1990s' Economic Performance: 1991-1994

#### 4.2.2.1 Monetary and Financial Development

Doubtlessly, the CBA was highly successful in restoring stable monetary conditions. Within three months, it managed to bring monthly inflation down from 27

---

[397] In effect, this scheme was a fiscal devaluation. See Pastor/Wise (1999), p. 496.
[398] See Pastor/Wise (1999), p. 486.
[399] See Heymann (2000), p. 61.
[400] Source: Oficina de la CEPAL en Buenos Aires, on data from INDEC.

percent (February 1991) to 2.8 percent (May 1991). The annual rate (average CPI growth 1990: 1,344 percent) reached single-digit levels in summer 1993 (1993: 7.4 percent), only to decrease further to near zero (and at times even into light deflation) and to remain low until the end of the CBA. As a result of the elimination of inflation, trust in the Peso and thus the demand for real Peso balances recovered, and the economy experienced a quick re-monetisation. M3 as a proportion of GDP, after having reached an all time low of five percent in 1990, rebounded to 10 percent in 1992, and steadily increased during the decade to reach more than 20 percent in 1997. An important characteristic of this re-monetisation was the massive growth in US-Dollar time deposits, while checking accounts, held mostly for transaction purposes, were held in Pesos[401]. Total (Peso and Dollar) deposits rose by 450 percent between April 1991 and November 1994[402].

Another indicator that the CBA enjoyed remarkable credibility right from the start is the rapid convergence of Argentine towards US interest rates. Mainly deposit rates and short term lending rates (such as money market and intercompany market rates) fell very quickly after the CBA was introduced, while long-term lending rates, reflecting also the conditions of the domestic banking system, were slower to converge towards US rates. The development of both currency and country risk, as measured by the differentials of Argentine Peso deposit rates and Argentine US-Dollar deposit rates over the US certificates of deposit rates respectively, was impressive. Measured this way, currency risk fell from roughly 50 percent in early 1991 to five percent in early 1993, and to one percent in early 1994, while country risk was valued even less than currency risk during most of the early 90s[403]. The high reserve requirements, imposed on the banking system mainly as a prudential provision, had the beneficial effect of keeping the money multiplier relatively low and dampening not only the expansionary effects of the strong capital inflows but also real activity and real exchange rate appreciation.

In November 1992, however, a minor run on the Peso occurred, interpreted unanimously as a kind of initial credibility test for the CBA which it passed as the government stuck to its rules[404]. It was small and transitory enough to affect only

---

[401] See Kiguel (1999), p. 15.
[402] See Schumacher (2000), p. 261.
[403] See Baliño/Enoch (1997), pp. 32f.
[404] See Pastor/Wise (1999), p. 497.

monetary variables. Interest rate spreads experienced temporary surges, but quickly returned to their previous levels.

### 4.2.2.2 Economic Activity

Equally impressive was the resumption of growth in economic activity once a stable monetary frame was established. Real GDP grew by 10.5 percent in 1991 and continued to grow fast in the following years, to average 8.2 percent in the years between 1991 and 1994[405]. This growth was created on the one hand by strongly growing investments, with increases by around 30 percent in the first two years after the CBA's introduction and somewhat slower growth thereafter. On the other hand, consumption grew in the first two years by well above 10 percent, and by above five percent until 1994.

The boom was accompanied by a deterioration in the current account, reflecting the increased demand for imports of goods and services, as well as strongly rising inflows of financial and physical capital. Imports of goods and services grew by nearly 70 and 60 percent in 1991 and 1992 respectively, and by 30 and 11 percent in the following years[406]. Exports were slower to recover; in 1991, there was still a slight reduction, and only since 1993 did exports grow markedly (by 8.5 and 17.8 percent in 1993 and 1994[407]). This can be explained partly with a sort of "crowding out" of exports by strongly rising domestic demand, and partly with the fact that, despite the immediate price stabilisation, Argentina's inflation continued to be higher than that of its trading partners until 1994, which resulted in a substantial real appreciation. Its effects on exports, however, were mitigated by productivity gains, the elimination of most export taxes, as well as some export subsidies.

As indicated, the massive increases in consumption and investment were financed to a large extent by foreign capital, attracted by lucrative privatisation offers and deregulation in many markets, as well as by low international interest rates. Net foreign capital flows into the country reached over 32 billion US-Dollars between 1992 and 1994, and about ten percent of GDP in 1994[408]. However, the current account deficit did not reach exorbitant levels: starting from 0.2 percent of GDP in

---

[405] Between 1991 and 1994, Argentina recorded the second fastest growth in Latin America (after Chile).

[406] Imports of consumer and capital goods grew strongly, at the expense of intermediate goods. See Pastor/Wise (1999), p. 483.

[407] See IMF Independent Evaluation Office (2004), p. 10.

[408] See Jonas (2002), p. 9.

1991, it reached 3.4 and 4.3 percent in 1993 and 1994 respectively, before being reduced again during the Tequila crisis.

### 4.2.2.3 Fiscal Development

The fiscal development of the early 90s stood in sharp contrast to anything Argentina had experienced since decades. Having averaged around five percent of GDP during the 1980s, the overall fiscal deficit fell to 0.4 percent in 1992 and reached a small surplus (0.1 percent) in 1993. 1994 saw a still moderate deficit of 1.4 percent which, as an effect of the Tequila crisis as well as the pension reform's additional fiscal burden, broadened to 3.2 percent in 1995[409]. Accordingly, with the exception of 1995, the primary balance was positive during the early 90s.

On the income side, some of the reforms put into place in the early 90s effectuated a reduction in public revenues (such as the modifications of foreign trade regulations that reduced tariff income, and the pension reform, that diverted social security contributions to the pension funds), while other reforms exerted an improving influence on the budget. These were, primarily, privatisations which, apart from generating extraordinary revenues, gradually eliminated the financing needs for public enterprises (in 1990 still having required around three percent of GDP) and the tax reforms, which increased tax rates and bases in the context of the expanding economy.

The budgetary improvement was not achieved by reductions of public expenditures. Indeed, these rose from 14.8 percent of GDP on average during the 1980s to 17.2 percent during 1991-98, reflecting, above all, increases in social expenditure and in transfers to the provinces. Expenditures were dented mainly by lower interest payments for the largely dollarised public debt.

Although the fiscal improvement was significant, it did not (except for 1993) amount to produce budget surpluses in times of a booming economy. As a result, public debt, after an initial decline from around 35 to 28 percent between 1991 and 1992, rose in the following years to nearly 37 percent in 1995 (to be reduced only temporarily during the second expansionary phase in 1997)[410].

---

[409] With the quasi-fiscal deficits of the central bank having fallen apart, the overall fiscal deficit was composed of the annual financing needs of the federal government and those of the provinces (averaging 1.0 and 0.7 percent of GDP respectively during 1991-98). See Heymann (2000), p. 63f.

[410] See IMF Independent Evaluation Office (2004), p. 24.

### 4.2.2.4 Unemployment and Income Distribution

The strong economic growth translated into slightly higher employment only initially. As early as in late 1992, the unemployment rate started to increase, from around seven to twelve percent in 1994, only to rise further strongly during the Tequila crisis and to reach more than 18 percent in May 1995. These levels were highly problematic given Argentina's history of very low unemployment, and, above all, the economic boom they accompanied. Never since did the unemployment rate decline back to pre-1994 levels: with the beginning 90s, a new era of high structural unemployment had emerged. Strikingly, the expansionary cycle between 1990 and 94 scored a rise in GDP by 35 percent, a rise in employment by only eight, and a rise in unemployment by 105 percent[411].

The very low employment elasticity of the early 90s[412] is the result of several factors. First, large fractions of both labour and capital resources were lying idle as a consequence of the 1980s, so that idle capacities were utilised before new demand for labour emerged[413]. Second, the important structural reforms such as trade liberalisation, privatisation, and deregulation, brought with them a relative cheapening of the production factor capital against labour, and hence a reduced labour demand for productive purposes. Third, the strongly recovering investment not only updated the country's obsolete capital stock but also introduced labour-saving technologies, bringing about important productivity increases: labour productivity rose in certain manufacturing sectors by 15 percent annually between 1991 and 94, and on average (excluding the primary sector) by 7.9 percent[414].

Thus, a relative increase in activities intensive in the use of capital, imported goods, and natural resources stood against a relative decline in labour intensive processes. As a consequence, the already existing commercial pattern of overwhelmingly exporting low value-added primary products, favoured by the widely

---

[411] See Waisgrais (2003), p. 28.

[412] Employment elasticity here means the relation employment/product, i.e. the change in employment a change in output brings about. As such, it is reciprocal to labour productivity. Employment elasticity was slightly above 0.2 for Argentina in the period 1991-4, indicating that a ten percent rise in GDP generated a rise in employment by around two percent.

[413] The existence of idle labour capacities after periods of recession is evidence of labour market regulations that make dismissals costly enough to avoid them even in bad times.

[414] E.g., textile and confections: +15.2%, metal and machinery: +15.1%, construction: +13.1%. See Altimir/Beccaria (2000b), p. 414.

undifferentiated progress in trade liberalisation, was intensified[415]. A process of de-industrialisation in labour intensive, import-competing sectors was the flip-side of this development. Labour intensive industries recording employment growth were those not exposed to international competition, such as tourism, financial services, and transport[416]. Mismatches between the skills supplies set free in the course of such de-industrialisation and the skills demanded by expanding sectors are a further factor explaining low employment elasticities.

In addition, an important increase in labour market participation added to the rise in unemployment. This was mainly due to women entering labour markets, above all in the district of Buenos Aires (where female participation increased from 28 to 33 percent between 1991 and 1995)[417]. Thus, the low employment elasticities of the early nineties made the strong economic growth fail to absorb the increase in the economically active population[418].

Not surprisingly, the rising unemployment contributed to a worsening distribution of income among private households and among the economically active population, continuing a trend that had been persisting since the 1970s[419]. Another important reason for rising inequality in the early nineties is the widening gap between labour productivity and wage development: real wages show negligible growth at best in times of soaring productivity, so that the profits of rising productivity largely benefited capital rather than labour[420]. In addition, in the early 1990s, all households experienced deteriorating "terms of exchange" with other economic agents, to the degree that, due to the pertaining inflationary inertia, the CPI rose by more (by 30 percent) than the total of prices implicit in GDP, mirroring

---

[415] Low value-added exports of natural resources (agricultural and energy products) rose from 25 percent of total exports in 1989 to 34 percent in 1994 – a development boding ill for the long-term perspectives of a country needing to industrialise to keep more value-added in the country and obtain more diversified production and trade patterns. See Pastor/Wise (1999), p. 486.

[416] See Frenkel/González Rozada (1999), p. 54.

[417] See Altimir/Beccaria (2000b), p. 405. This is part of a global trend since the 1960s, and, for the case of Argentina, largely also driven by the desire of women to supplement low household incomes. At the same time, an increasing female participation rate mirrors the changes in the economy's structure, from industry to services. See Waisgrais (2003), p. 25.

[418] See Waisgrais (2003), p. 28.

[419] The Gini coefficient for private households in the Gran Buenos Aires area, excluding households with zero income, rose from 0.416 in 1980 to 0.430 in 1991 and to 0.433 in 1994. See Altimir/Beccaria (2000a), p. 432, and González Rozada/Menendez (2002).

[420] See Waisgrais (2003), p. 31.

the relative rise in non-tradables' prices. Also, income distribution among the employed failed to improve, despite the strong economic recovery[421].

As for the functional income distribution, an initial slight rise of the share of wages in total factor income (from 35 to 38 percent between 1991 and 93) is explained mainly by rising labour costs in the first years of Convertibility. This trend was reversed after 1993, and the wage share went to decline under levels of 1991 in 1995[422].

Hence, the labour market reforms of the early 90s had, if any, very little effect on unemployment, and certainly none on income distribution[423]. This is partly because, as already mentioned, the need to adopt deeper labour market reforms was acknowledged only later in the decade, and partly because early measures (such as the modified labour contracts) were not, or only later, accepted to a substantial degree throughout the economy.

### 4.2.3 Coping with the Tequila Crisis: 1995

#### 4.2.3.1 The Tequila Effect

On December 20th, 1994, Mexico devalued its currency, giving in to intense pressure in the foreign exchange market[424]. This triggered the biggest crisis and challenge to the Argentine CBA during the 1990s.

Shunning Mexico, international investors became increasingly suspicious of other Latin American economies as well, and very much so of Argentina which was similarly dependent on foreign funds and had a fixed exchange rate as well. This made them doubt whether it would soon be forced to follow suit and abandon its CBA. The upcoming presidential elections of May 1995 reinforced this uncertainty. Shortly after the Mexican devaluation, a small Argentine wholesale bank with a large exposure to Mexican assets got insolvent, which proved to be the trigger for the crisis invading Argentina. Suddenly, Argentine banks were denied foreign funds

---

[421] See Altimir/Beccaria (2000a), p. 494.

[422] See Altimir/Beccaria (2000a), pp. 476f.

[423] See Fanelli/González Rozada (1998), p. 33.

[424] It was forced to do so (ending an era of fixed exchange rate that had lasted since 1987) after political and social unrest, as well as rising US interest rates, made foreign investors doubt about its economy's health. The withdrawal of their funds made Mexico's large current account deficit increasingly difficult to finance.

and faced liquidity problems, forcing them to call in loans, which negatively affected investment and growth.

In parallel to a massive outflow of international capital, a panicky flight from the domestic banking system unfolded. Argentine depositors, worried about the safety of their bank deposits, started to withdraw them, thus putting further pressure on the banks. Deposits were withdrawn in a speed and magnitude nearly unrivalled in history: between December 1994 and March 1995 (the most severe crisis months), the banking system lost 18 percent of its deposits[425]. Large parts of deposits withdrawn left the country. International reserves fell by 33 percent (or 6 billion US-Dollars) during those four months.

The crises' repercussions on the real economy were serious. Real GDP shrank by 2.8 percent in 1995 as a result of a drop of investment (by 13 percent) and of private consumption (by 4 percent). Unemployment skyrocketed to reach more than 18 percent in May 1995, and the proportion of households living below the poverty line increased from 13 to 17 percent during that year[426]. The current account improved by more than two percentage points (to a deficit of two percent of GDP) as exports grew strongly while imports fell by around five percent[427].

The crisis started to recede by mid-March, as a result of the government's active crisis management with the objective to defend the fixed exchange rate, and with assistance from the IMF which extended the existing arrangement in that month. Nevertheless, the decline in deposits stopped only after president Menem's re-election on May 14th, 1995, which renewed confidence in the domestic currency. The financial system's exhibited fragility, still considerable despite the strengthening measures taken in the years before, prompted the central bank to fully utilise the frame offered by the Convertibility law (in terms of approaching the lower limits of the backing rule and lowering reserve requirements), with the result that the crisis was eventually successfully managed, the CBA preserved, and the banking system thereupon equipped with further strengthening regulations. The following paragraphs focus on the characterisation of the crisis, its management, and on the measures taken subsequently to prepare for similar future events.

---

[425] In the Great Depression in the US, 35 percent of deposits were withdrawn, however over a period of four years. See Kiguel (1999), p. 17.

[426] See Jonas (2002), p. 10.

[427] See IMF Independent Evaluation Office (2004), p. 10.

#### 4.2.3.2 Currency and Bank Run

The structure and development of deposit withdrawals shows that the crisis was not only a currency run but also extended to a bank run. Withdrawals did not occur uniformly across banks, nor did they only affect Peso-denominated deposits. Depositors evidently were aware of the impact of the currency run on individual banks' solvency: first, they selectively withdrew deposits from "bad" banks and re-deposited them in "good" (predominantly foreign and large domestic) banks, often dollarising their Peso-deposits at the same time[428]. So, initially, only a few domestic wholesale banks with large operations in government bonds were affected by deposit outflows. Only later, as contagion within the financial sector took hold, did withdrawals spread to larger chunks and finally the whole of the banking system, including foreign, public, and large private banks.

Thus, the severity of the crisis cannot be explained exclusively with doubts about the sustainability of the exchange rate. Very clearly, additional factors were the limited lender of last resort capacity of the central bank (excess reserves amounted to only four percent of total deposits before the crisis), the lack of deposit insurance, as well as the fears that the government could react once more with a forced deposit restructuring, as had happened only five years ago with the Plan BONEX (which had inflicted heavy losses for depositors)[429].

The outflow of deposits exerted severe liquidity pressures on the banking system, while the central bank lost much of its international reserves (they fell by one third during Tequila) and was forced to defend the Peso parity by allowing interest rates to rise (short term interest rates exceeded 60 percent at the climax of the crisis), which further crippled banks' solvency and liquidity. The crisis made clear that the central bank's limited lender of last resort capacity had to be substituted by both the provision of systemic liquidity and strengthened regulation and supervision. The first issue had to be addressed in the midst of crisis, while the second was tackled after its retreat.

#### 4.2.3.3 Managing the Crisis

The central bank's first reaction to the run was to lower reserve requirements on bank deposits in order to alleviate banks' liquidity strains[430]. In January 1995, Peso

---

[428] See Schumacher (2000).

[429] See Kiguel (1999), p. 21.

[430] Between late December and late January, reserve requirements for checking and savings accounts, held both in Pesos and US-Dollars, were reduced in steps from 43 to 30 percent, and for

deposits of commercial banks held with the central bank were automatically converted to US-Dollars, thus signalling support to the CBA and increasing Dollar liquidity of the financial sector.

A revision of the central bank law, put on the way in the midst of crisis, in February 1995, stood at the centre of crisis management. It included various liquidity securing provisions. First, the creation of a new system of mandatory and privately financed deposit insurance was decreed (it was put into effect only a few weeks later), meant to enhance depositor confidence in the banking system and to protect small depositors. Under this scheme, 20,000 (later 30,000) US-Dollars per depositor had to be insured, with the effect that 75 percent of depositors (although only 25 percent of deposits) were covered[431]. Moreover, the law modified the central bank law in a way that, under extraordinary circumstances, rediscount and repurchase operations with financial institutions were allowed to be extended, so that the volume of such assistance was limited only by the reserves legally required to back the monetary base (i.e. 80 percent of the monetary base during the first central bank directory's term)[432]. At the same time, the central bank was given substantial power to restructure and to liquidate troubled banks, again with the objective to defend depositors[433]. Notably, the creation of two trust funds was decreed which intended to facilitate the necessary structural changes in the banking sector. One was founded to help in the privatisation of provincial banks, the other to help restructure or merge troubled private banks. Finally, the central bank enlarged its potential lender of last resort funds by opening contingent repo facilities with 13 private international banks, to be triggered at its discretion in case of need[434].

---

time deposits from three to one percent. In the following months, reserve requirements were again raised slightly, to 33 and two percent respectively. See Ganapolsky/Schmukler (1998), p. 5.

[431] See Canavese (2001), p. 10.

[432] See República Argentina (1995), articles 1 and 2. Some authors claim that, in effect, the rules of Convertibility were bent. See e.g. Pastor/Wise (1999), p. 484. However, nominally, the frames given by the Convertibility and central bank laws were maintained, and it is majority opinion that Convertibility in its core remained untouched.

[433] See República Argentina (1995), article 3. It allowed the central bank to split troubled institutions into a "good" and a "bad" bank, the first to be sold and the second to be liquidated. See Pou (2000), p. 14.

[434] This facility gave the central bank the option, in the event of a crisis, to sell Argentine public bonds denominated in US-Dollars and receive the proceeds in Dollars, thus enabling it to expand domestic money while using the borrowed reserves to back the monetary base, as provided for by

All of the provisions of the new legal frame were put into practice. The central bank's "hard" international reserves were allowed to melt down to the legal minimum of 80 percent required to back the monetary base. The central bank temporarily suspended the operations of 15 domestic financial institutions. During the crisis, out of a total of 137 private financial institutions, nine failed and 30 were either acquired or merged with another bank[435].

### 4.2.3.4 Financial Sector Reforms in the Wake of Tequila

Once the worst of the crisis was over, further banking regulations were enacted which aimed at better allowing markets to discipline financial institutions. Banking supervision introduced the so-called CAMEL system, by which it rated financial institutions, as well as a system that combines different sources of evaluation (called BASIC)[436], both ratings to be published and made available to each depositor upon request. Another, quite remarkable, rule to expose banks to market discipline was incorporated in the requirement for banks to issue subordinated debt, corresponding to two percent of their deposits. The market pricing of this debt was expected to provide valuable information about a bank's risk for depositors as well as regulators[437]. Intervals of banks' inspections were shortened. Also, a differentiation of capital requirements was introduced, whereby several risk dimensions were attributed to bank assets, namely counterparty risk, interest rate risk, and market risk[438].

A further important step was to replace reserve requirements by liquidity requirements, in August 1995, with the objective to make sure financial institutions had sufficient resources to confront possible deposit withdrawals. The new liquidity requirements applied to all bank liabilities (not just deposits), were differentiated according to their residual time to maturity, and remunerated. Four fifths of the

---

the Convertibility law. It comprised six, and was later extended to 7.1 billion US-Dollars. See Kiguel (1999), p. 28.

[435] See Schumacher (2000), p. 262.

[436] See Caprio (1998). CAMEL stands for capital, asset quality, management, earnings, and liquidity. Each aspect is rated separately, with the total rating of the bank resulting from the average – a system most central banks use to rate banks. BASIC stands for bonds, external auditing, supervision, information, and credit rating.

[437] See Kiguel (1999), p. 28.

[438] The inclusion of the indicator "interest rate" (higher interest rate implies higher loan risk) is remarkable; introducing the logic of risk premia in the banking supervision context is not international standard.

required liquidity was allowed to be held in safe and liquid international assets, with the remaining fifth to be channelled through the central bank. Average liquidity requirements amounted to 16 percent, and were increased over time to 20 percent[439].

The central bank's active liquidity management as well as the decisive actions in its supervising function limited the detrimental effects of the crisis on the banking system as a whole and contributed to dampen its transmission to the real economy[440]. While deposits fell by a total of 8.5 billion Pesos, total credit fell by just 1.1 billion Pesos (thereof credit losses to the private sector of 400 million). In the end, total credit, which had grown by over 23 percent in 1994, fell by 0.8 percent in 1995[441]. Only one percent of depositors eventually lost funds, amounting to 0.28 percent of total deposits[442].

After the implementation of the new liquidity requirements, and with the contingent credit lines of the central bank, systemic liquidity of the financial sector covered as much as 30 percent of total deposits, a proportion considered adequate to face future deposit outflows (and which would in any case have been sufficient to overcome Tequila)[443]. There is a broad consensus that the liquidity instruments and prudential banking regulations emerging from the Tequila crisis did much to moderate the impact of the external shocks that were to follow[444].

### 4.2.3.5 Fiscal Adjustment Following Tequila

In addition to strengthening the financial sector, further measures were necessary to better cope with similar future crises which could undermine confidence in the CBA. These concerned the fiscal sphere and included the intensification of fiscal adjustment and the improvement of debt management.

---

[439] Moreover, also in the wake of Tequila, Argentina's scattered and inefficient payment system was reformed to introduce a modern real-time gross settlement system, operated by the central bank, and three automated clearing houses. See Pou (2000), p. 15.

[440] According to Kiguel (1999), around three quarters of deposit losses were financed by liquidity instruments of the central bank (such as rediscounts, reduced reserve requirements, repos, and foreign credit lines). See Kiguel (1999), p. 22.

[441] See Schumacher (2000), p. 262.

[442] See Canavese (2001), p. 10.

[443] See Kiguel (1999), p. 28.

[444] In an IMF report on transparency practices, Argentina's monetary and financial policy as well as banking supervision receive substantial praise. See IMF Staff Team (1999), pp. 7ff.

Besides the immediate fiscal adjustment need evoked by the crisis, the necessity of further fiscal improvements arose from the impact of some of the reforms undertaken on public finances, such as, for the largest part, the pension reform which accounted for a revenue loss of three billion Dollars annually. Other reforms, such as the reduction in labour taxes and the absorption of provincial social security systems, as well as higher scheduled interest payments (that stemmed from old non-interest bearing debt, the "BOCONes", on which now interest started to be paid), added to the fiscal burden, with the mentioned positions accounting for additional five billion Dollars to be financed annually.

The immediate fiscal response to Tequila consisted mainly of a rise in the VAT rate by three percentage points, to 21 percent, in March 1995[445]. Later, in 1996, a fifth of the tax on combustibles was dedicated to prop up the ailing public pensions system. Finally, in 1998, on the background of high unemployment, the federal government introduced a tax reform to further lower labour taxes (not "coparticipated" with the provinces), but raised some other taxes (shared with the provinces)[446].

However, as the additional burdens mentioned above accounted for much of the actual fiscal deficits of the years following Tequila, those adjustment efforts failed to tackle these (more or less) "exceptional" expenditures[447].

With respect to financial management, the government focused after 1995 on lengthening the maturity structure of its bonds as well as on better synchronising bond sales and financing needs in order to prevent liquidity squeezes and emergency sales in turbulent times, and generally to reduce the vulnerability arising from potential refinancing risks[448]. As a result, the proportion of short term debt was reduced to around three percent of total debt, with the average maturity of government debt rising to around eight years in 1998[449].

---

[445] This increase was initially limited to one year, and exempt from „coparticipación". However, it continued to persist and was later included into the provincial transfer scheme. See Heymann (2000), p. 67.

[446] The federal government compensated the inflicted revenue losses by negotiating further "precoparticipaciones" with the provinces. See Saiegh/Tommasi (1999), pp. 188f.

[447] Many authors argue that, without these „exceptional" items, Argentina's budget would have been neutral or even in surplus in some years, which, however, in their view, was not correctly honoured by markets in the late 90s.

[448] See Heymann (2000), p. 54.

[449] See Kiguel (1999), p. 26.

**4.2.4    The Second Expansionary Phase after Tequila: 1996-1998**

The quick economic recovery from Tequila was widely seen as proof of the Convertibility regime's robustness and added massively to its popularity. Favourable external conditions such as the US-Dollar's relative weakness, as well as tariff reductions within MERCOSUR, facilitated a quick resumption of strong export-led growth. Argentina soon was a major beneficiary of strong capital flows to emerging economies again. Its development became widely viewed as a success story and a model for other emerging economies[450]. Again, it received support from the IMF with a new Stand-by Arrangement approved in April 1996.

As indicated, the financial sector recovered remarkably quickly from the severe crisis: the pre-Tequila level of deposits held in banks was reached again as early as in the first quarter of 1996 (45 billion Dollars), and mounted to 65 billion in late 1997[451]. Annual real GDP grew by 5.5, by 8.1, and by 3.8 percent between 1996 and 1998. Exports continued to contribute much to growth: they grew by 13.6 and 9 percent in 1996 and 1997, to be reduced, under deteriorating world market conditions, to a growth of 0.7 percent in 1998. Private consumption was again another driving force, recovering from its 1995 slump (when it had contracted by 4 percent) with growth rates around eight percent in the following two years, and with 2.5 percent in 1998. Likewise, real fixed investment saw its late 1990s peak in 1997 with a growth of nearly 18 percent. Inflation was now down at virtually zero (the CPI grew between 0.1 and 0.7 percent in 1996 to 98), at a time when rising foreign currency reserves automatically created more relaxed monetary conditions with declining interest rates and expanding credit.

However, strong domestic demand induced imports to grow much faster than exports (by 24 percent in 1997), causing a reversal of the current account's previous, Tequila-induced, improvement: it steadily deteriorated from a deficit of two percent in 1995 to 4.9 percent in 1998, willingly financed by international capital markets. Correspondingly, external debt continued its growth trend, uninterrupted since 1992 (from 28 percent then to 47.5 percent in 1998 as a percentage of GDP).

---

[450] The enthusiasm in and outside the country was such that, in October 1998, president Menem was invited to the annual meetings with the IMF Managing Director where "the experience of Argentina in recent years" was characterised as "exemplary". See IMF Independent Evaluation Office (2004), p. 12.

[451] See Canavese (2001), p. 10.

As to fiscal performance after 1995, 1996 was the second year when even the government's primary balance was negative (by 0.7 percent of GDP), and slight primary surpluses (of 0.3 and 0.5 percent) were reached in 1997 and 1998. Overall, the consolidated[452] budget deficit was reduced from the Tequila level by around one percent until 1997, to 2.1 percent in both 1997 and 1998. Public debt interrupted its upward trend (since 1992) only temporarily in 1997, to reach 40.9 percent of GDP in 1998 (thus crossing the forty percent-mark which, by some, is deemed the limit for sustainability in developing economies)[453].

Unlike the first expansionary phase of the early 1990s, the boom following Tequila was accompanied by considerable reductions in unemployment. After the 1995 peak of 18 percent, the open unemployment rate declined during the following years to reach 13.2 percent in 1998 (although this level was still nearly double that of the beginning decade). While during 1991-94, employment had grown by a meagre average of 0.8 percent annually, between 1995 and 1997 it did so by 3.9 percent. Employment elasticity was much higher now than before Tequila[454], thanks partly to strong growth in sectors with relatively low potential for productivity increases, such as services and construction, but partly also to the effects of labour market reforms: the reduction in non-wage labour costs and the increase in flexibility in labour contracts added to the better employment performance[455].

---

[452] The consolidated public sector includes national, provincial, and municipal levels.

[453] See IMF Independent Evaluation Office (2004), p. 10.

[454] Waisgrais (2003), p. 28, calculates employment elasticities of -1.61 for the 1980s, 0.23 for the period 1991-4, and 0.63 for 1995-8. This observation has led many to the assumption that the low employment elasticity of the early nineties was mainly of transitory nature, reflecting the restructuring of production in a sort of one-time technological catching-up. However, there were also reasons, such as ongoing concentration and rationalisation processes, to suggest that the higher post-Tequila employment elasticity would not stay that high either. See Altimir/Beccaria (2000b), p. 420.

[455] However, these reforms' effectiveness should not be overestimated given the high proportion of unregistered labour in employment growth (estimated at well over 40 percent between 1996 and 97; but parts of jobs classified as "unregistered" were again results of the new legislation exempting some employments during the probation period from social security contributions, which led to their classification as "unregistered" – a problem of inadequate statistics). It has been estimated that active labour market policies have resulted in the creation of around 52,000 jobs, corresponding to about 10 percent of total employment growth. See Altimir/Beccaria (2000b), pp. 383ff.

The labour market's relaxation, however, did not extend to reversing the trend of a steadily worsening income distribution. The Gini coefficient for private households in the Gran Buenos Aires area, excluding households with zero income, continued to rise from 0.433 in 1994 to 0.446 in 1997[456]. This is mainly considered the consequence of an increasing differentiation of employment by qualification, and thus of income by education, resulting in a polarisation in the labour market. This is to large parts attributable to a massive fall in employment within the manufacturing sectors as a result of the economy's commercial opening and its entering into a new phase of technological progress: the share of employment in the industrial sector fell from nearly 30 percent in the late eighties to a mere 20.9 percent in the late nineties[457].

### 4.2.5 The Late 1990s' Recession: 1999-2001

#### 4.2.5.1 The Asian, Russian, and Brazilian Crises

Within 15 months, a series of three financial crises hit the world, and most severely its emerging economies. The series started with the East Asian crisis, triggered by South Korea's devaluation on October 22nd, 1997, which hit the whole region with a largely unexpected severity. South Korea and Thailand, hitherto deemed creditworthy, approached the verge of default, and most East Asian currencies plummeted quickly. As international investors lost their appetite for emerging markets in general, the crisis started to spread beyond South East Asia. Only after large financial assistance was granted by multilateral organisations, under the lead of the IMF, did the crisis recede.

Ten months later, on August 17th, 1998, Russia declared a moratorium on its Rouble debt. The repercussions of the Russian default were much more serious for the world economy as a whole, as they not only spread quickly through emerging markets, but went well beyond, hitting also the financial systems of industrial countries to the degree that they were exposed to emerging market debt. The episode saw the failure of many hedge funds, as well as the spectacular rescue of Long Term Capital Management by the New York Fed.

Finally, on January 13th, 1999, Brazil floated its currency which had been under attack since the Russian default. It fell in early 1999 by 70 percent, from 1.2 to 2

---

[456] See Altimir/Beccaria (2000a), p. 432.

[457] See Waisgrais (2003), p. 24. The respective employment shares in services rose from 33.4 to 38.2 percent in that period, in the construction sector from 4.5 to 5 percent.

Reais per Dollar. Despite widespread fears, the Brazilian devaluation did not bring about major contagion among emerging economies and was relatively quickly under control, with turbulences receding after a few months.

From the emerging markets' perspective, the Russian crisis was by far the worst. Judged by the development of the EMBI[458], the spreads observed during the second half of 1998 (around 1,700 basis points) were the only to get near those recorded during Tequila (almost 1,900); the immediate effects of the Asian and Brazilian crises were considerably minor. For Argentina, the picture is similar; spreads of its government bonds over US treasuries took a largely parallel development.

Argentina's financial sector withstood these crises largely unaffected. Banks seemed to have gained in actual and perceived robustness, as to judge from the development of deposits (they increased by 15 percent during the Asian, and remained stable or increased modestly at the time of the Russian and Brazilian crises respectively). Equally, the development of domestic interest rates (they never exceeded 15 percent) and foreign exchange reserves (they stayed stable or continued to increase) show that even the Russian default did not get into the region of triggering a bank or currency run. The fixed exchange rate and its sustainability did not seem to be questioned, which was generally attributed to the improvements achieved in the areas of public debt, its amortisation structures, and the banking system[459].

However, beyond its immediate effects, the Russian crisis marked a turning point for Argentina and the end of the second expansionary phase of the nineties, as lasting higher international interest rates increased the debt service, and withering capital imports (the so-called "sudden stop" in capital flows) dried out the country's sources of liquidity.

### 4.2.5.2 More Adverse External Shocks

While Argentina's economic indicators took a turn for the worse in the wake of the Russian default (from the fourth quarter of 1998), this event was, as indicated above, by far not the sole culprit for the long downturn that was to follow. A series of further external shocks added to these crises, and they hit primarily Argentina's exports.

---

[458] Emerging Market Bond Index, which measures spreads of emerging market bonds over US treasuries, as published by J.P. Morgan.

[459] See Kiguel (1999), p. 32f.

These were, first, the weakening global economy which brought about a terms of trade shock for Argentina, as international prices for most of Argentina's export commodities, such as petroleum, soy beans, wheat, corn, and beef plummeted[460]. As a result, Argentina's terms of trade deteriorated in 1998 by 5.1 and in 1999 by 8.4 percent[461]. Second, as mentioned above, the recession of and devaluation in neighbouring Brazil made the most important trading partner (accounting for 30 percent of exports) fall apart and turn into a competitor dominating many sectors (although the much-feared scenario of cheap Brazilian imports inundating Argentina did not materialise)[462]. Third, the appreciating US-Dollar increasingly disadvantaged Argentina's exports to the Euro area (the second biggest export destination after Brazil) as well as, in competition with non-Dollar origins, those to the United States (Argentina's third biggest export market).

### 4.2.5.3 Recession cum Deflation

Being pegged to the US-Dollar now turned out increasingly counterproductive, as the imported tight monetary conditions meant high real interest rates that choked credit and investment in Argentina. The growing misalignment of the exchange rate impeded Argentina's export sector. Falling capital inflows and eroding international competitiveness resulted in reduced investment and economic activity. Real GDP fell by three percent in the second half of 1998, and thus cut the otherwise strong growth of 1998 to a total of 3.8 percent. It continued to fall by 3.4 percent in 1999, although increased government spending in the run-up to the presidential elections in 1999 temporarily improved economic activity in the second half of that year[463]. GDP shrank by 0.8 percent in 2000, to deteriorate to a negative growth of 4.4 percent in 2001[464].

---

[460] Petroleum and non-fuel commodities' prices plummeted, by 32 and 16 percent respectively, during 1998. Prices for oilseeds declined by around 25 percent between 1998 and 2000, beef prices fell by over 16 percent in the first half of 1999 alone, <http://www.imf.org/external/pubs/ft/weo/1999/01/0599ch2.pdf>.

[461] See IMF Independent Evaluation Office (2004), p. 10.

[462] See Nunnenkamp (1999), p. 9.

[463] See Powell (2002), p. 4. The reduction of world interest rates in the second half of 1999, itself the result of European governments striving to meet the Maastricht criteria in the run-up to the Euro's introduction, also helped facilitate an interim recovery through recovering capital flows to Argentina, as yield-seeking investors were attracted by new issues of Argentine high-yield government bonds denominated in Euros. See Dominguez/Tesar (2004), p. 10.

[464] See IMF Independent Evaluation Office (2004), p. 10.

The recession and fall in domestic demand did not produce a significant improvement of the current account, and international capital shied away from financing it. As the option of nominal adjustment to external imbalance, i.e. of devaluation, was barred by the CBA, adjustment had to occur "the hard way", i.e. over a shrinking monetary base and price and wage deflation. So, what seemed unthinkable for decades in Argentina now happened: prices started to fall in 1999 and continued to do so until the end of the CBA. The CPI shrank by 1.8, 0.7, and 1.5 percent respectively during those three years. Despite decreasing prices, however, real wages continued the downward trend they had initiated after the first expansionary phase of the early nineties. Thus, nominal wages fell faster than prices, defying the perception of downward rigidity of nominal wages. In addition, falling prices and wages increased the real value of domestic debt.

During the late nineties' recession, overall employment elasticity was reduced against its previously higher levels to near zero (i.e. employment did not fall with output), but this was mainly due to the effects of some employment programmes introduced from 2000. However, employment elasticity remained high in the manufacturing sector, partly due to institutional changes that facilitated dismissals for economic reasons, so that the crisis entailed increasing unemployment there[465]. Overall unemployment rose from its post-Tequila low of 12.9 percent in 1998 to 17.4 percent in 2001.

### 4.2.5.4 Real Appreciation of the Peso

Price and wage deflation caused the desired, however limited, real depreciation of the Peso against the US-Dollar[466]. But, as other currencies were nominally depreciating against the Dollar, Argentina's real effective exchange rate (i.e. the exchange rate against the basket of currencies that reflects trade patterns) continued to appreciate. Argentina's real effective exchange rate appreciated between 1998 and 2001 by more than 8 percent, and by 4 percent in 1999 alone[467].

The assessment whether, and by how much, the Peso was overvalued when the country entered recession, i.e. by how much it deviated at that time from its equilibrium exchange rate in real terms, was and still is a disputed issue.

---

[465] See Marshall (2004), pp. 22ff.

[466] Consumer prices fell by 1.3 percent on average between 1999 and 2001, while producer prices began to decline earlier (in 1997) and continued to do so much faster, by 4.5 percent in average during 1998 and 2001. See Schuler/Hanke (2002), p. 4.

[467] See IMF Independent Evaluation Office (2004), p. 10.

Estimations depend on how far productivity improvements are judged to have made up for the nominal effective appreciation against its trading partners' currencies during the 1990s. A judgement from the experienced trade performance is difficult because the effects of numerous liberalisation efforts of the 90s interfere with exchange rate effects[468].

So, estimations of the degree of overvaluation differed widely, and many of them ascribed the Peso only moderate overvaluation during 1999, or none at all[469]. In early 2000, published estimations of the Peso's real overvaluation against the US-Dollar ranged from a mere seven to more than 20 percent. To judge from estimations based on purchasing power parity, it seems that, at the turn 1999/2000, the Peso was indeed not that much overvalued[470]. There seems to be a consensus, however, that in the course of 2000 and 2001, with worsening economic and financial conditions in Argentina and a further weakening Euro against the US-Dollar, the real Peso exchange rate acquired a major misalignment[471].

### 4.2.5.5 Fiscal Atrophy

In the run-up to the presidential elections of 1999, the peculiar situation prevailed that the candidate from the incumbent Peronist party, Duhalde[472], publicly took into consideration the abolishment of the CBA and debt restructuring. In contrast, the opposition candidate from the Alianza, de la Rúa, committed himself to maintaining the CBA. Besides reflecting discontent with the Menem administration accused of corruption, which de la Rúa promised to fight, his clear victory was also proof of the CBA's far-reaching popularity[473].

---

[468] See IMF Independent Evaluation Office (2004), p. 23.

[469] See Schuler/Hanke (2002), p. 11.

[470] Judgement made by Roque Fernández, who sided with estimations of an overvaluation of around 7 percent, in an interview conducted by the author in Buenos Aires in November 2004. The famous "Big Mac Index", published by the Economist, and, to be sure, a mosaic piece only, calculated a real overvaluation against the Dollar of less than five percent in January, 2000, and of zero in April that year. See www.economist.com.

[471] The topic will be addressed in more detail in section 5.

[472] Duhalde has been a fierce opponent of his fellow party member Menem whose repeated attempts to gain political support for a constitutional reform allowing for a third presidential term failed in early 1999, but left the Peronist party deeply divided.

[473] Nevertheless, the Alianza government encountered much suspicion from the private sector, because the coalition partner FREPASO seemed not to share much of the Radical's positions, and, moreover, the coalition had no majority in congress.

Maintaining the Peso-Dollar parity required tight fiscal policies in order to restore confidence and appease capital markets. Restrictive budgets, however, fit ill with the prevailing recession, high unemployment, and rising poverty. The new government's priority was to get the fiscal stance back on track, while largely accepting the negative growth effects of fiscal restriction. This strategy was based on the expectation that fiscal discipline would regain access to cheaper and more abundant international finance, and that the rewards in terms of investment and growth would compensate for the contractive effects of fiscal restriction (and, ideally, that external conditions, such as the Dollar exchange rate and world market prices for primary goods, would improve in time to help pull the economy out of recession)[474]. Hence, everything depended on getting interest rates down.

Four measures were taken by the new government in the year 2000 to make up for dwindling tax revenues. These included a "Law of Fiscal Responsibility" that decreed, from January 2000, a gradual reduction in the federal deficit to reach zero in 2003, mainly via an increase in tax rates on incomes, personal net assets, and certain consumer goods (dubbed "el impuestazo"), as well as a ceiling imposed on federal revenues to be shared with the provinces[475]. Finally, in the attempt to reduce the budget deficit to appease capital markets, Argentina negotiated support from the IMF who granted a new Stand-by Arrangement amounting to seven billion US-Dollars (which later, in early 2001, was augmented, with other official and private sources, to a total of 39 billion US-Dollars[476], and then dubbed "el blindaje", or "armour"), as growth was expected to pick up later in the year and in 2001.

Initially, there were some encouraging results. The consolidated public deficit, at 4.2 percent in 1999, was reduced to 3.6 percent in 2000, year in which the GDP contraction decelerated to 0.8 percent (although a positive growth rate of approximately two percent had been expected). However, Argentina's access to international markets deteriorated again in the second half of 2000, and the government decided to draw a first tranche of the IMF's credit line in December 2000, which, with the "blindaje", was nearly doubled a month later. External

---

[474] See Jonas (2002), p. 13.

[475] See Pou (2000), p. 15. This ceiling tried to tackle the problem that the federal government was biased to cut expenditures in order to obtain a required fiscal improvement, as alternative tax increases only had to be "shared away" with the provinces.

[476] The package comprised 14 billion US-Dollars from the IMF, 5 billion from the Inter-American Development Bank, 1 billion from the government of Spain, and the rest from the private sector, on a market-based and voluntary approach.

conditions deteriorated further, with the Dollar again starting to rise against the Euro in early 2001, and the world economy sliding deeper into recession. The economy shrank faster again, and the consolidated public debt reached vexing 6.2 percent in 2001. Even the consolidated primary budget turned out negative in 1999 and 2001 (-1.4 percent in the latter year).

The usual Argentine pattern of the federal balance ending up better than the consolidated, i.e. the balance including provincial budgets, continued to persist, but the difference widened to a maximum of 2.4 percent of GDP in 2001, when, without the provinces, the federal deficit alone amounted to "only" 3.8 percent of GDP. Thus, the still existent structural shortcomings of the coparticipation scheme[477], above all the built-in incentives of provincial governments to spend generously while not having to stand up to their debt, strained the fiscal situation the more the economic situation deteriorated. In addition, owing to the only half-hearted reforms the years before, tax collection was still inefficient and evasion high, and interest obligations on public debt kept growing (in 2000, they reached 15 percent of total public spending)[478].

Accordingly, public debt as a percentage of GDP took off to reach more than 50 and 62 percent in 2000 and 2001 respectively[479]. As mentioned above, certain off-budget liabilities, such as the court-ordered payments of past pension benefits (averaging over two percent of GDP during 1993-99), added to the business cycle effects on public sector debt. Some characteristics of total federal government debt as of mid-2001 are that, on total, it was 90 percent above the level of 1994; approximately two thirds of it was owed to external creditors. As to its denomination, 70 percent were denominated in Dollars, 20 percent in Euros, 5 percent in Yen, and only 4 percent in Pesos[480].

### 4.2.5.6 Limited Financial Sector Robustness

During 1999 and 2000, the Argentine financial sector proved remarkably sturdy. It was undisputed that it was now better positioned to master external shocks than before 1995. As a result of the strengthening banking regulations following the

---

[477] Attempts to re-negotiate coparticipation continued to fail time and again.

[478] See Jonas (2002), p. 13.

[479] See IMF Independent Evaluation Office (2004), p. 10.

[480] See Schuler/Hanke (2002), p. 3.

Tequila crisis, as well as of mergers and closures of weak banks[481], the system was now generally well equipped with capital as well as liquidity-protecting regulations and devices. Moreover, to judge from the fact that in many cases banks exceeded minimum liquidity requirements substantially, it seems that they generally took over liquidity responsibility themselves and relied less on the limited bail-out capacities of the central bank, and hence, that moral hazard was reduced[482]. With the exception of a new anti-bubble rule for mortgage loans, introduced as a reaction to the Asian crisis in 1998[483], no changes were made in the financial sphere until events started to accelerate in spring 2001.

By 1999, monetisation had advanced such that M3 surpassed 30 percent of GDP, reflecting the advanced size of the financial system[484]. Notably, despite the significant rises in country risk premia during the Asian, Russian, and Brazilian crises, the fall in asset prices, and the prolonged recession, the banking system did not register shrinking deposits for a surprisingly long time. While the high degree of dollarisation certainly also contributed to keeping depositors calm for a long time, the strengthening, Tequila-induced, reforms as well as the higher prevalence of foreign-owned banks made the financial sector seem firm.

Yet, with deteriorating public accounts, the probability of default increased, and so did the awareness that banks, left with batches of then worthless government bonds in their balance sheets, in the case of a public default would follow the government into insolvency. So, finally, when confidence in the Dollar peg was shaken by a series of heterodox policy measures in early 2001, a first, albeit limited, bout of deposit withdrawals set in, with the banking system losing about three billion Pesos, or four percent of total deposits, within a few days[485].

---

[481] Between 1991 and 1999, the number of banks shrank from 167 (35 of them public) to 119 (16 public). Further 16 government-owned banks, as well as the national mortgage bank, were privatised. See Pou (2000), p. 15.

[482] Of course, the flip side of the more active liquidity policies of banks was an increased reluctance to lend to the private sector and, correspondingly, a bigger share of bond holdings in their balance sheets. See Caprio et al. (1996), p. 629.

[483] It increased capital requirements for new mortgages as soon as a defined real estate price index surpassed a certain threshold.

[484] To be sure, the financial sector was still small by international standards, but it compared highly favourably with the state it was in after the era of high inflation.

[485] See IMF Independent Evaluation Office (2004), p. 47.

### 4.2.5.7 Further Labour Market Reforms

After long political battles between the ruling Peronist party and the opposing Alianza[486], a new labour market reform was proposed in 1998. The plan included further gradual reductions in non-wage labour costs, but failed to reduce the predominance of collective bargaining. Also, with the consent of trade unions and against entrepreneurial resistance, some of the non-traditional contracting variants created in 1991 were to be eliminated (the rationale behind this move being to gain union support and workers' votes for the presidential elections in late 1999), and the probation period shortened to one month[487]. At the same time, the regime for indemnity payments after dismissals was planned to be modified (reducing indemnities for those dismissed after short periods of service)[488]. The reform code failed to pass Congress and was postponed until after the elections of 1999.

In May 2000, a labour code reform was finally agreed (after continued urging by the IMF). It fixed the minimum probation period at three months (extendible to six months via collective bargaining, and to twelve months in the case of small companies), limited the automatic extension of collective bargaining agreements and of decentralised collective bargaining, and restricted the use of probation contracts, while offering incentives (in terms of reduced social security contributions and wage subsidies, differentiated according to social status, sex, and age of the employed) for replacing probation contracts by permanent employments[489].

As a result of these reforms, labour markets were increasingly characterised by flexible, short-term, and precarious contractual arrangements[490], the latter understood as not complying with labour and social security regulations. The share of temporary employment more than doubled between 1996 and 1998 (from 8 to 17

---

[486] The Alianza was created in 1997 as a coalition of the centrist Radical ("Unión Cívica Radical") and the centre-left FREPASO ("Frente País Solidario", founded in 1994) parties, to confront the Peronists' lock on power.

[487] The probation period was planned to be freed from pension contributions. It should be allowed to be lengthened to six months via collective bargaining.

[488] While dismissal costs of junior employees were planned to be reduced substantially, the costs of dismissals due to economic reasons were to be raised in relation to those of unfair dismissals (from one half to two thirds of the latter). See Marshall (2004), p. 14.

[489] This labour reform was starkly combated by labour unions, and answered by several national strikes. In its wake, vice president Carlos Álvarez resigned in protest over allegations that the government had paid bribes to senators to get the labour reform approved.

[490] See Altimir/Beccaria (2000b), p. 392.

percent), but decreased following the 1998 reforms to some five percent[491]. In contrast to what had been expected by the reforms, they did not succeed in reducing non-registered employment: while, in the early 90s, employment "en negro" (i.e. not registered with the social security system) had been about 25 percent of total wage employment, it rose to 31 percent after 1997, and, after the elimination of special temporary contracts in 1998, to about 33 percent (in the private sector alone to around 40 percent) at the beginning 2000s[492]. Thus, unregistered employment continued to rise largely without visible connection to changes in regulations or costs on the one hand, or to economic activity on the other.

In sum, the whole of labour market reforms and interventions of the 1990s left the country in the early 2000s with employment regulations that were not decisively different from those that had prevailed before these reforms. Essentially, only reduced dismissal costs for workers with less seniority, the option to extend probation contracts beyond three months, and, in general, more freedom to change regulations through collective bargaining remained. Probably the most important achievement was the reduction of non-wage labour costs, for the most part obtained in the first half of the decade. It left the country with non-wage costs for permanent contracts of around 47 percent of hourly wages at the end of the decade (as opposed to 65 percent in 1991)[493].

## 4.2.6    The Run Up to the Collapse: 2001

### 4.2.6.1 Meddling with the CBA

During 2000, the hopes of an economic revival triggered by fiscal rectitude had eroded. The country was trapped in a vicious circle that ran from recession to dwindling tax revenues, worsening fiscal deficits, deteriorating fiscal sustainability, higher risk premia[494], higher interest rates, and reduced investment feeding back on

---

[491] See Marshall (2004), pp. 17f.

[492] Few labour inspectors, negligible control of compliance, and low penalties facilitated this development. See Marshall (2004), p. 21.

[493] See Marshall (2004), p. 14.

[494] The messy collapse of Turkey's crawling peg exchange rate in February 2001 was reflected in an increase in spreads for the Argentine sovereign, though the deteriorating fiscal situation, as well as the political discord about fiscal consolidation, contributed most to the surge in spreads, from around 650 to 850 points in February and to over 1,000 points in the following weeks. See Mussa (2002), p. 22.

economic activity. With the increasingly fragile state of the governing coalition, a second, politically determined, vicious circle developed and aggravated the economic one, in a way that political quarrels over the fiscal adjustment further increased country risk premia, as markets increasingly doubted the ability of Argentine politics to bring forth fiscal sustainability[495].

After the resignation of the minister of economy in March 2001[496], his successor, Ricardo López Murphy, proposed a plan of immediate cuts in public sector expenditure, but failed to convince his own party of their necessity and was forced to resign after only two weeks in office.

De la Rúa appointed no lesser than Domingo Cavallo, the "father of Convertibility", as his successor. Within the frame of granted "emergency powers", in spring 2001, he initiated a series of mainly heterodox measures which intended to directly revive the ailing economy. Most of these measures worked in effect to weaken the CBA, and were increasingly perceived as delaying its end at best[497]. In addition, they suffered from a crumbling governing coalition whose left-wing member, FREPASO, abandoned the commitment to the CBA.

Mr Cavallo's first major action, in April of that year, was to announce a modification of the Convertibility law, such that the US-Dollar was to be replaced as an exchange rate anchor by an equally weighted basket of the Euro and the US-Dollar, to be put into force from the time both currencies reached parity[498]. While intending to make the CBA more flexible and to increase trade competitiveness[499], this announcement, and its final political approval in June, proved to cause major harm to the CBA's credibility, as the markets' interpretation was that, if this modification of the CBA could be made so swiftly, other changes, such as devaluation, could follow with the same ease. Spreads on government bonds at that time exceeded 1,000 basis points.

---

[495] See Powell (2002), p. 8.

[496] The reasons for the resignation of José Luis Machinea, who had negotiated the "blindaje", remain opaque. His abdication certainly did not help foster confidence in the country's recovery.

[497] "Cavallo's economic principles were [...] as fluid as the assets in a well managed bank. This fact, combined with his hyperactivity, was a deadly cocktail." Hanke (2002), p. 2.

[498] Mr Cavallo had proposed this move towards a basket peg already in 1998. See interview <http://www.pbs.org/wgbh/commandingheights/shared/minitextlo/int_domingocavallo.html>. Parity between the Euro and the US-Dollar, however, was not reached until July 2002.

[499] The Brazilian Real would have been a key currency to include in a peg that intended to increase Argentina's international competitiveness.

Also weakening the CBA, though less publicly perceptible, was a decree which allowed pressed banks to meet their liquidity requirements with government bonds up to a maximum of two billion Dollars. Also, a financial transactions tax was introduced. The forced resignation of the well-respected central bank governor, Pedro Pou, who opposed any weakening of the CBA, in late April, was a further blow to confidence in the CBA[500].

Moreover, in the face of increasing rollover risks, given reluctant domestic credit markets, a voluntary, market-based restructuring scheme for government debt held by Argentines, the so-called "mega canje" (mega swap), was carried through and completed by June 2001. With this swap, government bonds maturing between 2001 and 2005, worth about 30 billion US-Dollars in face value (including 8 billion held externally), were exchanged against bonds with longer maturities. As a result, the average maturity of Argentina's public sector debt was lengthened from 7.5 to 8.2 years, and interest obligations were reduced by 1.7 billion US-Dollars until 2005. However, yields had to be high enough (between 14 and 16 percent) to entice bondholders to accept the offer, so that short-term reductions in interest payments were bought at much higher future obligations[501]. To judge from the development of risk spreads, markets appreciated the improvement of immediate liquidity, but moderately enough to suggest limited enthusiasm[502].

Under the heading "Plan de Competitividad", a package of protectionist policies was implemented in June, 2001, including tax and trade measures in favour of exporters. The most important feature of this package was the introduction of a dual exchange rate. It was realised via a fiscal compensation mechanism (called "factor de convergencia") which mimicked the hypothetic exchange rate on the basis of the Euro-Dollar peg as long as it was not yet in force. Accordingly, exporters were paid

---

[500] Mr Pou not only objected looser "monetary policy" but also the introduction of the Euro into the peg, and preferred a move towards dollarisation rather than more flexibility. He was removed of office after a legally dubious procedure, as a result of which a congressional committee charged him of "misconduct" and recommended his removal to the President. With his removal, the central bank's independence was removed as well. See Powell (2002), p. 12.

[501] Interest rates at this level were not consistent with growth expectations and debt sustainability calculations. "By pursuing and accepting a debt swap on such onerous terms, the Argentine government was effectively declaring that it shared the market's assessment that sovereign default was virtually inevitable. Thus, the debt swap on these terms is properly viewed as an act of desperation by a debtor who is prepared to promise almost anything in the longer term for relatively modest debt service relief in the nearer term." Mussa (2002), p. 24.

[502] See Powell (2002), p. 13.

a subsidy, while importers were charged a duty. With this measure, in effect, a devaluation of the Peso of about eight percent[503] was undertaken by fiscal means, in order to stimulate exports, discourage imports, and thus to reduce the needs for external finance. This measure was received very unfavourably by the markets, as it put at risk the already strained relation with the IMF.

So, in July, presumably to appease the IMF, the "Plan Déficit Cero" (zero deficit plan) was announced and made law, by which the federal government (but not the provinces) was prescribed drastic across-the-board cuts in expenditures with the goal to balance the federal budget from August on. Expenditure cuts were decreed such as to equal available revenues. They included a 13 percent salary and pension cut for all public sector employees (of the federal government only)[504]. Although the wage cut was justifiable in the sense that private sector nominal wages had been falling as well during the recession[505], it caused social and political unrest. Markets reacted very negatively to the zero deficit plan, with risk spreads climbing to 1,600 basis points[506]. Despite the cuts, the weakening economy made budget revenues fall faster than government spending. The announcement of the zero deficit plan in effect triggered a bank run, as mostly institutional investors and larger private depositors started to withdraw deposits.

After some tense weeks with falling bank deposits, risk spreads approaching 1,700 basis points, and negotiations with the IMF, a second augmentation of IMF assistance (to SDR 17 billion, equalling about 22 billion US-Dollars) was negotiated in August[507]. The agreement was only moderately successful in persuading investors that the crisis was one of liquidity and not of solvency, and in pushing interest rates down: the bank run came to a halt and spreads went down, although only to 1,400 basis points.

---

[503] See Calvo/Izquierdo/Talvi (2003), p. 46.

[504] This cut was later (in August 2002) declared unconstitutional by the supreme court.

[505] See Jonas (2002), p. 16. Apart from that, federal employees were generally paid much more than private sector employees (45 percent more, comparing the average wages of federal and private sector employees for the year 1998). See IMF Independent Evaluation Office (2004), p. 27.

[506] The unexpectedly negative market reaction has been explained by either the perception that the zero deficit plan was not credible, that it did not include a big enough adjustment, or that it was perceived to reveal a situation much worse than expected, with the implicit admission that private sector funding was not expected any more. See Powell (2002), p. 15.

[507] The conditions included a renewed attempt to reform federal fiscal relations, and preparations for a voluntary swap programme for foreign debt.

Yet, the deposit losses already incurred (over 10% of total deposits), as well as the still very high risk spreads, caused a credit crunch that hit a private sector already deprived of access to international capital markets. With the suffering economy, fiscal revenues continued to fall short of any targets, and of course of the "déficit cero". A new debt restructuring that had to include foreign investors, i.e. default, was increasingly perceived as unavoidable[508].

Messy politics added to the increasing uncertainty. The ruling Alianza coalition was in disarray over the fiscal austerity measures, as well as over Convertibility, which was proposed to be abandoned by the left-wing member FREPASO in September. After the Lower and Upper House elections in October 2001, which gave the Peronist Party a majority in both houses, the coalition finally broke.

The announcement and implementation of another policy package on November 1st included a two-phase debt exchange for both local and international bondholders (called "orderly" instead of "voluntary"), further "competitiveness plans", VAT reductions on debit card payments, temporary rebates on employees' social security contributions, a corporate debt restructuring scheme, as well as an amnesty for accrued interest and penalty payments on outstanding tax obligations[509].

Although phase I of the debt exchange, aimed at domestic creditors[510], was completed by November 30, risk spreads reached 3,000 basis points. As bond prices fell, it got ever more widely realised what a default on sovereign debt would mean for heavily exposed domestic banks' balance sheets, and in turn, what failing banks would mean for the government's solvency position. A directive by which the

---

[508] Interestingly, despite IMF pressure to do so, the authorities did not seriously consider drawing on the contingent repo lines negotiated with a consortium of private banks after Tequila, for several reasons: first, parts of the government securities that had been agreed to collateralise these credits had been retired from the markets as a result of the previous debt exchange so that the potential credit line was in effect reduced to a fraction of the negotiated value; second, it was feared that drawing on these lines would alarm investors; and third, the expected reaction of the potential creditor banks of throwing other government securities on the markets would have made bond prices collapse. See Eichengreen (2001a), p. 26.

[509] See Dominguez/Tesar (2004), p. 25.

[510] It included the exchange of old government debt for guaranteed loans to the federal government at lower interest rates and longer maturities, collateralised by revenue from the financial transactions tax. Phase II was meant to be directed at international creditors, but never came to be realised. See IMF Independent Evaluation Office (2004), p. 56.

central bank effectively capped interest rates paid on deposits[511] eventually triggered a full-scale run in the financial system. Within three days, 3.6 billion Pesos were withdrawn, bringing the cumulative decline to 15 billion, or 20 percent of total deposits since the beginning of the year.

So, on December 2nd, in an effort to confront intensifying deposit withdrawals and capital flight, the government enacted far-reaching interferences in banking and foreign exchange transactions, such as a ban on granting loans in Pesos (and a forced conversion of existing Peso loans into Dollars), restrictions in transferring Dollars abroad, as well as a decree by which deposit withdrawals in cash were limited to 250 Dollars per week for each individual bank account (the so-called "corralito")[512]. In a desperate step a few days later, the government forced pension funds to buy government bonds.

Financial markets were appeased neither by the government's activism, nor by the IMF's financial support[513]. Argentina completely lost market access as the spreads on its bonds continued to rise, to exceed 5,000 basis points towards that year's end. Finally, with Argentina continuously failing to comply with the fiscal targets agreed, the IMF decided in early December not to clear a disbursement scheduled for that month.

### 4.2.6.2 Emission of Quasi-Monies

As neither the IMF's financial assistance nor various demand-stimulating measures were successful in restoring investors' confidence, the liquidity-pressed federal government resorted to printing small-denomination bonds, the so-called "Lecops" ("letras de cancelación de obligaciones provinciales"), with which it paid its tax obligations to the provinces. Many provinces followed suit and issued their own provincial bonds, such as e.g. the "Patacón" of Buenos Aires province, or the

---

[511] On November 23rd, a 100 percent liquidity requirement was imposed on deposits paying an interest rate higher than one percentage point above the average of all local banks. See IMF Independent Evaluation Office (2004), p. 61.

[512] After a sudden increase in the number of new bank accounts, the government quickly changed the decree to limit deposit withdrawals per person rather than per account. – Payments with cheques, credit and debit cards, and electronic payment were left unrestricted. Deposits could be exchanged against federal bonds (BODENs) with different maturities. See Dominguez/Tesar (2004), pp. 14 and 26. – "Corralito" means "little fence", alluding to a corral where cattle are herded into in order to transport them to the abattoir.

[513] Most of the described measures were introduced by the Argentine authorities without prior consultation with the IMF. See IMF Independent Evaluation Office (2004), p. 61.

"Lecor" of Córdoba, to pay wages, pensions, and unemployment grants[514]. These quasi-monies were accepted for tax payments and went to be broadly accepted also for every-day consumer transactions. The amounts issued rose quickly during the second half of 2001, to exceed 24 percent of total Pesos in circulation in December[515].

### 4.2.6.3 Social and Political Overflow, and the End of the CBA

After three years of recession and severe wage cuts, the deposit freeze was just what confiscation-experienced Argentines needed to lose patience. The corralito deeply outraged Argentine depositors, and especially the middle classes, who took to the streets and staged the so-called "cacerolazos"[516], to join the more serious demonstrations, riots, and lootings going on in the streets of Buenos Aires.

After the IMF's decision, on December 5th, to withhold a scheduled loan instalment of 1.24 billion US-Dollars because of Argentina's fiscal non-compliance, the authorities announced that payments on foreign debt could no longer be guaranteed. A national strike was called in protest against the corralito and pension payments delays, and a series of demonstrations against the government's economic policies followed. Violent social unrest unloaded. The state of emergency was declared, as well as the closing of banks for several days. The president resigned, on December 20th, after the riots had cost human lives[517]. The country sunk into chaos, with the following twelve days seeing four new presidents in office[518].

On December 23rd, 2001, the then president Rodríguez Saá declared default on Argentina's federal and provincial external debt (worth 81 billion US-Dollars in face value). While sticking to Convertibility, he announced the creation of a new, parallel

---

[514] The issue of these parallel currencies generated real seigniorage revenue for the federal and provincial governments. See Roubini (2001), p. 15.

[515] See Dominguez/Tesar (2004), p. 12.

[516] "Cacerolazo" refers to the noisy beating of casserole pans in an otherwise peaceful demonstration.

[517] Over twenty demonstrators died in the riots.

[518] After Fernando de la Rúa's resignation, in accordance with the constitution, the president of the Senate, Ramón Puerta, became interim president. Adolfo Rodríguez Saá was elected president by the legislative assembly on December 23rd, only to resign seven days later. Eduardo Camaño, head of the lower house, became the new interim president (as Ramón Puerta had resigned as senate president). He was replaced when the legislative assembly elected Eduardo Duhalde on January 1st, 2002.

and inconvertible, fiat currency, the "Argentino"[519], as well as a new job creation programme. He left the "corralito" untouched, announcement which set off new street riots on December 29th. His resignation was forced on December 30th by Peronist provincial governors not agreeing with his emergency measures. Finally, on January 3rd, 2002, the new president, Eduardo Duhalde, announced the end of the CBA (to introduce a dual foreign exchange regime), and thus put an end to more than ten years of guaranteed one-to-one convertibility between the Peso and the US-Dollar.

### 4.2.7    A Sketch of the Post-Collapse

Convertibility was replaced by a dual exchange rate regime, by which the Peso was devalued to the relation 1.4 Pesos to 1 Dollar for foreign trade transactions, and floated for all other transactions. In February, the exchange rate was unified, and asymmetric pesification of bank balance sheets was decreed: all debts up to 100,000 Dollars were converted to Pesos at 1:1, while larger loans and deposits were converted at the "official" exchange rate of 1.4 Pesos to the Dollar. Creditors were decreed to be compensated for the devaluation costs from the revenues of a new tax on oil. Capital and bank account controls, including the "corralito", were stuck to and intensified (the "corralito" was finally abolished after one year, on December 2nd, 2002). Though banks were formally compensated with special government bonds (the so-called BODENs), asymmetric pesification commanded the financial sector into bankruptcy. In March, the pesification of government debt issued under Argentine law was decreed[520].

During the first weeks of 2002, the Peso market exchange rate jumped to reach its peak in late march at 4 Pesos in the Dollar. It later stabilised to 3 Pesos per Dollar and was kept there since then. However, the pass-through on inflation stayed moderate, thanks to idle capacities and low wage pressure, with prices rising by 40 percent in 2002. A complete credit crunch, diving consumption (minus 13 percent) and investment (minus 36 percent), soaring unemployment (it reached 25 percent in

---

[519] The "Argentino" was intended to act as a "consumption currency", officially to replace the variety of quasi-monies that were circulating in the economy, but probably rather another short-circuit attempt for printing-press financed spending. It did not rise above the announcement level. See Krugman (2001b).

[520] See IMF Independent Evaluation Office (2004), p. 100.

the second half of 2002[521]), and a fall of GDP by 11 percent marked the year 2002, with the result that per capita income by that time was 22 percent below its 1998 level. Real wages fell by 30 percent in that year, and 56 percent of the Argentines were counted as living below the official poverty line[522].

Economy minister Roberto Lavagna, brought in by Duhalde (and kept by his successor Kirchner[523]), is widely credited for having engineered the following swift recovery, which started in the second half of 2002 and brought strong growth (plus 8.7 percent) with low inflation (4 percent) in 2003 that continued to approach the 1998 GDP level again in 2005. Inflation, however, has risen with the tightening capacity constraints, to surpass 10 percent in late 2005.

The devalued Peso entailed a dramatic shift in relative prices in favour of tradables, thus stimulating exports and import substitution. Exports rose by 15 percent in 2003[524], imports decreased, foreign reserves grew, and the current account moved into surplus – helped, of course, by soaring world market prices for farm products and the weakening Dollar.

The relative cheapening of labour reduced unemployment fast (to around 11 percent in 2005, or 13 percent including those receiving welfare payments), but also, besides the severe credit restriction, helped discourage investment in capital intensive sectors. The investment drought has been especially severe in the infrastructure and energy sectors, where tariffs have been pesified and frozen in early 2002, pushing the privatised utilities into default on their dollar debt. Looming energy shortages, endangering growth, are the result of the investment standstill.

Absent domestic and foreign credit, and precluded the money printing option, public and private saving remained as the only sources of finance. The fiscal situation has vastly improved (with primary budget surpluses of over 3 percent annually), thanks above all to the stop in servicing debt (except the debt owed to the IMF and other multilateral institutions, "guaranteed" debt, and the bank

---

[521] The official number is 21 percent, but does not include those receiving minimum income payments under a new welfare programme ("jefes y jefas de hogar desocupados") which supports unemployed heads of households with a monthly stipend (150 Pesos as of late 2004). The programme is widely perceived as being manipulated by local political bosses who are suspected of handing out the money in exchange for political support. See e.g. N.N. (2004), p. 7.

[522] See Gerchunoff/Aguirre (2004).

[523] Though Kirchner has sacked him in November 2005.

[524] However, only half of export growth reflected changes in volume, and half was due to higher prices.

compensation bonds) and new taxes on exports and on financial transactions. Despite fears of capital flight and re-dollarisation, a slight rise in Peso savings occurred, albeit deposited only short-term. Thus, a slow stabilisation of bank's liabilities has been taking place, though their assets side is still crunched, with credit amounting to only 8 percent of GDP in 2004 (compared to 22 percent in 2000), all of it short-term[525].

The debt restructuring, finally completed in early 2005, imposed a 65 percent haircut to international creditors' titles, reflecting cuts in principal, lengthenings of maturity, and reductions in interest. This restructuring was without precedent in terms of the harshness with which the government confronted creditors, the size of the haircut and total debt write-down achieved (almost 70 billion US-Dollars out of more than 100 billion outstanding), the number of bondholders having not signed up (holding together 26 percent of the defaulted bonds, or 25 billion US-Dollars in value), the dispersion of titles (152 bonds), creditors (over 500,000), currencies (six), and jurisdictions (eight) involved, and also in being carried through without IMF involvement.

Important areas have remained untackled as yet, among them the recapitalisation of the agonal banking system (only a few banks have closed their doors), the reforms necessary to rationalise the tax system and the federal redistribution scheme, the overdue re-negotiation of tariffs with most foreign-owned privatised utilities, and the promotion of capacity maintaining and increasing investment in infrastructure and the tradables sector. Uncertainty about the future macroeconomic course, repeatedly fed by the populist and left-leaning rhetoric of President Kirchner, is also standing in the way of badly needed bigger investment. The benefits of the recovery seem, once again, not to trickle down equally, and poverty is still rampant: though unemployment has come down, nearly 40 percent are still living below the poverty line, and seventy per cent of the employed earn less than the minimum required to cover an average family's food expenses[526]. All of this is boding ill for the long-term prospects of the country.

---

[525] See BIS Review 62/2004, <http://www.bis.org/review/r041028c.pdf>.
[526] See http://web.amnesty.org/report2005/arg-summary-eng.

# 5 What Went Wrong?

Pointing to convertibility or dollarisation as basic explanations of the crisis, in order to downplay structural problems in fiscal institutions, overlooks the fact that they were precisely chosen after decades of fiscal mismanagement.[527]

## 5.1 The Main Suspects

After the CBA's collapse at the turn of the year 2001, obituaries mushroomed. A multitude of factors was made responsible for Argentina's latest crisis, factors of external or internal origin, solely or jointly in a variety of combinations. Many of them had been the subjects of ever-repeated warnings since the CBA's inception.

Fiscal imbalances as well as the overvalued real exchange rate, clearly inter-related as they are, figure most prominently among the culprits. These predispositions made the country extremely vulnerable to external shocks. Accordingly, the "sudden stop" hypothesis has gained some prominence; an approach focussing on adverse policy constellations within MERCOSUR sheds further light on the issue. Important co-factors of the crisis are, undoubtedly, various institutional deficiencies, tackled little or not at all during the 1990s, as well as political economy in a country that, for many, seemed improbable to bring forth durably coherent politics, given its track record. Other blames extend beyond the country's sole responsibilities, and point at international financial organisations, in their vanguard the IMF, as having helped bring about the unfortunate outcome. In the same vein, the liberal policy recommendations labelled "Washington Consensus" find themselves made responsible for the disastrous outcome. Finally, the much-repeated argument that the CBA itself contained the conditions of its own inevitable destruction has to be addressed.

### 5.1.1   Fiscal Imbalance

The foremost explanation for the CBA's fall relates to large and persistent fiscal deficits. As has been shown, Convertibility made fiscal policy extremely important, as it was, due to the reserve backing rule which constrained monetary policy, the only tool of macroeconomic management. This required budgets balanced over the business cycle, but in any case levels of public debt low enough to maintain

---

[527] López Murphy/Artana/Navajas (2003), p. 23.

borrowing capacities that would be large enough to allow for sufficient deficit financing during downturns and for lender of last resort assistance in case of banking crises. Moreover, credibility of the Dollar parity required the government's unquestioned capacity to borrow in Dollars, itself again dependent on fiscal solvency, in order to guarantee unrestricted convertibility.

As has been shown, fiscal deficits persisted, and were massively financed by borrowing on domestic and, increasingly, international capital markets[528]. Though Argentina's debt management was quite sophisticated (it avoided excessive dependence on short term or floating interest rate debt and sought to discharge it from the dominance of Dollar denominated debt[529]), the rapid growth in public indebtedness resulted in serious rollover problems when the external shocks of the late 90s pushed the country into recession and encumbered access to capital markets. However, the core of fiscal problems was widely, and for too long, seen as lying in the flow variable, the budget deficit. Only after a lengthening row of failed attempts to redress the fiscal deficit did it become undeniable that the problem was much harder to come by, as it had developed into a stock problem: total debt was far too high to be sustainable under other than very favourable conditions.

Thus, fiscal profligacy seems to stand at the centre of Argentina's crisis, giving perfect credit to traditional, fundamentals oriented, crisis explanations. Both the flow and stock determinants of debt sustainability will be dealt with in what follows.

### 5.1.1.1 Persistent Budget Deficits

The federal primary balance averaged, over the period 1992-2001, 0.73 percent of GDP. It was in deficit once (in 1996) and usually, with the exception of the early 90s, amounted to a surplus of less than one percent. Including the provinces, the record deteriorates, with an average of 0.03 percent, and four years of negative

---

[528] Despite the growth in domestic financial markets (Argentina started with very small domestic markets in 1991, due partly to Argentina's low savings rate of hardly 15 percent of GDP), domestic sources (mostly banks and pension funds) amounted, in late 2000, to only roughly half of the financing, with the rest stemming from external sources. 90 percent of total public debt was foreign currency denominated. By late 2000, Argentina was the largest emerging-market borrower on international capital markets (accounting for a fifth of the entire asset class). See IMF Independent Evaluation Office (2004), p. 86, and Mussa (2002), p. 15.

[529] During much of 1999 and early 2000, Argentina issued Euro bonds, taking advantage from the decline in European interest rates, induced by the advent of the Euro, and serving the preferences of yield seeking investors.

primary balances (1995/96, 1999, and 2001)[530]. Interest payments averaged 2.8 percent of GDP during 1991-2001[531]. The resulting overall fiscal balance was negative, both with and without the provinces, throughout the whole period, with the single exception of the year 1993. Argentina entered the recession of the late 1990s with an overall fiscal deficit of 2.1 percent of GDP in 1998 (1.3 percent excluding the provinces), which, taken at face value, does not seem too worrying. However, several facts have to be taken into account to judge these deficits adequately.

First, a simple exercise in summing-up reveals that the accumulated budget deficits do not correspond, as one would reasonably expect, with the rise in public debt. Taking the period between 1993 and 1998 (which largely excludes the initial stabilisation boom, but still incorporates, despite the Tequila interruption, strong average growth with virtual zero inflation), the difference between the two amounts to more or less one percent of GDP[532]. The explanation for this difference is that a substantial portion of public debt incorporated borrowings to finance off-budget-liabilities (such as the court-ordered payments of past obligations to pensioners, to government suppliers, and to provincial governments)[533]. Budget deficits therefore never represented a complete measure of fiscal performance. The debt to GDP ratio rose by around 12 percent during six years – six years in which growth would have been strong enough to allow for a constant ratio of indebtedness.

Second, the comparatively favourable official deficit figures included two major sources of non-recurring relief. One was the Brady restructuring of 1993 which incorporated a significant upfront relief in interest payments against a back-loading of payments due in later years. So, the 1993 fiscal surplus was aided by proceeds from the Brady bond restructuring entering the books of that year[534]. The other boost was given by non-recurring privatisation receipts, amounting to around 24 billion Dollars until 1998[535].

---

[530] See IMF Independent Evaluation Office (2004), p. 10.

[531] See López Murphy/Artana/Navajas (2003), p. 24.

[532] On basis of the data given by the IMF Independent Evaluation Office (2004), the difference amounts to 1.3 percent of GDP. Mussa (2002) uses slightly different numbers and arrives at 0.6 percent. See Mussa (2002), p. 8.

[533] Mussa (2002) reckons that, without the off-budget-liabilities, the strong GDP growth (by 26 percent in nominal terms between 1993 and 1998) should have made the debt to GDP ratio result seven percent below the sum of declared yearly deficits. See Mussa (2002), p. 8.

[534] See Mussa (2002), p. 8.

[535] See Heymann (2000), p. 55.

On the other hand, the extraordinary burden on the public budget arising from the social security reform of 1994, i.e. the upfront transfer of funds from the public to the private pension scheme (equalling about one percent of GDP in the years following the reform), although promising long-term relief, worsened the short-term fiscal situation. Yet, it should have been possible to neutralise this effect with the extraordinary receipts and back-loaded obligations sketched above.

Thus, looking behind the mere numbers of seemingly modest fiscal deficits, the fiscal performance of the nineties clearly does not look like the reflection of disciplined fiscal policies. What is more, such record obviously defies the notion of the CBA disciplining fiscal policy, as well as of privatisations helping restore fiscal balance. Tellingly, as soon as 1994, one of the early expansionary years (with 5.8 percent GDP growth), Argentina missed, for the first time in a lengthy row, a fiscal target set by the IMF[536].

### 5.1.1.2 Total Indebtedness

Total public sector debt was less than 30 percent of GDP in 1992, and reached 41 percent in late 1998, to rise faster during the following recession years. The absolute level of indebtedness, however, was not perceived as worrying until well into 2000, when the debt to GDP ratio surpassed 50 percent. From an industrial country's perspective, and to judge from the Maastricht criteria, such ratios might seem not alarming. Yet for Argentina, the case has to be judged differently for several reasons.

First, emerging market economies, with the typically low degree of trade diversification, are in general far more susceptible to real external shocks than industrialised countries, even more so when they have fixed exchange rates and lack the option to devalue. Such susceptibility requires much lower debt levels ex ante, so as to dispose of a broader margin of debt sustainability in the light of a more volatile GDP.

Second, a country which, like Argentina, depends on foreign capital to finance its current account deficit needs to insure not only against a cut-off of market access in case of deteriorating fundamentals, but also against changes in general market sentiment due to contagion[537]. The only insurance against the latter risk is

---

[536] This stayed without consequences only because of Mexico's devaluation a few days later, which necessitated fresh assistance.

[537] See IMF Independent Evaluation Office (2004), p. 26.

creditworthiness to a degree that expectations of default never emerge, and never become self-fulfilling.

Third, Argentina's both public and private sector debt were for the largest part denominated in foreign currency and contracted with creditors abroad. This required, for the public sector, enough fiscal revenues available as well as the maintenance of convertibility (so that one Peso of these revenues was always convertible into one Dollar to service debt), and, for the private sector, enough foreign exchange earned out of exports to service the debt. While industrial countries raise tax revenues of 40 to 50 percent of GDP, Argentina's tax raising capacity rarely exceeded 20 percent of GDP. As, due to Argentina's peculiar federal fiscal relations, most of the tax receipts were sucked into the coparticipation scheme, only a small proportion of these tax revenues was available for debt service. As for the private sector, by 1998, the ratio of total external foreign currency debt to export earnings in foreign currency was 500 percent. Such ratios necessarily imply a high risk of an external financing crisis[538].

Fourth, beyond any static measure of indebtedness, debt dynamics over time should have given enough reason for concern. As already noted, the strongly growing indebtedness over years of generally strong economic growth is clear proof of a deficient fiscal performance[539].

After Argentina's collapse, efforts were made to develop tools to identify benchmarks for sustainable debt-to-GDP ratios for developing countries, both for public debt and for total external debt. The IMF arrived, in 2003, at a 40 percent threshold for Argentina's external debt to GDP with the CBA, at which point the probability for a crisis was estimated at 15-20 percent. Such diagnostics, if in place, would have rung alarm in 1998 the latest (factual external debt surpassed 50 percent of GDP in 1999 and would have required, depending on projections, a

---

[538] Eichengreen/Hausmann/Panizza (2003) depict currency mismatches as a consequence of two distinguished phenomena responsible for developing countries' financing difficulties: "original sin" and "debt intolerance", the first comprising problems arising externally, through realities on international capital markets (especially the impossibility for a country to place debt in local currency), and the latter describing internal problems such as weak institutions and unreliable policies.

[539] An analysis of the dynamics of debt towards unsustainability is undertaken in the paragraph dedicated to the sudden stop thesis below.

turnaround of up to 2.5 percent of GDP in the non-interest current account balance)[540].

Reinhart et al. argue that Argentina, with its five defaults since 1820, had developed higher debt intolerance through the accumulation of payment difficulties over time. With this level of debt intolerance, acquired before the 1990s already, they estimate a threshold where markets start ascribing the country a risk of default at a total debt to GDP ratio of only 25 to 30 percent (the 30 percent mark was surpassed since 1993)[541]. Consistent with that view is Argentina's estimated "revenue-equivalent debt-to-GDP Maastricht target" of 30 percent[542]. In late 2000, the factual public debt to GDP ratio of 47.6 percent would, according to retrospective IMF estimations, have required a primary surplus of 1.6 percent, while the actual balance was in deficit by 0.5 percent[543].

### 5.1.2 Overvalued Exchange Rate

The second common view of the single most important cause of the CBA's end is the growing real exchange rate misalignment, developing as a result of the Peso appreciating significantly against the Dollar in real terms, first, between 1991 and 1993, and, second, from 1998 onwards. In between, the real exchange rate showed smaller movements, showing both phases of mild depreciation (above all in 1994 and 1995) and of slight appreciation.

#### 5.1.2.1 Real Appreciation before 1998

The Peso's real appreciation of the early 1990s can be explained as the result of several factors. First, as a legacy from the high inflation years during the 1980s, the Argentine currency started, in 1991, with a value significantly below its long-term equilibrium level, so that the post-stabilisation appreciation partly reflected an overdue correction. One estimate is that, while the Peso appreciated in real terms by about 50 percent in the early 90s with respect to its 1980s average (admittedly a doubtful benchmark, but at least giving a clue), half of this appreciation represented a catch-up of the previous undervaluation, so that "only" 25 percent of the Peso's

---

[540] The external debt to GDP ratio jumped to over 140 percent in 2002, displaying the Peso's previous degree of overvaluation. See IMF Independent Evaluation Office (2004), p. 88.

[541] See Reinhart/Rogoff/Savastano (2003).

[542] See Guidotti (2004), p. 17.

[543] See IMF Independent Evaluation Office (2004), ibid.

appreciation originated in the 1990s[544]. Second, in the aftermath of hyperinflation, price movements took time to stabilise. While inflation inertia was, to a limited degree, calculated into the choice of the exchange rate fixed in 1991, it was well known and accepted that disinflation would create additional real appreciation of the currency. It took until 1994 for Argentine inflation to fall to international levels, and much of the rise in the real value of the currency occurred until that time. Third, in addition to the real appreciation of the early 1990s, the US-Dollar started, in 1995, to continuously revalue against the European currencies (and later the Euro) which meant that the Peso likewise revalued against the currencies of Argentina's trading partners[545].

Pastor/Wise undertook, in 1999, an estimation of the Peso's equilibrium exchange rate, via regression of the real exchange rate since 1960. They found that its equilibrium value rose over time, which justifies the view of the Peso's real appreciation partly as a long-term and sustainable trend[546]. Nevertheless, they find that, in 1993, the Peso was already about 25 percent above its estimated equilibrium value, though this gap was narrowing somewhat due to subsequent real depreciation via low (and even negative) inflation towards the end of the decade[547].

### 5.1.2.2 The Real Exchange Rate after 1998

Inescapably, the order of magnitude of a real exchange rate misalignment is a controversial issue, due to the impossibility to exactly detect the equilibrium (or "fair") value of an exchange rate at any point of time[548]. Hence, it is disputed

---

[544] See Pastor/Wise (1999), pp. 480 and 496, as well as Dominguez/Tesar (2003), p. 12.

[545] The US-Dollar's surge lasted from August 1995 to February 2002, during which period the US-Dollar appreciated by 34 percent. See Joint Economic Committee (2005), p. 2.

[546] See Pastor/Wise (1999), p. 498. It is, however, questionable to conjecture a stable trend in equilibrium values, given the highly volatile economic development in the period considered.

[547] "If we generously assume that: (a) zero inflation continues, (b) international inflation stays at around 3%, and (c) the equilibrium currency value continues to drift upward, then the actual real exchange rate will arrive within 5% of its equilibrium value by the end of 2001." Pastor/Wise (1999), p. 498.

[548] There are three theoretical concepts to gauge the "fair" or equilibrium value of a currency. These are, first, the notion of purchasing power parity (PPP) which holds that, in the long run, exchange rates should equalise the prices of a common basket of tradable goods and services in any two countries, but which itself is reduced in its operability by its inherent long-term perspective. Second, the concept of the fundamental equilibrium exchange rate (FEER) holds that the fair currency value would be consistent with external (current account) and internal balance (full

whether, and to which extent, the Peso was overvalued before the series of external shocks hit Argentina from 1998 onwards.

The most evident operational criteria from which to gauge the approximate position of the equilibrium exchange rate are, on the one hand, the current account balance (a deficit would argue, prima facie, for an overvalued real exchange rate), and on the other, the development of foreign exchange reserves (declining reserves would suggest overvaluation). The current account aspect, especially the strong rise in imports, might support the notion of a real overvaluation of the Peso during the whole of the 1990s, both in relation to the main trading partners and to the US. However, evident counterarguments are, first, the equally (if less than imports) rising exports (which, granted, are difficult to interpret, given the low initial base, the trade liberalisation efforts, and the impact on trade flows of MERCOSUR), second, the notion that trade does not have to be perfectly balanced to be "fair", and, third and probably more important, that the deficits might mainly have reflected differences in national savings and investment rates: given the low domestic savings rate (less than 15 percent of GDP during the 1990s on average[549]), the investment growth, primarily of the early 1990s, was largely financed out of vigorous capital inflows, themselves validating the exchange rate[550]. As to the international reserves criterion, these were built up strongly to back the currency and to remonetise the economy, so that they can be referred to as a symptom of overvaluation only from late 2000, when they ended their strong and almost uninterrupted rise during the 1990s.

A further important argument as to why the real appreciation of the Peso might be judged as more of a natural and potentially beneficial process is the rapid productivity growth. This is supported by calculations which find the real Peso-Dollar

employment with low inflation), but again, this concept is not an operable guide. Third, the idea of the behavioural equilibrium exchange rate (BEER) examines which economic variables (such as productivity growth or budget balances relative to other countries, or net foreign assets) have determined the exchange rate in the past and compares them with current values of these variables and the current exchange rate, assuming stable relationships. While, e.g., Argentina's strong productivity growth in the early 1990s can be argued to take the edge of much of overvaluation concerns, its overall turbulent past disqualifies any such serious analysis from the start.

[549] Argentines thus saved nearly 10 percent of GDP less than emerging economies on average. See IMF Independent Evaluation Office (2004), p. 86.

[550] Both FDI and portfolio investment showed sound term structures, so that the suspicion of a prevalence of short-term, easy-exit, positions of investment which would reflect doubts about exchange rate sustainability does not hold. See Pastor/Wise (1999), p. 481.

exchange rate based on unit labour costs depreciating by almost 50 percent between 1991 and 1998[551].

Thus, it is far from clear whether, or to which degree, the Peso's real appreciation up to 1998 was an equilibrium phenomenon, reflecting a necessary and positive course of events, or rather was the result of the fixed exchange rate (i.e. of economic parameters inconsistent with the hard peg). Accordingly, views on the Peso's overvaluation in 1998, when the series of external shocks started to hit the country, vary widely. Estimations ranged, in 1999, from zero (held, understandably, by government officials) to about 25 percent. In early 2000 (the period before economic and financial conditions worsened further, and before the Euro further weakened against the Dollar), the Peso's overvaluation was still gauged highly differently by economic researchers, ranging from a mere seven to over twenty percent[552].

### 5.1.3    Sudden Stop

The sudden stop interpretation of the CBA's collapse focuses on the unforeseen standstill of capital inflows, provoked by the Russian crisis in August 1998, and its detrimental effects on an economy with the peculiar characteristics of Argentina[553]. The sudden stop came, in its severity, to most as a surprise, as the speed and extent of contagion was hitherto unseen, and as it also hit countries that had little or no economic relations to Russia – such as Argentina. Thus, the crisis did not fit well with traditional explanations of financial crises, which is why it led to an intensified focussing on capital market behaviour as an autonomous trigger of crisis[554].

Besides having been unexpected, the sudden stop also failed to meet expectations that it would stay, as the Tequila crisis had been, only short-term, and that markets would recover quickly. Tellingly, the spreads on Argentine government

---

[551] See IMF Independent Evaluation Office (2004), p. 20.

[552] See IMF Independent Evaluation Office (2004), p. 23.

[553] This paragraph draws mainly from Calvo/Izquierdo/Talvi (2003).

[554] The most important arguments are derived from the assumption of asymmetric information: given the relatively high fixed costs of obtaining information about a country to invest in, only the largest investors will be able to specialise and to be well informed. The remaining, less informed, investors in the market tend to observe the informed leaders' market transactions to the minute, in order to derive from these a directive for their own behaviour. Seeing a presumably informed investor selling assets, but not being able to deduct his motives with certainty, can lead to supersensitive behaviour of other investors, and a spreading of asset sales through the market on the grounds of reasons possibly not related to the country's fundamentals.

bonds over US treasuries remained lower than average emerging markets' spreads until August 2000, which can be interpreted as capital markets considering Argentina's fiscal situation sustainable until then. The provision of multilateral institutions' (IMF) financing during that time obviously made up for the missing private capital flows and their negative impact on the economy and government finances. Hence the conjecture that, would the shock have been less long-lived, default could have been avoided[555]. However, the capital stop's persistence and the subsequent adaptation of expectations about Argentina's fiscal solvency worked to render the fiscal situation unsustainable.

The following calculations depict the magnitude of derogation of fiscal sustainability after the sudden stop. While it can be argued that, in the absence of the sudden stop, Argentina's fiscal position was not unsustainable in 1998, there is no doubt that it was highly vulnerable to real exchange rate swings.

### 5.1.3.1 Leveraged Argentina

The large and unexpected withdrawal of international capital from the current account and the corresponding rise in interest rates met a country with the three well-known fatal characteristics of relative closedness, high public and private indebtedness, and high liability dollarisation. Being closed meant that the share of exported tradable goods in total output was small in relation to the domestic absorption of tradables (i.e. of imports or exportable goods of domestic origin), and that, consequently, a high proportion of domestic absorption (consumption and investment) had to be financed by capital imports (rather than by export revenues)[556]. High liability dollarisation, on the other hand, implied large currency mismatches in the public as well as the private non-tradables sector (Dollar debts to be serviced out of Peso incomes). These mismatches in both output and debt composition potentialised the sudden stop's devastating effects.

The sudden stop withdrew the current account deficit's financing. With the exchange rate fixed, the corresponding improvement of the current account had to occur via a fall in the domestic absorption of tradables. This fall required a fall in the prices of non-tradable relative to tradable goods, i.e. domestic deflation, or, put

---

[555] See Calvo/Izquierdo/Talvi (2003), p. 35.

[556] Put differently, the more closed an economy, i.e. the smaller the share of tradables in domestic production in relation to the domestic absorption of tradables, the higher is the country leveraged towards the exterior, i.e. the higher are the domestic adjustment needs following external shocks.

differently, an increase (depreciation) in the real exchange rate. The more closed an economy, the higher the real exchange rate adjustment required to compensate for the withering capital inflows.

Calvo/Izquierdo/Talvi (2003)[557] quantify Argentina's economic characteristics and the effects of the sudden stop. According to their computation of an "un-leveraged absorption coefficient", Argentina ranked, in 1998, comparatively low within a group of Latin American economies, signifying that its absorption was higher leveraged, i.e. its economy significantly more closed, than, say, that of its neighbour Chile. From this they derive the required real exchange rate depreciation to bring the current account to balance: it would have been 46 percent. As it turned out, according to their calculations, Argentina's real exchange rate depreciated by only 14 percent between 1998 and 2001, which accordingly did not suffice to close the current account gap.

### 5.1.3.2 Debt Sustainability

Taking high liability dollarisation into the picture, it gets clear that Argentina's debt composition added to its unfavourable output composition to aggravate the consequences of the sudden stop. Thus, besides the immediate recessionary impact of the required rise in the real exchange rate, its effects on debt sustainability were detrimental.

Debt sustainability requires a minimum primary surplus to service a constant debt to GDP ratio. The debt to GDP ratio is determined by debt (Peso debt, and Dollar debt times the real exchange rate) and output (output of non-tradables, and of tradables times the real exchange rate). When, as in the case of Argentina, domestic output is dominated by non-tradables, while total debt is dominated by Dollar debt, the real depreciation necessary to restore external balance has to be comparatively large, and thus breaks through heavily on the debt component: the revaluation effects of the real exchange rate depreciation undermine debt sustainability.

Calvo/Izquierdo/Talvi (2003) quantify Argentina's "public sector debt mismatch measure" for the year 1998, and find that its value was one of the lowest in Latin America[558], and very close to zero, i.e. close to the worst case where a real

---

[557] See Calvo/Izquierdo/Talvi (2003), pp. 15ff.

[558] Calvo/Izquierdo/Talvi (2003) calculate Argentina's „public sector debt mismatch measure" at 0.01, the worst (together with Ecuador) of the sample of Latin American countries, compared with the highest sample measure of 0.45 for Chile. See Calvo/Izquierdo/Talvi (2003), p. 22.

exchange rate depreciation fully hits upon debt sustainability. With this mismatch, under the (unrealistically optimistic) assumption of both constant interest rates and GDP growth, the required 46 percent rise in the real exchange rate would lead to a revaluation of debt such, that Argentina's debt to GDP ratio would jump from 36.5 (the observed value of 1998) to 49.7 percent, increasing the primary surplus required for debt sustainability by 0.7 percent of GDP to 1.6 percent.

Allowing for the more realistic conditions of increased interest rates and slower GDP growth, as well as for the inclusion of those contingent liabilities which reflect the fiscal cost expected to be incurred by the government eventually bailing out the financial sector, the post sudden stop-debt to GDP ratio approaches 59 percent, so that the required primary surplus rises to 3.6 percent of GDP (from an observed primary surplus of 0.9 percent in 1998), itself requiring, e.g., a 13.5 percent cut in total expenditures, or, alternatively, a debt reduction by 75 percent[559].

### 5.1.3.3 The Sudden Stop in the Region

A comparison of the different outcomes of the sudden stop within Latin America sheds further light on Argentina's unfavourable predispositions.

Figure 27: Capital Flows to Latin America between 1998 and 2001 (% of GDP)

|                         | II/1998 | III/2001 | Reversal |
|-------------------------|---------|----------|----------|
| Total Capital Flows     | 5.6     | 1.6      | -4       |
| Non-FDI Capital Flows   | 2.0     | -0.9     | -2.9     |
| FDI                     | 3.6     | 2.5      | -1.1     |

Includes: Argentina, Brazil, Chile, Colombia, Mexico, Peru, Venezuela.
Source: Corresponding central banks.[560]

Figure 27 reflects the dimension of the reversal in capital flows for the biggest Latin American economies between the 2nd quarter of 1998 and the 3rd quarter of 2001. This sample of countries experienced an improvement in their consolidated current account from a deficit of almost five to one percent of their cumulative GDP during the same period.

---

[559] Interest rates were chosen at 200 basis points above the 1998 average, and GDP was assumed to slow down by one percent. Contingent liabilities were estimated at 19 billion US-Dollars. See Calvo/Izquierdo/Talvi (2003), pp. 27 and 31.

[560] See Calvo/Izquierdo/Talvi (2003), p. 11.

Argentina and its biggest neighbours, Brazil and Chile, confronted the sudden stop quite differently. Chile had a higher share of tradables in GDP and a lower share of Dollar denominated debt in total debt. Consequently, it required a smaller real exchange rate adjustment (32 percent) to close its current account gap, and the debt revaluation effects were smaller (its public sector debt mismatch measure being much higher – see figure 28). Effectively, between 1998 and 2001, Chile's currency depreciated by 45 percent in real terms (as opposed to Argentina's 14 percent), and its debt to GDP ratio remained largely constant.

In fact, Chile closed its current account gap (which amounted to nearly 19 percent of its imports in 1998) completely within one year. Besides import reductions, a production shift towards exports (induced by the real exchange rate depreciation) contributed to closing the current account gap: as figure 28 shows, the change in exports relative to the current account change was positive both until 1999 and for the period until 2001. In contrast, Argentina's comparatively small increase in the real exchange rate delivered no similar incentive to shift production, and exports collapsed in 1999, helping further deteriorate the current account.

Brazil provides another contrasting example. It started from a worse position in two respects: its economy was even more closed than Argentina's (its un-leveraged absorption coefficient was 0.56), and its debt to GDP ratio already very high at 51 percent. However, its public debt was to a far smaller degree dollarised than Argentina's, which compensated for the unfavourably high absorption of tradables. Two other factors contributed to Brazil's more favourable development. First, the devaluation of the Real in January 1999 made investments in Brazil highly attractive, which obviously managed to quickly overcome international investors' general caution (FDI flows increased by 80 percent between 1998 and 2001), and second, Brazil undertook a severe fiscal adjustment in 1999, resulting in a strongly increased primary surplus and improved debt sustainability.

Figure 28: The Sudden Stop in Argentina, Brazil, and Chile

|  | Argentina | Brazil | Chile |
|---|---|---|---|
| **Current Account** | | | |
| Current Account Balance 1998 (% of GDP) | -4.9 | -5.0 | -6.0 |
| Current Account Balance 1999 (% of GDP) | -4.2 | -4.7 | 0 |
| Current Account Balance 2001 (% of GDP) | -1.7 | -4.6 | -1.4 |
| Current Account Change between 1998 and 1999 (% of 1998 imports) | 6.1 | 10.6 | 18.8 |
| Current Account Change between 1998 and 2001 (% of 1998 imports) | 21.1 | 13.5 | 14.9 |
| Exports Change / Current Account Change between 1998 and 1999 (%) | -127.5 | -47.6 | 11.1 |
| Exports Change / Current Account Change between 1998 and 2001 (%) | -1.8 | 82.7 | 79.1 |
| Exports Change between 1998 and 1999 (%) | -10.6 | -6.5 | 2.4 |
| Exports Change between 1998 and 2001 (%) | -0.5 | 14.3 | 13.4 |
| | | | |
| **Public Sector** | | | |
| Debt to GDP Ratio 1998 (%) | 36.5 | 51.0 | 17.3 |
| Primary Surplus 1998 (% of GDP) | 0.9 | 0.6 | 0.6 |
| Primary Surplus 1999 (% of GDP) | 0.4 | 4.1 | n.a. |
| Primary Surplus 2001 (% of GDP) | 0.1 | n.a. | n.a. |
| | | | |
| **Debt Sustainability Measures** | | | |
| Un-leveraged Absorption Coefficient | 0.66 | 0.56 | 0.81 |
| Required Real Exchange Rate Depreciation (to close the current account gap, in %) | 46.2 | 52.5 | 32.4 |
| Observed Real Exchange Rate Depreciation between 1998 and 2001 | 14 | n.a. | 45 |
| Public Sector Debt Mismatch Measure | 0.01 | 0.14 | 0.45 |

Sources: Calvo/Izquierdo/Talvi (2003); World Economic Outlook (IMF), April 2002; Economist Intelligence Unit.

## 5.1.4 Shock Exacerbation within MERCOSUR

In the debate of the reasons for Argentina's collapse, the focus on MERCOSUR, and especially on policy interdependencies within the common trade area, is highly relevant[561].

It might seem that the exchange rate systems of the most important MERCOSUR members, Argentina and Brazil – at least until Brazil's devaluation in early 1999 – were conducive to the integration of their economies and trade: in July 1994, Brazil, after several less than successful stabilisation attempts, had pegged its new currency, the Real, to the Dollar at a 1:1 exchange rate. Thus, the Argentine Peso and the Brazilian Real were, via the parallel Dollar peg, effectively pegged to each other. Such monetary integration should, as one would expect from the theory of optimal currency areas, and especially the argument of economic integration being endogenous to monetary integration, foster economic integration between the two countries, i.e. within MERCOSUR[562].

However, though the fixed exchange rate required that the money supply in both countries be kept in line with Dollar reserves, there was still scope for differences in the monetary policies of both countries, as the Real exchange rate was allowed to move within a target band. This opened the possibility for the Brazilian central bank to sterilise reserve shocks, in order to not let them pass through to the domestic money supply. That this scope for different monetary policies actually mattered can be shown empirically: monetary base and foreign reserves moved nearly completely in parallel in Argentina, mirroring the strict currency board rule, while the Brazilian monetary base was only to a small degree dependent on the development of Dollar reserves[563]. In other words, Brazil, despite its fixed exchange rate regime, pursued an independent monetary policy within its

---

[561] This paragraph draws largely from Andrade/Falcão Silva/Trautwein (2005).

[562] For the purpose of this analysis, Argentina and Brazil are taken as equivalent with MERCOSUR, while the two other members, Paraguay and Uruguay, are ignored. This is because, together, Argentina and Brazil represent the bulk of MERCOSUR: both their combined GNP and population figures account for more than 96 percent of the respective MERCOSUR totals. The shares in total MERCOSUR GNP are 70.8 and 26.5 percent for Brazil and Argentina, respectively. 79 percent of the total MERCOSUR population are Brazilian nationals, and 17.3 percent are Argentines.

[563] Andrade/Falcão Silva/Trautwein calculate a cointegration vector, which describes the relationship between monetary base and reserves between 1991 and 2001, of 0.915 for Argentina and of 0.186 for Brazil. See Andrade/Falcão Silva/Trautwein (2005), p. 68.

scope for sterilisation of reserves changes (and continued to do so after its move to floating the Real) while Argentina closely followed the currency board rule.

It can be shown that these differences in monetary policies mattered with respect to the efficacy of economic policies in both countries, on the one hand, and to the transmission of common external shocks, on the other[564]. Since Argentina's economy is only roughly a third of its neighbour in size, Brazilian policies generally could be expected to have a bigger impact on Argentina than vice versa. As to the particular effects of policies and external shocks, the Mundell-Fleming framework[565] is adequate to highlight the implications for both the period between 1994 and 1998, when both countries had fixed exchange rates, and the period between 1999 and 2001, after Brazil had moved to floating.

### 5.1.4.1 1994-1998: Fixed Here, Fixed plus Sterilisation There

In the described fixed-fixed-scenario of the years between 1994 and 1998, the Mundell-Fleming analysis yields the following effects of macroeconomic policies and external shocks on Argentina:

First, Argentina is positively affected by expansionary monetary policies in Brazil, insofar as they lower equilibrium interest rates and increase equilibrium income levels in both countries. Second, Argentina is negatively affected by Brazilian expansionary fiscal policies, since, while Brazil's higher demand for exports from Argentina increases also the income of the latter, this effect is outweighed by interest rate-induced capital flows from Argentina to Brazil, which are sterilised by the latter, so that the Brazilian restrictive monetary antidote again reflects negatively back to Argentina, in the end raising Argentina's equilibrium interest rate and lowering its equilibrium income. Third, Argentina's fiscal policies (monetary policies are precluded) experience an amplification through Brazilian sterilisation: an Argentine fiscal expansion leads to higher, income-induced, demand for imports of goods and services from Brazil, as well as to higher, interest rate-induced, capital imports from Brazil. Brazil sterilises its reserve outflows through expansive open-market operations, which in turn reinforce the expansionary effect of Argentina's fiscal policies, delivering a process that ends when, due to continuing capital imports from Brazil, Argentina's interest rate reaches its original equilibrium level.

---

[564] See also Mussa et al. (2000), p. 51f.
[565] For a concise summary of the Mundell-Fleming model, see e.g. <http://cepa.newschool.edu/het/essays/keynes/international.htm>.

The third of the described policy interactions within MERCOSUR is highly relevant for the understanding Argentina's fiscal performance during the years 1994 to 1998. According to this analysis, Argentine fiscal expansion did not crowd out private investment, since the equilibrium interest rate level remained unchanged due to the Brazilian sterilisation policy[566]. Fiscal policy, the only remaining macro policy tool for Argentina, was thus, as both theoretical analysis and empirical evidence suggest, highly effective because it was boosted by its neighbour's monetary policy[567].

For common external shocks, the analysis yields a mitigating effect of Brazil's sterilisation policy on both countries. For the case of symmetric negative reserve shocks (like, e.g., the Tequila crisis), Brazilian sterilisation of its reserve outflows to the rest of the world works, first, to lower Brazilian interest rates and induce arbitrage capital movements towards Argentina, and second, to keep up Brazilian income and demand for imports from Argentina. Of course, there are limits to sterilisation, which did materialise in the wake of the Asian and Russian crisis, when reserve outflows in Brazil reached levels which the Brazilian central bank could no longer neutralise. Brazil's move to floating and inflation targeting changed the described policy interdependencies profoundly.

### 5.1.4.2 1999-2001: Fixed Here, Floating plus Sterilisation There

For the new constellation (CBA in Argentina and floating exchange rate in Brazil), the analysis yields a drastic exacerbation of the impacts of external shocks on Argentina, as follows:

A common negative reserve shock in both countries now leads to a devaluation of the Brazilian currency. This reduces Brazilian demand for imports from Argentina, and increases Argentine demand for imports from Brazil. Thus, the Argentine economy is hit twice: first by the reserve shock itself (representing, in the Mundell-Fleming framework, a left-shift of the LM curve), and second, by Brazil's depreciation (which induces a left-shift of the IS curve). Possible sterilisation in Brazil now changes little, as a sterilisation-induced interest rate differential commands arbitrage capital from Brazil to Argentina (thus correcting the LM curve again a bit to the right), but thereby also works to further depreciate the Brazilian currency (and so to command the IS curve further to the left). The degree of the

---

[566] Andrade/Falcão Silva/Trautwein (2005) give empirical evidence, using filter analysis and a structural VAR model.

[567] Of course, the same would have been true for the case of fiscal restriction.

negative reaction on goods markets (left-shift of the IS curve) depends on the degree to which Brazil sterilises the reserve shock.

### 5.1.4.3 Exposed within MERCOSUR

As has been shown, even before 1999, monetary policies of Argentina and Brazil were different enough to be responsible for various asymmetries in the absorption of internal and external shocks. Moreover, while the "fixed / fixed plus sterilisation" constellation before 1999 favoured the effects of monetary expansion in Brazil and fiscal expansion in Argentina, and mitigated the effects of negative external shocks in both countries, this was a double-edged sword: the highly effective expansionary policies undermined the fixed exchange rates and led to increasing devaluation pressures in the wake of the massive external shocks of the late 1990s. So, the lack of monetary policy coordination before 1999 contributed to the vulnerability of the fixed exchange rate regimes and to their ultimate collapses. After Brazil's move to floating, the disintegrated monetary policies brought the existing asymmetries to their extremes, so that common external shocks hit Argentina twice, while the impact on the Brazilian economy was buffered by the depreciation of the Real.

Andrade/Falcão Silva/Trautwein (2005) substantiate the above analysis with empirical evidence. They find that, as was to be expected, the asymmetries in the transmission of domestic and external shocks were strongest when both countries pursued extremely different exchange rate and monetary policies[568]. In particular, their correlation analysis of Argentine and Brazilian economic indicators yields evidence of increasingly different reactions to exogenous variables: Argentina's vulnerability to changes in foreign interest rates and Brazilian output doubled after 1999, while Brazil was affected less, after 1999, by changes in foreign interest rates or Argentine output than before.

Thus, the diverging monetary policies of Argentina and Brazil have not only undermined economic integration within MERCOSUR[569], but also aggravated its member countries' vulnerabilities and, ultimately, helped evoke their deep crises.

---

[568] They examine the correlation of the output cycles of both countries and find significantly less synchronised cycles after 1999. See Andrade/Falcão Silva/Trautwein (2005), pp. 74-5.

[569] A further symptom for disintegrating monetary policies in MERCOSUR can be found in decreasing trade between the countries. As, according to the endogeneity argument of the theory of optimal currency areas, monetary integration is expected to foster economic integration, diverging monetary policies within a currency area are, conversely, expected to result in less,

## 5.1.5    Institutional Defects

Given the impressive growth and disinflation results of the CBA, but the disturbing employment and distributional developments, it is argued that the failure to co-ordinate macro and micro reforms were also decisive in contributing to the CBA's collapse. In other words, the macroeconomic framework, defined by the rigid monetary regime and accompanied by the simultaneous trade liberalisation and privatisation policies, would have called for deeper institutional changes to help the economy adjust to the new conditions. As the argument goes, the lack or incompleteness of such microeconomic reforms worked to undermine economic performance and social peace, and thus lastly the per se successful macroeconomic reforms.

### 5.1.5.1 Insufficient Labour Market Reforms

With a fixed exchange rate, the burden of adjustment of an overvalued real exchange rate falls on domestic prices, the flexibility of which can be ensured only by, especially downward, flexible wages. Thus, theory has it that flexible labour markets have to act as the substitute for a flexible exchange rate. No one would sincerely contest the verdict that the labour market reforms Argentina implemented were insufficient and sometimes contradictory, often performed in a stop & go mode, and often paid heed more to political constraints than to fundamental economic necessities.

One flaw was that the main incentive for, and measure of, the realised labour market reforms was always the high unemployment rate[570]. While the combat of unemployment clearly need not run against the objective of more labour market flexibility, there was a neglect and failure in politics to acknowledge, internally and publicly, the need for reforms due to other, more fundamental, economic reasons. From the start, no serious efforts were made to make the public familiar with the thought that higher labour market flexibility was the price to pay for the cherished "Convertibilidad". Hence, a lack of consistency and of political courage to market and promote labour market deregulation with the parallel goals of reducing

---

especially intra-industry, trade. This is confirmed by empirical data: intra-industry trade between Argentina and Brazil increased substantially until 1997, and declined afterwards. This development can be explained econometrically by macroeconomic policy variables. See Andrade/Falcão Silva/ Trautwein (2005), pp. 80ff.

[570] Other motives for reform were, occasionally, also industrial and sectoral policies, while distributional aspects never featured as goals of labour market policies.

unemployment and "insuring the economy against devaluation" is a serious blame the Menem administration has to bear. Clearly, the main factor behind this neglect were the trade unions, traditionally strong and the Peronists' fundus, anything but weakened from the inflationary past, and generally more worried about preserving regulatory achievements than about unemployment.

Apart from this basic neglect, the reforms enacted can for the biggest part be labelled as "too little and too late". What happened during the early 1990s' reforms has to be judged partly as steps, if small, into the right direction (above all the denting of non-wage labour costs, especially of indemnity payments after dismissals), partly as neutral or potentially beneficial but running into the void because not achieving sufficient coverage (the employment insurance scheme), and partly as complicating and strengthening the regulatory framework while serving neither the employment nor the flexibility goals (such as the changes in working time and vacation regulations, the frequently altered and diluted rebates on social security contributions, or the to and fro manoeuvres with probation period length). The record of the reforms of the late 90s can be judged only slightly better: some mixed and counterproductive measures (such as the shortening of probation periods) were purely politically motivated, meant to secure trade unions' support in the elections of 1999. Further gradual reductions in non-wage labour costs and very limited freedom to change regulations through collective bargaining were the most important achievements. But while the need to adopt deeper labour market reforms generally got more acknowledged towards the end of the decade, chronic political opposition stood in the way of realising them.

Potentialising a sufficient adjustment mechanism via labour and goods markets would have required more deregulation, especially a weakening of the dominance of sectoral collective bargaining in favour of an encouragement of wage negotiations on enterprise levels, much further reductions of contractual regulations (instead of introducing new, highly regularised, contracting variants), and, especially, more easing of the very strict hiring and dismissal regulations[571]. Certainly, an agreed and socially acceptable level of labour regulations would have had to be respected, with the safety nets provided by employment insurance and cash transfer programmes for the unemployed, both of which the foundations were laid for. Very importantly,

---

[571] Likewise, institutions such as "special labour statutes" (giving some workers favoured status over others) and union-run health plans sheltered from competition should have been abolished. See IMF Independent Evaluation Office (2004), p. 32.

qualification measures would have been needed to reduce the mismatches between labour demand and supply, and especially to improve the employability of blue collar workers, who were hit unproportionately by rising unemployment and by the rise of sectors like financial services that favoured workers with higher skills[572].

Perhaps the most severe failure is that the labour market policies of the 90s did not succeed in reducing unregistered employment (to the contrary, they seemingly helped drive registered employment into the "black" sphere). The expectation was that dented non-wage labour costs and more short-term labour contracts would bring about a higher propensity to formalise employment (which measures, to be sure, would certainly have helped, but were far from sufficient), but there was no (accompanying) direct targeting of the problem[573]. While one can cynically comment that more "black" labour means more overall labour market flexibility, the growth of unregistered labour during periods of strong growth is a testimonium paupertatis, and proof of labour market regulations still highly burdensome.

### 5.1.5.2 Insufficient Diversification of Production

Argentina's productive structure is also made responsible for standing in the way of smoother adjustment to changes in external conditions. In the tradables sector, limited progress was made in reducing the dominance of low value-added production in favour of the higher value-added export products needed to trigger future development and thus income and employment growth. Though various measures were taken to subsidise exports of higher value-added products (such as tax reimbursements on such exports), the industry's response was weak. The reason was the strong Peso which increasingly overlay these incentives by discouraging production for foreign and stimulating production for domestic markets[574].

Diversification of production and trade was also encumbered by the relative cheapening of capital relative to labour, itself again a consequence of brakeless capital imports and of strong trade unions. It entailed growing capital intensity, declining employment, and an ongoing process of industrial concentration in capital intensive sectors, mirrored by a process of de-industrialisation in labour intensive, import-competing sectors. Small and medium sized companies were squeezed out

---

[572] See Pastor/Wise (1999), p. 490.

[573] Direct measures would have included, e.g., systematic compliance controls and the enforcement of penalties.

[574] See Pastor/Wise (1999), p. 486.

of markets by growing industrial conglomerates, which were financed by foreign capital and enjoyed better access to the technologies, skills, and market information necessary to compete on world markets[575].

Concentration took place in the financial sector as well, with bank closures and takeovers in the wake of the Tequila crisis. Segmented credit markets reinforced industrial concentration: small enterprises were demanded interest rates for business loans easily double or triple those demanded from large companies[576]. A further factor in the thinning base of small and medium sized companies was that few traditional links between small and large firms existed, partly a consequence of the economy's capricious and inflationary past where inter-business relations were kept as small as possible in order to minimise cost and delivery risks.

Arguably, MERCOSUR also contributed to spare Argentina from more competitive pressure from the rest of the world: most (about two thirds during the early 90s) of total export growth resulted from intra-industry trade with Brazil. Exports to Brazil consisted overwhelmingly of products from the motor vehicles industry, the sector still most regulated through exemptions from trade liberalisation, and thus least based on competitive advantages. As a result, Argentina's trade got increasingly concentrated on one partner (Brazil) and one sector (motor vehicles)[577].

A further disappointing trait of Argentina's industrial development is that privatised firms, overall, failed to fulfil the expectations of more dynamic production and investment activities: neither R&D activities nor export orientation increased by much. This was clearly also the failure of the bodies regulating privatised utilities, the work of which partly was influenced by lobbying and corruption rather than by efficiency considerations[578].

The sketched problems could have been tackled primarily by improving the business environment much more than actually happened. Though, during the

---

[575] Some numbers illustrate the concentration and labour saving process: in 1994, the biggest 30 export firms, belonging to just four sectors, covered 55 percent of total exports; the biggest 500 companies accounted for 30 percent of GDP, but employed only 20% of the workforce; both the number of small enterprises and of workers employed by them had fallen during the previous 10 years by 21 percent. See Pastor/Wise (1999), p. 486.

[576] See Pastor/Wise (1999), p. 487.

[577] While trade with MERCOSUR partners was 20 percent of Argentina's total in 1991, it rose to 45 percent in 1998, with the bulk of exports going to Brazil. See Dominguez/Tesar (2004), p. 12.

[578] "The picture is more of oligopolistic rent-seeking than of dynamic enterprise [...]." Pastor/Wise (1999), p. 489.

1990s, the physical infrastructure got, via utility privatisation, vastly better, and the legal framework also improved (with, e.g., a world-class bankruptcy law adopted in 1991), judicial as well as political imponderabilities remained (or even increased in the late 1990s). As for the human resource base, this essential part of a forward-looking business environment was vastly neglected. Striving for higher value-added production would have necessitated policies to promote qualification measures and the diffusion of technological and marketing skills, as well as measures to expedite R&D activities, to encourage venture capital and possibly the growth of industrial clusters, in order to facilitate horizontal and vertical integration between smaller and larger firms[579]. Very importantly, these measures should have been designed explicitly to promote industrial development in the provinces. After all, "market reform in and of itself is not a development strategy"[580].

With these cornerstones of a successful industrial policy missed, the final goal, an increase in Argentina's openness via a higher share of non-traditional exports, was also missed, which helped undermine the macroeconomic framework.

### 5.1.5.3 Banking Sector Reforms Impaired

As indicated above, the banking sector reforms, especially those carried through after 1995, concerning banking supervision and prudential policies, were considered one of the most successful reform areas within the Convertibility Plan, and praised as a model for emerging economies. Together with the encouraged entry of foreign-owned banks, assumed to diversify risk away towards their owners abroad, the swiftly widening and deepening Argentine financial sector was thought healthy and able to match the requirements of an open market economy[581].

However, some concerns remained about credit policies. The first concern was the strong segmentation of credit markets, reflected in wide gaps between the interest rates charged small as opposed to large industrial borrowers, and between interest payable on Peso as opposed to Dollar loans[582]. This segmentation

---

[579] See Williamson (2003), p. 12.

[580] Pastor/Wise (1999), p. 494.

[581] Banking assets doubled between 1991 and 1999 (from 20 to 40 percent of GDP), and the percentage of banking system assets held with foreign banks rose from 15 percent in 1994 to 73 percent in 2000. See Dominguez/Tesar (2004), p. 12.

[582] Small enterprises were demanded interest rates for business loans easily double or triple those demanded from large companies. See Pastor/Wise (1999), p. 487. Interest rate spreads between Peso and Dollar currency transactions, often exceeding two percent p.a., reflected not

persisted even in times of strong growth, low inflation, and high confidence, such as during 1997, when risk spreads of government bonds over US treasuries reached their minimum. In discriminating against small businesses and low income earners, this partly excessive segmentation fostered industrial concentration and a deteriorating distribution of wealth. Second, in the effort to catch up and gain market shares in the field of consumer credit, financial institutions embarked on aggressive consumer credit policies. Increasingly, credit cards were pushed into a retail banking market that just started to develop and largely consisted of over-confident consumers, with the result of ever more indebted private households[583]. Arguably, these developments mirrored neglects in the otherwise successful implementation of banking regulations. On the whole, though, and to judge from the weak financial constitution the country had started from in 1991, the elaborate prudential standards after 1995 represented a huge progress, and, above all, they largely satisfied the regulatory needs for a banking sector operating under a currency board, i.e. without a lender of last resort.

But any regulatory framework, however fit, is useless if subject to political influence. Several instances of political meddling exposed Argentine banks to additional risks. These were, first, the forced resignation of the supposedly independent central bank manager, Pedro Pou, in April 2001. Second, the politically encouraged, and later openly imposed, massive purchases of government bonds by public and private banks (as well as by private pension funds) loaded the banking sector with assets of dubious worth. The permission for banks, in April 2001, to include government securities up to 2 billion Dollars to meet liquidity requirements was thus only the first formal political abrogation of prudential standards, in a row of several factual violations before[584]. With the growing weight of government bonds in banks' balance sheets, the financial sector was exposed to a broadened cluster of risks: not only was it vulnerable to economic downturn (non-performing loans) and

primarily devaluation risk, but also a lack of competition among banks in a regional context, enabling banks to exert some degree of monopoly power on nontradables producers and households with a lack of access to international capital markets. See Catão (1998), p. 22.

[583] Payments via bank accounts were also politically encouraged as a means to reduce tax evasion.

[584] See Dominguez/Tesar (2004), p. 13. The banking system's exposure to the public sector doubled between 1995 and 2001, from 10 percent of total banking assets constituted by public debt to 20 percent.

to the risk of devaluation (currency mismatch), but also to default by the public sector (worthless assets)[585].

The third blow to the financial sector's constitution came, finally, with the "corralito" in early December 2001. The drastic violation of property rights destroyed any reputation the banking sector had enjoyed before[586]. The financial sector was dealt the fourth and final blow after default and the end of the CBA had been sealed, with asymmetric pesification in February 2002, which entailed a massive redistribution of wealth between depositors, lenders, and financial institutions, as well as a cauda of court injunctions and legal action that should occupy banks and courts for years, and which left the banking system in shatters.

What remains is that banking sector reforms of the early and mid-1990s basically deserved their reputation as having been apt and well implemented, and served the financial sector and the economy well – so long as banks remained free from fiscal desires[587]. With the central bank, in its supervising and regulating function, captured by politics, and the banking system saddled with worthless assets, the financial sector was directed towards the utmost exposition to devaluation and public default.

### 5.1.5.4 Other Deficient Reforms

The single most neglected area of reform undoubtedly has been (it still is) the sphere of federal fiscal relations. Though the damaging nature of the existing regulations has always been recognised, political intricacies constantly stood in the way of approaching more rational norms. Even the constitutional commitment of 1994 to redefine the coparticipation scheme until 1996 failed to produce a result: no

---

[585] Public sector banks (such as the federally owned Banco de la Nación, the Banco de la Provincia de Buenos Aires, and a few other provincial banks) were particularly vulnerable to reduced confidence in the government, as they were especially exposed to political influence. This perception affected the banking system as a whole. See IMF Independent Evaluation Office (2004), p. 35

[586] Though meant to dam capital flight, the corralito contained a loophole that facilitated a legal transfer of funds abroad for the financially versed. It worked via so-called "ADRs" (American Depository Receipts), shares of Argentine companies also listed in the US. The corralito allowed depositors to use funds in excess of the monthly 1,000 Dollars withdrawal maximum to buy either government bonds or shares of Argentine companies. Shares of Argentine companies cross-listed in the US could be legally converted into ADRs, sold in the US, and the Dollar proceeds deposited on a US-account. See Dominguez/Tesar (2004), p. 15.

[587] See Calvo/Mishkin (2003), p. 4.

fundamental reform passed the fierce resistance of the main beneficiaries of the existing regulations, the provincial governors. To the contrary, the few realised modifications, such as the introduction of "precoparticipaciones", or the guaranteed fixed transfer sums, made the system even more complex and, above all, counterproductive in creating additional moral hazard and procyclical fiscal outcomes. The effects of several sensible fiscal reforms realised in the areas of tax compliance and tax structure effectively got stifled by the increasingly perverse fiscal redistribution process[588]. Besides a rationalisation of federal fiscal relations, the fiscal task would have also been to reduce the reliance on regressive taxes, above all VAT, in favour of higher direct taxes on income, and, generally, to improve tax compliance and tax administration[589].

The social security reform, while completely necessary and broadly judged as a success, proved to create a massive burden on the government's borrowing requirements. Its consequences for the public purse should have received greater consideration, as a result of which the financing of reform costs via taxes or expenditure cuts, rather than via borrowings, should have been envisaged[590].

Generally, social policy is a field massively disregarded during the whole of the 1990s. As Argentina disposed of a highly educated population and comparatively wide welfare coverage, the market reforms of the early 90s were implemented without social compensation schemes. But as the described productive changes, such as increases in low value-added production and industrial concentration, took hold and the employment and distribution situation continued to worsen, it would have been necessary to boost and coordinate industrial and social policies. Better targeting of social expenditures to high risk groups on the one hand and, as indicated above, more active industrial policies (favouring higher value-added production and educational training programmes) on the other would have been needed to tackle the increasing social problems. Again, a shift in taxes towards more taxation of income (which is typically at least mildly progressive), away from regressive VAT, would also have created an element of redistribution.

As for commercial policies, apart from the proposed measures to promote trade diversification, limited capital controls, such as, e.g., reserve requirements on external debt by firms, or minimum stays of FDI, could have been used to encounter

---

[588] See IMF Independent Evaluation Office (2004), p. 30.
[589] See Pastor/Wise (1999), p. 494.
[590] See IMF Independent Evaluation Office (2004), p. 34f.

short term and volatile capital flows. As long as the repatriation of profits from FDI is not restricted, the experience shows that such measures can be implemented without discouraging long-term capital inflows, and without compromising trade liberalisation[591]. Such limited capital controls could, at the same time, have been tailored to bring up "infant" industries, i.e. to confront the dominance of low value-added primary production by supporting investment in a broader spectrum of higher value-added production for export purposes[592].

In parallel, Argentina's trade policies should have been aimed more at diversifying not only the basket of traded goods but also of its trading partners. Negotiations within MERCOSUR, though essentially rational in terms of boosting intra-industrial trade, have always been hampered by lack of bilateral and industrial commitment, and should have been in any case complemented by efforts to deepen trade relations with industrial, but also with other developing countries. With the latter, the development of trade patterns beyond Argentina's traditional patterns would possibly have been easier to stimulate, and possible common exchange rate links to the US-Dollar would have reduced the exposedness of trade to Dollar appreciation.

Finally, several public sector institutions, such as the judiciary, regulatory commissions, social ministries, the civil service, police, and provincial governments, remained prone not only to lobbying interests and corruption, but also to political pressure. They would have needed a thorough remake to comply with the requirements imposed by an efficiency seeking market economy. Instead, state institutions continued to justify the suspicion it was viewed with by the Argentine public, in times when their conduit should have been targeted at fostering greater equality in the benefits of market reform[593].

The described failure to co-ordinate macro and microeconomic reforms, with macroeconomic stabilisation highly successful, but micro reforms failing to help the economy adjust to the rigid macro conditions, was, as late as 1999, generally viewed as still curable. Accordingly, a "second generation of reforms" was urgently called for, in order to secure the successes of stabilisation and growth and to shield

---

[591] Chile successfully implemented such capital controls in the 1990s. See Rojas-Suárez (2003), p. 151.

[592] Capital controls are in any case preferable to the more protectionist stance of import tariffs and duties, which make counteractions from trading partners more probable.

[593] See Pastor/Wise (1999), p. 495.

the economy against external shocks[594]. Such a second generation of reforms should have been designed to confront the described inadequacies of institutional defects, broadly along the proposals made above.

### 5.1.6    Politics

While thorough political analysis is beyond the scope of this investigation, the field of politics cannot be left out in the search of explanations for the Argentine CBA's fate. The analysis shall be confined to some conspicuous traits of Argentine politics during the 1990s and their relation to economic outcomes.

Though next to unbelievable with a view to its roots, Peronism has, by its figurehead Carlos Menem, got inseparably linked to Convertibilidad. Among Menem's merits was, in the late 1980s, the broadening of the Peronist electoral base, to add larger business and middle class segments to the traditional backbone of working classes, and thus turn Peronism into a grantor of majorities[595]. While this was a precondition for the agenda of market-oriented reforms to realise, it also entailed ample potential for intra-party rivalry, which favoured autocratic governing, corruption, and the turning of a blind eye towards the country's military past. A symptom of this is the massive "governing by decree" the President took recourse to in order to overcome anti-market sentiments within party and government. Topics such as the revision of tax and labour laws, the setting of the trade regime, or the modification of public contracts were settled autocratically, by executive decree, and the core of the reform programme comprised in the Convertibility Plan was realised as decrees of "necessity and urgency"[596]. Circumvention of the parliament, defiance of the constitution, and biased nominations for the Supreme Court were customary traits of the Menem governing style, the legitimacy of which got additionally undermined by personal charges of corruption. While autocratic tendencies may be justified in case of economic emergency, the danger is that they persist and get routine; a country subscribing to market economy needs fundamentally free

---

[594] See Pastor/Wise (1999).

[595] According to Pastor/Wise, another tactic to grant majorities was the initial sparing of the provinces from fiscal tightening, and the maintenance of "clientelistic and traditional networks of power and mobilization in the periphery". Pastor/Wise (1999), p. 492.

[596] Between July 1989 and December 1993 alone, over 12,000 executive decrees and 308 decrees of "necessity and urgency" were passed. The number of presidential emergency decrees passed by Menem exceeds the total number issued by all constitutional presidents in the past 130 years. See Pastor/Wise (1999), p. 492f.

"political markets" for successful development. The persisting lack of factual democracy fit badly with the country's late 1990s' image of a poster boy among emerging economies, and inevitably turned against the government as soon as luck ran out[597].

The constitutional reform of 1994, launched to allow for a second term of President Menem, entailed political deals with the opposition, as well as with provincial leaders and organised labour, which softened fiscal discipline and stalled or even rolled back the structural reform process. To the merits of the Peronist government, much of this languishing was corrected soon after, under the pressure of the Mexican crisis. Equally, Menem's attempt to get admitted as a candidate seeking a third term caused, as long as the case was not yet settled, the competition for nominations within the Peronist party, which entailed again increased public spending for political reasons[598].

A clear political fault of the Peronists in the mid to late 1990s, in terms not only of securing majorities, but also of ensuring sustainability of the per se necessary and successful macroeconomic reforms, was the apparent lack of concern for the employment and distributional consequences of reform. As indicated above, turning a blind eye to the increasing social malaise did not only defy the Peronist stance but also destabilised the country politically and socially, and thus undermined the whole stabilisation success.

As to the Alianza government, the coalition faced extremely difficult tasks while having to cope with widely diverging political positions internally. In sticking to the CBA and setting to increase the primary surplus to regain debt sustainability, it struggled with the fierce redistribution conflict which arose over who was to bear the adjustment costs. Since taxes and spending cuts hit predominantly the non-

---

[597] One popular suspicion runs as follows: when political support from the traditional Peronist voter bases, increasingly hit by unemployment and declining real wages, wore thin in the run-up to the 1999 presidential elections, and the economic and fiscal situation deteriorated, the calculation of the ruling Peronists was to "leave the bomb to the Alianza". The bomb would be left to "explode" under the Radicals, and to interrupt their constitutional term, so that the Peronists could take over early again (of course never taking responsibility for the existence of the bomb). With hindsight, the course of events can be interpreted to match this assumption, with the cynical aftertaste that it would have been, for political reasons, perfectly consistent with such a strategy to avoid minimising the costs related with the end of Convertibility. Opinion expressed by Fernando Navajas during an interview conducted by the author on November, 18th, 2004, in Buenos Aires.

[598] See IMF Independent Evaluation Office (2004), p. 16.

corporate sector[599], the coalition risked its main constituency, the middle class. Under accusations of leaving external creditors unscathed, the Alianza finally broke into pieces over the redistribution conflict[600]. Certainly, the chances of succeeding in turning the rudder and installing debt sustainability would doubtlessly have been higher had the government, taking over from the Peronists in 1999, appeared a unified whole.

As to opposition to the Convertibility regime, there has always been some, mainly from the left, which criticised the negative effects of the radical liberalisation and privatisation policies on employment, distribution, and industrial structures[601]. Such opposition remained marginal until the late 90s' recession exposed more of the CBA's vulnerabilities and led even major candidates in the 1999 elections to call it into question publicly. However, such criticism could not dent the CBA's popularity with the vast majority of the public.

### 5.1.7    The IMF

Almost continuously involved in Argentina during the whole of the 1990s, the IMF ("the Fund") inescapably played a role in the developments that led to the devastating crisis in 2001[602]. The IMF's attitude towards the CBA, its engagement during the CBA's existence, as well as the role it played before and during the crisis are the issues addressed in what follows[603].

---

[599] With the "impuestazo", taxes on income, personal net assets, and some consumer goods were increased in early 2000. The "plan déficit cero" of July 2001 included a cut of salaries and pensions of public sector employees by 13 percent.

[600] "Coalition governments almost never succeed in implementing long-lasting fiscal adjustments of the sort that are likely to have short-run expansionary effects". Eichengreen (2001a), p. 18.

[601] See, e.g., Rofman (1997), or, written in 2001 with the claim to offer a plan for the Argentine economy to arise from the ashes of convertibility: Universidad de Buenos Aires, Facultad de Ciencias Económicas (2001): "Hacia el Plan Fénix - Una Alternativa Económica".

[602] Indeed, Argentina is different from most other cases where the IMF has provided extraordinarily large support in that the IMF was strongly involved in the country for many years before the emergence of the crisis. See Mussa (2002), p. 2.

[603] The Evaluation Report "The IMF and Argentina, 1991-2001", issued in 2004, is the result of the Independent Evaluation Office's (IEO) investigations into the Fund's role in Argentina. This recently installed office operates under the authority of the IMF's Executive Board, independent of staff and management, so that, though ultimately responsible to the Fund's membership, it is thought to be relatively free of bias. This paragraph draws in many, though not all, aspects from this candid analysis.

### 5.1.7.1 The IMF and the CBA

The Convertibility Plan of 1991, implemented by the Argentine government without consultation with the IMF, was initially treated with scepticism but, with a view to the broad agenda of market-oriented and efficiency-enhancing reforms, basically welcomed by the latter. The quick and impressive defeat of inflation and the stabilisation boom of the early years did their part to mute occasional concerns about the medium-term viability of the programme within the Fund[604].

During the Tequila crisis, the Fund supported Argentina's efforts to maintain the CBA. The decisiveness shown by the Argentine government pushing through tax and financial sector reforms in the eve of presidential elections impressed even sceptics within the IMF. The success in mastering the crisis proved very important in that it brought the IMF to unambiguously endorse the fixed exchange rate regime as "both essential for price stability and fundamentally viable"[605]. After Tequila, the CBA experienced a veritable credibility thrust which encouraged public and private spending and drove critics of the CBA into the background[606].

During the expansionary period after Tequila, Argentina and its Convertibility Plan were even praised by the IMF as a model for developing countries. Remarkably, the IMF continued to provide funds even though there was no longer an immediate balance of payments need, and even when the political preconditions for the implementation of policies needed to sustain the exchange rate regime had broken away. When recession and a loss of access to international capital markets followed the shocks of the late nineties, the IMF stepped in with a new arrangement in early 2000 in support of the newly elected government's effort to halt the recession and redress public finances, in order to maintain the CBA. Even after repeated instances of non-compliance with fiscal and policy targets agreed with the Argentine government, and with ever smaller chances of avoiding default and collapse of the CBA, did the IMF stick to its support of the CBA, and granted

---

[604] "Little substantive discussion took place with the authorities on whether or not the exchange rate peg was appropriate for Argentina over the medium term, and the issue received scant analysis within the IMF." IMF Independent Evaluation Office (2004), p. 3.

[605] IMF Independent Evaluation Office (2004), p. 8.

[606] Daniel Heymann minted the expression "excess credibility" of the Convertibility Plan, responsible for a collective overestimation of Argentina's potential and long-term growth expectations. Expressed during an interview conducted by the author on November 16th, 2004, in Buenos Aires.

extraordinarily large sums. Thus, the Fund knowingly pursued a high risk strategy in support of the Argentine CBA until things could not turn to the better any more.

### 5.1.7.2 Outline of the IMF's Engagement 1991-2001

During the decade between 1991 and 2001, Argentina maintained five successive financing arrangements with the IMF (see figure 29). These included three Stand-by Arrangements, one approved in 1991 after the introduction of the CBA, one in 1996 in the midst of the Tequila crisis, and one in 2000 to replace and continue the previous arrangement. In addition, two Extended Fund Facility arrangements were agreed upon in 1992 and in 1998, the latter of which was treated as precautionary, with no funds actually drawn. Accompanying the financial support, the Fund gave technical assistance, mainly in the fiscal and banking sphere, to support the objectives of the programmes.

Figure 29: IMF Financing Arrangements with Argentina 1991-2001

| | Type of Arrangement | Approved | Expired/ Cancelled | Amount Agreed (million SDR) | Amount Agreed (million USD) | Percent of Quota | Amount Drawn (million USD) |
|---|---|---|---|---|---|---|---|
| 1 | Stand-by Arrangement | 07/1991 | 03/1992 | 780 | 1,065 | 70.1 | 600 |
| 2 | Extended Arrangement | 03/1992 | 03/1996 | 4,020 | 5,661 | 361.2 | 5,661 |
| 3 | Stand-by Arrangement | 04/1996 | 01/1998 | 720 | 1,045 | 46.8 | 890 |
| 4 | Extended Arrangement | 02/1998 | 03/2000 | 2,080 | 2,820 | 135.3 | 0 |
| 5 | Stand-by Arrangement | 03/2000 | 01/2003 | 16,937 | 22,315 | 800 | 12,854 |
| | *Of which Supplemental Reserve Facility* | *01/2001* | *01/2002* | *6,087* | *7,961* | *287.5* | *7,684* |

Source: IMF Independent Evaluation Office (2004), p. 77. SDRs converted to US-Dollars at the respective yearly average exchange rates, with exception of the 2001 Supplemental Reserve Facility which is converted to USD at the exchange rate of the day of approval.

The first two arrangements were designed to support the structural reforms undertaken, while the third arrangement (of 1996) supported Argentina in coping with the Mexican crisis. The three-year Stand-by Arrangement of early 2000, originally amounting to SDR 5.4 billion (around USD 7 billion), was designed to address the worsening recession as well as, from early 2001, when it was augmented by an additional SDR 5.2 billion, to help Argentina regain access to international capital markets. Additional financing from official and private sources was arranged at the same time, so that the total package was announced to comprise USD 39 billion ("el blindaje"). IMF assistance was further augmented in late 2001 by an additional SDR 6.4 billion, so that the IMF's total exposure amounted to around SDR 17 billion (USD 22 billion), with USD 3 billion earmarked for a planned debt restructuring. With the non-completion of the scheduled fifth programme review in December 2001, IMF support was effectively cut off.

### 5.1.7.3 The Role of the IMF during 1991 to 2000

Criticism of the Fund's role for the Argentine CBA concentrates on the areas of exchange rate policy, fiscal policy, and structural reforms.

As to exchange rate policy, the Fund had, following its statutes, to accept any member country's prerogative to choose an exchange rate regime of its own liking. However, it clearly failed to examine the consistency of the chosen exchange rate regime with other policy choices[607]. Explanations for this failure are, first, a reluctance to discuss Convertibility for fear of upsetting financial markets and triggering self-fulfilling speculations (though this was not an argument for refraining from undisclosed discussion with the Argentine authorities), second, a lack of analytical tools to objectively evaluate the sustainability of a chosen exchange rate regime[608], and third, the difficulty to address the topic, in light of repeated public statements by the IMF supportive of the CBA. In any case, this failure "must be read as a weakness of [the Fund's] surveillance over exchange rate arrangements"[609].

A similarly disappointing assessment has to be made of the IMF's stance with respect to fiscal policy. First, the IMF focused too much and for too long on flow variables without considering the year-to-year changes in the debt stock. Only in 2000, when the debt to GDP ratio approached fifty percent, did overall indebtedness become an issue[610]. A second critique refers to the IMF's failure to pay sufficient attention to provincial finances. Until 1998, formal fiscal conditionality included only the federal government budget, so that provincial profligacy remained largely unmonitored. Finally, partly due to the absence (or non-application) of diagnostic tools, and partly also due to neglect, the sustainable level of debt was overestimated by the IMF. Thus, the IMF's fiscal analysis underestimated the vulnerabilities emanating from Argentina's peculiar set of economic policies in the

---

[607] "Yet, IMF staff devoted only limited resources to determining whether the exchange rate regime adopted in Argentina was consistent with other policies and institutional constraints and, if not, what possible exit strategies Argentina should consider." IMF Independent Evaluation Office (2004), p. 22.

[608] "The IMF lacked a forward-looking concept of exchange rate sustainability and failed to use the best analytical tools." IMF Independent Evaluation Office (2004), p. 66.

[609] IMF Independent Evaluation Office (2004), p. 23.

[610] Primarily focussing on annual deficits, unmet fiscal targets remained mostly without consequence, or were loosened when growth fell below forecasts, but not strengthened when growth exceeded forecasts. See IMF Independent Evaluation Office (2004), p. 25.

case of potential external shocks, with the effect that the required degree of fiscal discipline was underestimated.

In the area of monitoring structural reforms, the IMF's credentials are not much better. First, fiscal reforms, i.e. reforms of federal fiscal relations, of the tax structure, and of tax compliance, were only moderately successful in the latter two cases, and a complete failure in the former. Political and cultural (tax evasion!) realities may exonerate the IMF from much of the blame, but "it can be argued that the IMF did not employ all the available tools to bring about reform in some critical areas. Despite the rhetoric about the importance of structural fiscal reforms, there was only one structural performance criterion (on tax reform) included in all of the successive IMF-supported programs in this area."[611] A similar judgement has to be made with respect to labour market reforms, rightly emphasised as crucial by the IMF but not followed up consequently enough, as from 1998, when political obstacles increasingly foiled their implementation.[612] As to social security reform, the IMF erred in the same way as did most other observers, in overestimating the potential benefits of the new system and underestimating its fiscal consequences by far[613]. Finally, while the financial sector reforms, carried out with limited IMF assistance, were supported and recognised to be favourable with respect to prudential regulations and supervision, the IMF failed to address the vulnerabilities emanating from extensive liability dollarisation early enough. Likewise, it did not press the government to tackle the weaknesses of the banks still owned by the state.[614] One general feature of the IMF's programmes with Argentina was their brevity with respect to structural conditionality, and "what little conditionality the programs contained was not rigorously enforced."[615]

---

[611] IMF Independent Evaluation Office (2004), p. 31.

[612] "However, this forbearance on an issue that was ultimately central to the viability of the convertibility regime had its costs, because policies that a few months earlier were meant to be at the core of the IMF-supported program would be delayed to the point where they would have little impact on the economy's ability to respond to the shocks of 1999-2000." IMF Independent Evaluation Office (2004), p. 33.

[613] "The IMF, among others, did not fully grasp early on the conceptual weaknesses of the way the transition to the new system was financed, which together with other accompanying policy changes implied a flawed reform with serious long-term consequences." IMF Independent Evaluation Office (2004), p. 35.

[614] See IMF Independent Evaluation Office (2004), p. 36.

[615] IMF Independent Evaluation Office (2004), p. 36. And: "Stronger conditionality would be unlikely to have brought greater change in the absence of domestic ownership, but the IMF did not

The findings about the Fund's internal decision making process shall not be dealt with here[616]. As to the general mood, "the record suggests that the staff's generally upbeat public assessments were shared by most of the Executive Board", and "there was almost universal confidence expressed in the [Argentine] authorities' ability and willingness to implement the appropriate policies. Voices expressing serious doubt about the overall logic of the actions of the IMF or the authorities became rarer as the decade wore on."[617]

With hindsight, the rationale for maintaining a programme relationship with Argentina after the Mexican crisis had been overcome does not seem justified, given the country's access to relatively cheap international capital and the absence of an immediate balance of payments need. Yet, although fiscal adjustment and structural reforms stalled during the second expansionary phase due to political obstacles, and ever more of the targets of IMF-supported programmes were missed, IMF support was continued, and an Extended Fund Facility approved in 1998, while there would have been sufficient reason to end the programme relationship. However, markets' perception of the sustainability of policies was still favourable, which is why the Fund's confidence was viewed as justified[618].

### 5.1.7.4 The Role of the IMF in the Crisis

IMF support during the years 2000/2001 consisted in a new Stand-by Arrangement, agreed in early 2000 to replace the Extended Arrangement of 1998, which was reviewed four times and augmented twice until late 2001.

Initially, the Fund's support was based on the assumption that Argentina's recession and loss of market access were mostly the result of a combination of

---

adequately identify the structural measures that were key to longer-term success and then make adequate progress in those areas a prerequisite for its continued program relationship with the country."

[616] Yet, the report's criticisms concerning the decision making process (both the outspoken and the implicit) offer lessons of a more general nature. While some of the tangible findings may lead to improve the working of the institution in the future, other indications point at external political and market pressures that influenced decision making, which are inevitably harder to detect and to tackle. See IMF Independent Evaluation Office (2004), p. 63.

[617] IMF Independent Evaluation Office (2004), p. 37.

[618] See IMF Independent Evaluation Office (2004), p. 38.

adverse, but temporary shocks, and thus constituted primarily a liquidity crisis[619]. Hence, fiscal adjustment and measures increasing international competitiveness were expected to suffice to restore confidence and restart growth. A need for fundamental changes in the exchange rate regime and/or the debt structure was not recognised, as both external and public debt levels did not seem alarming, and no estimations were made as to the degree of misalignment of the real exchange rate. The provision of large Fund support therefore was viewed as justified "on catalytic grounds", i.e. to help build confidence in order to (re)gain complementary financing from capital markets[620].

This was the also rationale of the augmentation decision in December 2000 ("el blindaje") which was complemented by financing assurances by the private sector, to amount in total to 39 billion US-Dollars. Programme conditionality was based on a combination of slightly relaxed fiscal deficit and debt targets (meant to limit contractionary effects) and intensified structural reforms aiming at promoting competitiveness and investment (subject to benchmarks, not to targets). Although the risks faced by the programme were acknowledged to be "significant" with a view to possible adverse external developments and the political constraints the government faced, the benefit of doubt was given to the Argentine authorities, referring to the excellent track record of the CBA as well as to the high potential costs of its collapse and/or a debt default, including fears of international contagion[621].

This stance was basically kept through the following reviews which included a scheduled disbursement (of 1.2 billion USD in May 2001) and a second augmentation (by eight billion USD in September of that year)[622]. Despite

---

[619] An interim improvement in external conditions during 2000 (above all growth in global commodity prices) seemed to justify this stance and nourished expectations of further improvement of external conditions.

[620] See IMF Independent Evaluation Office (2004), p. 40.

[621] In an internal briefing paper, possible exit options (move to floating, dollarisation at par, dollarisation at a depreciated rate) were discussed by IMF staff, but without stating the Peso's overvaluation or debt sustainability as fundamental problems, and without seriously pressing for considerations of exit strategies in IMF support. See IMF Independent Evaluation Office (2004), p. 42.

[622] "In fact, even within the IMF, there was an increasing recognition that Argentina had an unsustainable debt profile, an unsustainable exchange rate peg, or both. Yet no alternative course of action was presented to the Board, and the decisions were made to continue disbursing funds to Argentina under the existing policy framework, on the basis of largely noneconomic considerations

continuously missed targets (partly due to political opposition, partly to deteriorating market access), and despite a departure from the agreed policy mix and deteriorating cooperation with the IMF since the advent of Minister Cavallo, the Fund approved continuance of the programme, at the same time recognising its low probability of succeeding in staving off crisis. The need for stop-loss rules for the Fund as well as for alternative approaches to crisis resolution was an issue in internal memoranda, but was not seriously followed up for fear of the catastrophic consequences of an exit from the CBA, and also because the Argentine authorities' refusal to discuss the topic was accepted.

During 2001, the economic policy agenda was almost entirely set by the Argentine government without prior consultation with the Fund[623] (instead sometimes furnished with premature public statements of allegedly secured IMF support[624]) and consisted largely of increasingly desperate and unorthodox measures which effectively urged the IMF to put a good face to things if it did not want to "shy[ ] away" from its mandate and to "effectively surrender[ ] to the same procyclical influences that are driving market behaviour"[625].

Without straight assessment of the risks and costs of possible alternatives, there was, in the decision process for the augmentation of September 2001, only the choice between supporting a programme with a low probability of success (estimated internally at 20-30 percent at best) and withdrawing support entirely, with the consequence of triggering a catastrophic collapse, and without any idea of what should follow. The IMF was well aware that the money would, at best, buy a few months, and "would be more likely to disappear in capital flight"[626].

Even after it had become clear, by late October, that the augmentation of the SBA had been a failure, the IMF continued to defer to the Argentine government's

---

and in hopes of seeing a turnaround in market confidence and buying time until the external economic situation improved." IMF Independent Evaluation Office (2004), p. 5.

[623] Among the measures taken are the "competitiveness plans", the financial transactions tax, the modification of the Convertibility law towards a Dollar-Euro basket peg, the pertinent "convergence factor" installing a dual exchange rate by fiscal means, the "mega swap", the "zero deficit plan", the planned debt exchange, and, finally, the "corralito".

[624] See Mussa (2002), p. 25.

[625] IMF Independent Evaluation Office (2004), p. 49.

[626] IMF Independent Evaluation Office (2004), p. 53.

refusal to discuss alternative policy frameworks[627]. The conviction that the fifth review would most likely not be going to be completed spread within the IMF, but stayed without communication to the Argentine authorities. Finally, during the corresponding negotiations, on the background of the accelerating bank run and the single-handed introduction of the corralito, differences in the Fund's and the Argentine authorities' assessments on the prospects of the CBA became overwhelming, and the non-completion of the review was decided. Given the acceleration of social and political turbulence in December, the stance of the IMF was to wait for a new government in order to offer fresh assistance for a comprehensive medium-term solution, including debt restructuring and either floating or devaluation cum dollarisation. The introduction of the dual exchange rate regime to replace Convertibility in early 2002, however, plainly excluded further IMF support[628].

### 5.1.7.5 The Fund's Responsibilities

From the above, it becomes apparent that the IMF has to bear some responsibility for Argentina's crisis. This is not to say that the Fund was completely wrong with its support for the CBA, or that it was the main responsible for the outcome (this position is incontestably reserved for the Argentine authorities[629]). But it is important to detect the instances where serious errors have become obvious. Clearly, in retrospect things are easier to put into context than in the middle of an inextricable situation.

Of course, the Argentine authorities' non-compliance as well as unfavourable external developments cannot be laid at the IMF's door. What can be laid there, however, are two fatal failures: first, the failure to press more for policy consistency, i.e. for much more conservative fiscal policies, during the whole of the 1990s (especially during the second expansionary phase), and second, the continuance of

---

[627] However, IMF staff had finally outlined a strategy to move to an alternative setting. It included further fiscal adjustment, debt restructuring with a reduction in the NPV by 40 percent, dollarisation at par (paying heed to the assumed preferences of the Argentine government), and full disbursement of undrawn balances under the existing SBA. The proposal was overtaken by events, as yet another stance of single-handed action by the Argentine government made it irrelevant. See IMF Independent Evaluation Office (2004), p. 56.

[628] See IMF Independent Evaluation Office (2004), p. 58.

[629] All the more so since the Argentine authorities "owned", i.e. stood firmly behind, virtually all of the key policies adopted during the decade.

support after mid-2001, when it had become obvious enough that efforts to maintain the CBA and avoid default had no reasonable chance of success. The first failure is nothing less than astonishing, given the Fund's usual standards, while the second, a reflex of lacking adequate risk assessment and contingency planning, is more of an embarrassment.

Citing these two failures implies that the IMF was basically right in all the other instances of its relationship with Argentina. This includes its support of the CBA in principle, being a regime sovereignly chosen by an IMF member, with a reasonable chance of success, as well as its support of the attempts to stick to the CBA through shocks and recession up to, and including, the financial package of December 2000 (the "blindaje"), which could be ascribed a reasonable chance of success in helping avert a major crisis[630].

There are some conspicuous and ill-omened characteristics of the Fund's second failure, the protracted support. These are, first, the Fund's obedience to increasingly being taken hostage by a perceived "take it or leave it" situation with assumedly only two options, namely to unambiguously endorse the CBA or to take responsibility for triggering a crisis (this, often enough, went in parallel with being taken hostage by a non-complying government)[631]. While such a bipolar approach, clearly to a large extent dictated by the centrality of credibility for the arrangement, may be viable under fundamentally sustainable conditions (witness the Tequila experience), it is clearly not in case of a severely misaligned exchange rate and/or an unsustainable fiscal stance. As indicated, the Fund failed for too long in recognising this, at the cost of a needed proactive approach to crisis resolution[632].

---

[630] See Mussa (2002), p. 3. Also: "Given the probabilistic nature of any such decision, the chosen strategy may well have proved successful if the assumptions had turned out to be correct (which they were not) and if the agreed program had been impeccably executed by the authorities (which it was not). The critical error was not so much with the decision itself as with the failure to have an exit strategy, including a contingency plan, in place, inasmuch as the strategy was known to be risky. No serious decision of alternative strategies took place, as the authorities refused to engage in such discussions and the IMF did not insist." IMF Independent Evaluation Office (2004), p. 5.

[631] "… it may be difficult to understand how great a perversion of [the Fund's] policies and principles was perpetrated in this incident." Mussa (2002), p. 25.

[632] However, "… it is quite possible that a situation in which some groups in Argentina viewed a devaluation/debt restructuring as having been "forced" by the IMF would have been associated with even greater political disruptions and short-term policy choices that would have made the situation worse. In other words, there may well have been no feasible actions by the IMF that would

Second, as a consequence of the Fund's failure to correctly judge the situation (namely to detect that the problem had developed into a solvency problem), it overestimated its leverage with respect to market sentiment[633]. The policy of private sector involvement which stood behind the "blindaje", effectively linking official support to voluntary finance from domestic and international private markets, was based on the assumption that official finance had to be only as large as to create enough confidence to catalyze further private finance which would, in turn, restart economic growth. As it turned out, correspondingly limited further official finance, as delivered with the augmentation decision of September 2001, worked to puzzle markets more than to reassure them, because they rightly judged the situation worse than the IMF implicitly signalled[634]. This is not to say that the Fund's support for Argentina was not enough; rather, that any sums granted after the failure of the "blindaje" were, in retrospect, doomed to be futile. Indeed, the Fund's exposure to Argentina had become exceptionally large after the subsequent augmentation, which created serious concerns of the country's capacity to repay[635].

The most severe reproach, however, is fed by the circumstances of the augmentation decision of September 2001, when the money, as even admitted by those responsible, was expected to buy a few months at best and to disappear in capital flight. This, together with the ambiguity inherent in the augmentation itself (the provision of funds to mend what was labelled a liquidity crisis, with parts of

---

have enabled the adoption of a meaningful Plan B. But this possibility is not an adequate justification for failing to think about, let alone design and actively promote, such a plan." IMF Independent Evaluation Office (2004), p. 69.

[633] The catalytic approach suffers, above all, from free rider and first mover problems, i.e. from the fact that for individual investors it is rational to wait and see whether the government's commitment, together with other investors' new funds, brings about the hoped-for consolidation, before they themselves put in new money. See Eichengreen (2001a), pp. 24ff.

[634] At the same time, the 3 billion Dollars as part of the augmentation earmarked for debt restructuring in effect was an unambiguous warning to markets that a restructuring including a loss in creditors' NPV was unavoidable.

[635] Certainly, it belongs to the nature of a crisis lender to assume "beyond-market" credit risks (and, after all, IMF credit enjoys seniority). However, internally there seems to have been a lack of focus on financial risk: "It is still striking how few Directors raised this issue as a concern during Board discussions, especially given the lack of conditionality on net international reserves (in view of what was considered to be a functioning currency board arrangement) and, in September 2001, the absence of standard assurances in the staff report concerning Argentina's ability to repay the IMF." IMF Independent Evaluation Office (2004), p. 61.

those funds earmarked to facilitate a debt restructuring), worked to feed the suspicion that external interests, political and economic alike, might have been unduly involved[636]. The potential motives would not be hard to conjecture, as, in the last weeks of the CBA, what remained of big and sophisticated investors' capital had time to leave the country[637].

One positive thing may be derived from the Fund's travails in Argentina, and this is the supposition that contagion remained limited after Argentina's collapse because the crisis was so protracted as to be widely anticipated by market participants in the end. The IMF has rightly emerged deeply damaged from the Argentine crisis. It has since tackled some of the identified shortcomings, and accordingly revised some policies and procedures.

### 5.1.8    The Washington Consensus

The term "Washington Consensus" was coined by US-economist John Williamson after a conference held in 1989 in Washington, DC, with economists from both the World Bank and the IMF, on policy reforms in Latin America. It was subsequently understood to stand for a set of free-market economic policies meant, after the debt crisis of the 1980s, to chart a path for restoring sustained prosperity in the region, or, in other words, "to refer to the lowest common denominator of policy advice being addressed by the Washington-based institutions to Latin American countries as of 1989"[638].

The Washington Consensus comprised a set of ten reforms to create growth on the basis of a commitment to macroeconomic discipline, market economy, and openness to trade. These reforms focused on fiscal discipline, a reordering of public

---

[636] "In fact, the practice of certain prominent shareholders [in the IMF] of bypassing the Board raises serious transparency concerns in the decision-making process, not only as to the negative effect on the lack of proper and adequate debate in the Board as the natural "locus" for discussions, but also as to the "agenda" – other than finding the best possible alternative in specific crisis prevention or crisis resolution scenarios – that such shareholders might be advancing." Lavagna (2004), p. 119. And, referring to shortcomings in governance and transparency in the handling of the Argentine crisis: "These shortcomings are indeed compounded by the fact that representation at the Board does not adequately reflect the importance of emerging economies in the global economy." Ibid.

[637] "Argentina's program was explicitly tailored to take the country out of the capital market through the end of 2001. That is to say, it allowed creditors with maturing claims to exit without losses. It was the opposite of a bail in." Eichengreen (2001a), p. 28.

[638] See Williamson (2000), p. 251.

expenditure (towards more spending on primary health, education, and infrastructure) and revenue (tax reforms that combine a broader tax base with moderate marginal tax rates), financial and interest rate liberalisation, a competitive exchange rate[639], trade liberalisation (replacement of quantitative restrictions with low and uniform tariffs), liberalisation of inward FDI, privatisation, deregulation (to abolish barriers to entry and exit), and secure property rights. The Washington Consensus has become to be viewed by its critics as a manifesto of neoliberalism and market fundamentalism.

Clearly, the policy set around the Argentine "Convertibilidad" was in line with the recommendations formulated in the Washington Consensus. Although the choice of exchange rate regime did not explicitly form part of them[640], being claimed by the IMF as a "poster boy for emerging economies" was tantamount to being praised as a "poster child for the Washington Consensus"[641].

There are (apart from, first, piles of mainly ideologically founded anti-capitalist, anti-US, and anti-globalisation criticisms, and second, claims that the Washington consensus neglected environmental and political issues[642]) basically three areas where the Washington Consensus ideas arguably were too blunt. These are, first, the requirement of financial liberalisation, which seemed to require completely open capital accounts and thus the encouragement of foreign capital to flood in without restraint. Together with fixed exchange rates and/or irresponsible fiscal policies, this inevitably led to overvaluation and/or fiscal unsustainability, and so made countries vulnerable to the vagaries of international capital markets[643]. Second, it can be

---

[639] "The term 'competitive exchange rate' [...] signifies a rate that is either at, or undervalued relative to, its long-run equilibrium." Williamson (2000), p. 263.

[640] Williamson noted on the recommendation of "competitive exchange rates" in 2002: "I fear I indulged in wishful thinking in asserting that there was a consensus in favor of ensuring that the exchange rate would be competitive, which implies an intermediate regime; in fact Washington was already beginning to subscribe to the two-corner doctrine." Williamson (2002).

[641] See Eichengreen (2001a), p. 1.

[642] See Stiglitz (1998).

[643] "Too many countries encouraged money to flood in and overvalue the currency when the capital markets were throwing money at the region, or used a fixed or crawling exchange rate as a nominal anchor, or pursued a procyclical fiscal policy. They thereby made themselves vulnerable to "sudden stops" in capital inflows, and they left themselves no scope to relax fiscal policy in difficult times. The policy agenda of a decade ago certainly did not warn countries against such foolish acts, and indeed in certain cases countries may even have been encouraged to do some of those things." Williamson (2003), p. 5.

argued that the Washington Consensus did not emphasise sufficiently the importance of institutional (later called "second-generation") reforms which are necessary to make any "first-generation" reform (i.e. the original policy set) work[644]. With incomplete or neglected fiscal and labour reforms, and other, complementary, institutional preconditions lacking (e.g. on fields such as the judiciary, civil service, tax collection, fiscal federalism, education), advantage could not be taken from the per se beneficial "first-generation" reforms[645]. The third critique is that policies shaped after the Washington Consensus were too narrowly focussed on growth, instead on "growth plus equity"[646]. There was little concern for income distribution or the social agenda, relegating to the conviction that the proposed reforms were generally pro-poor in being pro-growth. The prevalence of an already relatively unequal income distribution and of different income elasticities with respect to aggregate growth across different layers of income was not taken account of, with the effect that income distribution even worsened during growth phases.

The proponents of the Washington Consensus have largely, and productively, accepted such criticism[647]. The position claiming that, in Argentina, "the neo-liberal economic model was never implemented or, if it was, it was half-baked"[648] contains both aspects of the Washington Consensus' responsibility for Argentina's experience: on the one hand, the Washington Consensus represented a paradigm that seemed to fit ideally with Argentina's needs at the beginning 90s, and so (irrespective of the fact that, anyway, the stabilisation need made a very hard external anchor, and thus an economic alignment somewhere along the Washington Consensus proposals, unavoidable) offered a perfect ideological backing for the Convertibility Plan (which also helped in the relationship with the IMF). On the other hand, Argentina proved to comply least with the most important, namely the fiscal,

---

[644] See Burky/Perry (1998).

[645] See Huber/Solt (2004), p. 162.

[646] "My version quite consciously eschewed redistributive policies, taking the view that Washington had not reached a consensus on their desirability". Williamson (2000), p. 258.

[647] They have made a variety of proposals to tackle the post-1990s' problems of Latin America, paying heed to some lessons they, along with many economists worldwide, have learned from the experience with Latin America during the past 15 years. See Kuczynski, P.-P., and Williamson, J. (eds.): After the Washington Consensus. Restarting Growth and Reform in Latin America, Institute for International Economics, Washington, D.C., March 2003.

[648] Hanke (2002), p. 2.

policy requirements of the Washington Consensus, and so clearly disqualifies as a case study, and therefore also as a prey, of the Washington Consensus.

### 5.1.9   The Currency Board Itself

A popular attitude is that the 2001 crisis was a direct and necessary consequence of the chosen monetary constitution, i.e. of the CBA itself. The arguments are obvious: both the straitjacket the CBA imposed on monetary policy and the dollarisation it encouraged left the country without the flexibility to adequately respond to external shocks. The fiscal dimension plays, for the "culprit CBA" advocates, no independent role in causing the crisis.

Prima facie, there is little to oppose. However, such argumentation goes easy in fading out the very origins and the purpose of the CBA, i.e. the historical dependencies any responsible analysis cannot avoid bothering with. It is a fact that the CBA precisely was chosen as a last resort from chaos owed to decades-long macroeconomic mismanagement. There is no doubt that it was initially, and could well have been for a longer term, good at rectifying this. The true mistake was the failure of those responsible to acknowledge that, beneath its immediate effectiveness, the CBA, if it was to be viable in the medium to longer term, needed making the economy compatible with the CBA's functioning principles and limits, i.e. with restricted policy options, with harder adjustment processes, and with the elementary obligation to balance public budgets[649]. Beyond a wholesale condemnation of a potentially beneficial monetary constitution (which has been amply tested in history, and not only in pre-globalisation times), therefore, it is imperative to investigate into the defects in the Argentine CBA's gearing – as has been done above. Such investigation inevitably suggests that Argentine politics did not live up to their own commitment, to the CBA[650]. Thus, the CBA cannot per se be made responsible for the crisis.

A slightly more acceptable variant of the "culprit CBA" thesis is that the CBA obviously failed to fulfil expectations of its disciplining effect on fiscal policy[651]. However, such expectations enjoyed very little justification from the start: the

---

[649] "But surely, the ultimate tragic collapse was not preordained from the time that Argentina's stabilization and reform efforts began a decade earlier." Mussa (2002), p. 30.

[650] See e.g. Lavagna (2004), p. 116.

[651] Calvo/Mishkin claim that hard pegs may even weaken governments' incentives for fiscal rectitude, as they make foreign borrowing easier and thus allow them to delay necessary reforms. See Calvo/Mishkin (2003), p. 25.

Convertibility regime hinges on an open economy, and an open capital account, wherefrom deficits were financed, is a necessary precondition for the choice of an external nominal anchor. So, expectations of the CBA disciplining fiscal policy could realistically be based less on some sort of built-in restraints than on hopes that either responsible policies or, if not, rational capital markets would take over the disciplining role, in providing funds to a debtor just as much and as costly as sustainable. However, as long as international capital markets can reasonably expect international financial institutions to eventually bail out the country, the latter hope is ill-founded – moral hazard makes the provision of unserviceable finance a perfectly rational act[652]. So, there has never been a way around responsible fiscal policies.

## 5.2  Taking Stock

So far, the different factors that contributed to the collapse of the CBA have been examined. It has become evident that many of these factors have their origins well before the advent of crisis, some of them even before the CBA's inception. Just as in medical sciences where it is well known that pathogens unfold their worst effects when coming across a weak physical constitution, one has to distinguish here between the factors that created vulnerabilities (invaliding factors) and other factors that evoked crisis when encountering the vulnerable constitution (triggering factors). This implies the notion that, in the absence of triggering factors, the crisis would not (yet) have unfolded, and on the other hand that, in the absence of vulnerabilities, the triggers would have met a much more resistant environment and thus not have been able to do so much harm. Categorising and weighing the individual factors is what remains to be done.

### 5.2.1  Vulnerability

The uncontested lead in the ranks of the invaliding factors is held, not surprisingly, by fiscal profligacy. The most serious mistake made was that the high growth years, especially the post-Tequila years, were not used to generate fiscal surpluses in order to potentialise anticyclical fiscal policies, and to moderate later

---

[652] There are hopes that the hitherto unseen losses investors incurred in the aftermath of Argentina's sovereign default (the haircut was by 70 cent on the Dollar) will discipline future lending. History, as well as the fact that international capital quickly returned to Argentina, however, suggest otherwise.

liquidity constraints[653]. Mussa (2002) argues that an improvement of the primary fiscal balance by two percent on average since 1991, or, alternatively, a roughly equivalent improvement starting after Tequila (of one, two, and three percent in 1996, 97, and 98 respectively, and the subsequent maintenance of this improvement) would have been sufficient to cumulatively reduce Argentine sovereign debt in 2001 by enough as to reduce concerns about sovereign default. Such fiscal performance would have been imaginable in political as well as economic terms, and would have allowed lower interest rates and better conditions for economic recovery[654]. The chronic fiscal deficits, financed largely by Dollar-denominated government bonds placed on international capital markets, facilitated domestic absorption financed from abroad and persisting current account deficits, and left public accounts heavily currency mismatched[655]. Fiscal irresponsibility is thus the root cause for the triple macroeconomic vulnerability Argentina developed up to the late 1990s, consisting of high indebtedness, high leverage towards the exterior, and vast currency mismatches in public balance sheets. Thus, fiscal profligacy is also co-responsible for the increasing gap between the Peso's nominal exchange rate and its intrinsic, i.e. fundamentals oriented, value, i.e. for much of its overvaluation. Clearly, not all of the blame is with the public sector: the private sector equally borrowed freely from abroad, and/or incurred Dollar liabilities while its revenues were in Pesos (as in the nontradables sector). However, in doing so, it responded to the framework, policies, and mood set by the authorities.

Correspondingly, among the institutional weaknesses, those were most damaging that were responsible for the vast, especially non-discretionary, portions of federal public spending. As has been shown, the counterproductive rules that govern federal fiscal relations bear significant responsibility for the fiscal outcome. Had the provinces been prompted to balance (or improve) their budgets, the overall

---

[653] See Galiani et al. (2002), p. 22.

[654] "Thus, the margin between sustained success of Argentina's stabilization and reform efforts of the past decade and the tragic collapse at the end of last year was far from insurmountable." Mussa (2002), p. 31.

[655] "The combination of a weak fiscal policy and heavy reliance on external borrowing within the constraint of the Convertibility regime became a recipe for disaster, when the country was hit by the prolonged adverse shocks." Independent Evaluation Office (2004), p. 15. Thanks to careful management of maturity structure, the impact of the sudden stop on the public sector's immediate financing needs was not as bad as it could have been with shorter maturities; but this only meant that the crisis took a few years to develop.

fiscal stance would have been easier to keep sustainable (between 1992 and 2001, the combined annual provincial deficits added on average 1.1, and in 2001 alone 2.4, percent of GDP to the federal fiscal deficit[656]). Other traits, such as the generally weak tax administration, persisting loopholes, widespread tax evasion, as well as the corrupt judiciary, added to fiscal morbidity. The social security reform cannot be left unmentioned here as the single most fiscally burdensome, because blatantly ill-financed, institutional reform.

Very importantly, economic policy constellations within MERCOSUR were highly adverse in boosting expansionary Argentine fiscal policies before 1999, and in aggravating the effects of external shocks after 1999. MERCOSUR thus acted, for Argentina, as an amplifier of unsound policies and negative shocks, and thus added massively to its vulnerability.

Next come the much-lamented labour market rigidities. Undoubtedly, the labour market reforms stayed insufficient, and the regulatory burden was anything but helpful for the needs of structural change and wage flexibilisation. Nevertheless, the argument of rigid labour markets preventing the "automatic adjustment mechanism" is dented by the observation that the deflationary process significantly reduced nominal wages in the private sector as from 1998. This suggests that market pressures did pass through on wages, but that the degree of deflationary adjustment could not make up for the massive overvaluation[657]. Thus, maybe labour markets were not as flexible as they could have been, but they would have been in any case vastly overstrained if they had been expected to bring about the whole of the required real exchange rate adjustment[658]. Hence the reluctance to place labour market rigidities at a more prominent place in the score of culprits.

Other neglects follow, with declining importance as to their contribution to Argentina's crisis (though not necessarily for the country's long-term perspectives). Though the country made big efforts to move away from inward orientation and improve efficiency, and, overall, the realised privatisations brought significant efficiency gains and improved supply, in several cases, unduly monitored privatisation processes and deficient regulatory institutions, as well as generally insufficient industrial policies stood in the way of better meeting the demands of the new economic alignment. The educational system continued to deteriorate

---

[656] See IMF Independent Evaluation Office (2004), p. 10.

[657] See Lavagna (2004), p. 116.

[658] See Williamson (2003), p. 4.

throughout the 1990s, while it would have been crucial to match it with new qualification needs of those set free in privatised state companies. The complete lack of concern for social and distribution policies went largely unpunished during the high growth years but turned into a curse during the protracted recession.

## 5.2.2 Triggers

It is well known which factors triggered the crisis and exhibited Argentina's vulnerabilities. However, as will be argued, they are not exclusively of external origin.

First comes, now proceeding chronologically, the Dollar appreciation, which started in 1995 and unexpectedly continued even in the wake of the high-tech bubble burst, to appreciate, in total, by 34 percent between 1995 and early 2002. It contributed to the overvaluation the Peso entered the crisis with (the Dollar had appreciated by roughly 18% between 1995 and early 1999), and helped slow down export growth and attract international capital. However, as Argentina's trade share remained comparatively low, the appreciated Dollar's impact on growth stayed limited, which is also why Argentina's problem was not predominantly one of competitiveness. More important than the Dollar's rise was that part of the Peso's overvaluation that developed as a consequence of country risk considerations, i.e., of Argentina's increasingly unsustainable fiscal situation given its characteristics of relative closedness and of currency mismatched balance sheets. In the absence of other external shocks, the Dollar's appreciation could plausibly have been compensated via deflationary adjustment (the Dollar's rise between 1999 and late 2001 was by roughly another 12 percent[659]). Given the high credibility of Convertibility, the Dollar's rise alone would, with sounder fundamentals, probably not have evoked speculative attacks of the CBA, even though the external shocks of the late 90s would have put the economy under strain (as they did with other emerging economies).

Clearly, the sequence of emerging economies' crises between 1997 and 1999, starting with the Asian crisis, among them most severely the Russian crisis that dried out international capital markets, as well as the Brazilian devaluation that hit Argentina's trade balance, were the most fatal triggers for Argentina[660].

---

[659] See Joint Economic Committee (2005), p. 2.

[660] Turkey and Brazil also suffered major crises induced by the sudden stop. Uruguay's crisis, however, was the reflex of Argentina's collapse; contagion remained limited to Argentina's highly dependent neighbour.

It has been said that until some point in 2000, Argentina's fiscal situation seemed not unsustainable. As has been argued, even the "blindaje", disbursed in early 2001, still had a reasonable chance of success, as there were still ample international reserves available in the vaults of the central bank, the banking system was as yet unaffected by confidence losses, and there was the hope that the slowing US economy would weaken the Dollar[661].

This implies an additional category of trigger, pulled by the Argentine authorities themselves. Arguably, two events within just four weeks sealed Argentina's fate, the first of them by perforating hopes that politics could bring about the necessary fiscal redressing, and the second by lancinating the exchange rate peg. The refusal of the Argentine government to embark on the fiscal consolidation measures, as proposed by the new economy minister Ricardo López Murphy, and his forced resignation in March 2001, was the first of these fatal triggers[662], while the second completed the damage with what has been called above "meddling with the CBA", i.e. with the announcement in April 2001 of a change to a basket peg. This worked to actively undermine the CBA, in demolishing confidence into the peg and thus destroying any hope of avoiding default, and was helped by the violation of central bank independence a few days later when the central bank governor was removed from office[663]. To be sure, the change to a basket was, in principle, a fundamentally rational goal, and could have been envisaged in a fundamentally stable economic environment, but in the prevailing situation, the softening of support for the Dollar parity that had been firmly held up since ten years could not do other than upset markets as well as the Argentine public, accelerate bank runs and bankruptcies, and ultimately provoke the end of Convertibilidad[664]. Subsequent measures such as

---

[661] "While skeptical that the chance of success was as great as 50 percent, my view was that in late 2000 there still was a reasonable chance that tragedy could be avoided – if the Argentine government assiduously implemented fiscal measures that reassured private creditors about longer-term debt sustainability." And: "An interest rate spread of 750 basis points indicated concerns in financial markets about debt sustainability, but not yet firm conviction that sovereign default was virtually inevitable." Mussa (2002), p. 19.

[662] "In my view, this event marked the effective end to any realistic hope that the Argentine government would address its fiscal difficulties with sufficient resolve to avoid sovereign default and its attendant chaos." Mussa (2002), p. 22.

[663] See Guidotti (2004), p. 22.

[664] Of course, the „convergence factor", tied to the hypothetical Euro-Dollar basket and, in effect, a devaluation by fiscal means, worked to reduce the real exchange rate misalignment, but

the "mega canje" and the competitiveness and zero deficit plans, therefore, were deprived of any chance of success. Advancing these two events as the ultimate triggers (the second pulled, ironically, by the "father of Convertibility" himself) implies the conviction that until early 2001, and with López Murphy's fiscal programme, the collapse could have been avoided, the CBA could have stayed in place, and the economy could have adjusted in the required, although painful, manner to the external shocks. With the ensuing recovery of the world economy and the finally falling US-Dollar, Argentina would have been likely to recover as well, with its CBA in place (and possibly preparing for a softer exit at a later stage).

So, well aware of the unabated populist attitudes that still accuse the IMF, the Washington Consensus, or even, for that matter, globalisation as such of being accountable for Argentina's recent tragedy, any responsible analysis must arrive at Argentine politics as lastly having spoiled its own success. Sure, the Washington consensus was too sweeping in several aspects, and the IMF can be blamed for serious misjudgements long before, as well as during, the crisis. Also, external developments were extremely unfavourable, and it can, by extension, even be argued that, again, the IMF and its ideological alignment had contributed to the occurrence of these external shocks (especially the Asian crisis, from which the other crises spread). But, even when all these findings are acknowledged, Argentine politics cannot be spared from the verdict that they bear the ultimate responsibility for having failed to pursue the policies necessary to sustain its chosen macroeconomic framework, the CBA.

## 5.3 Missed Opportunities?

Considerations of possible opportunities to exit the CBA hinge upon the prevailing political and economic constellations. In retrospect, there would have been basically two time windows where an exit from the CBA, after having reaped its stabilisation benefits, towards a more flexible exchange rate would have been possible out of a position of strength ("soft exit"). The years immediately before, and those after, the Tequila crisis would have offered such opportunities, with the latter period certainly more apt, given the greater distance from, and thus assumedly lesser fear of a relapse into, high inflation. Though more painful and unavoidably implying a degree of expropriation (with the inevitable consequences for further

---

not enough by far, and at the cost of undermining credibility and thus the complete macroeconomic framework. See also Calvo/Izquierdo/Talvi (2003), p. 47.

policy credibility), an exit towards a flexible exchange rate would have been conceivable even after the advent of external shocks and recession at the end of the decade ("hard exit"). Fleeing ahead, i.e. taking the exit towards full dollarisation, would have been feasible basically anytime and in several variants. Contrary to an exit towards flexible exchange rates, official dollarisation would not have included a reneging on past commitments, but could have been viewed as a logical sequel of the CBA.

Of course, the assumption that any of these options, if realised, would have been preferable to the factual outcome is derived from hindsight. While it might be thought pointless to engage in hypothetical contemplations of past opportunities, such considerations help not only to assess factual developments but also to draw some important lessons. In what follows, these possible exit opportunities, as well as the facts that stood in the way of seizing them, will be addressed.

### 5.3.1 Soft Exit during 1993/1994

Once the economy was stabilised, with single-digit and continuously falling inflation rates and strong growth, the period 1993/1994, in retrospect, could have looked like an opportune time to exit the hard peg. The fiscal improvement of 1992/93, the US-Dollar depreciating in 1994 against Argentina's main trading partners and taking off pressure from the Peso, as well as improvements in competitiveness due to deregulation and privatisation, made existing concerns about the large current account deficit look less worrying.

As indicated, neither the Argentine authorities, nor economists (including those of the IMF) seriously considered the issue of an exit at the time. One part of the explanation is that the CBA was still considered mainly as a stabilisation tool, and attention was focused on its immediate success at that. Considerations of its medium or long term viability had not been undertaken at its inception, and only slowly started to enter analysis after the advent of stabilisation.

Moreover, memories of hyperinflation were still fresh. Raising the topic of exiting the peg and risking a relapse, at a time when things went well, was next to unthinkable. Such an exit, "soft" how it might have been (in terms of the economic environment and the distance between real and equilibrium exchange rate), would have implied the nullification of the law that was at the core of Argentina's revival. Thus, even if the Peso were not overvalued at that time, there would probably have been fears that, in the absence of the Convertibility law, the government would, at the first incidence of stress, take control of the central bank, which would soon lead into new self-reinforcing inflationary dynamics. This is why, despite a fairly favourable economic environment, an exit towards floating or a more flexible peg at such an early stage would almost certainly have been counterproductive in reviving inflation expectations – regardless of whether the replacement of the external anchor by another monetary rule (which would in any case have been necessary to show commitment to further stability) would have accompanied the move.

Perhaps the only advantage of the extremely hard exit actually seen in early 2002 over the discussed hypothetical exit at some time during 1993 or 1994 was its distance from the year 1991: inflation allergy had time enough to subside, and economic agents time enough to get accustomed to the new macroeconomic and institutional framework, so that, even after the traumatic parting from the CBA, fears of a relapse into old inflationary habits, or even of endangered democracy, were not paramount, and the country's basic economic alignment was not seriously questioned.

### 5.3.2    Soft Exit during the Second Expansionary Phase

With hindsight, the years 1996, 1997, or even 1998 offered the last, and at the same time best, opportunity for a "soft" exit from the CBA. At that stage, the main benefits of exchange rate-based stabilisation had been reaped, and many preconditions for monetary stability without a fixed exchange rate seemed reliably installed, such as a government professedly devoted to stability, a (still) bearable fiscal stance, an independent central bank, and a robust financial sector. Overall confidence into the economy was high, and growth was expected to stay high. Strong growth, receding unemployment (from 17 to 13 percent between 1996 and 1998), zero inflation, and a favourable external environment stood positively against the only worrying facts that the current account gap was quickly widening (from 2.5 to 4.9 percent between 1996 and 1998), due to strongly rising imports and less strongly rising exports. The real exchange rate appreciated only mildly over the period, and spreads between Dollar and Peso interest rates were small throughout 1996 and 1997 (never surpassing 200 basis points), indicating that the markets did not gauge the nominal exchange rate far from the equilibrium rate[665].

Although in this phase some economists raised the issue of considering an exit from the CBA, the topic did not seem pressing. There are several reasons why an

---

[665] It has even been claimed, e.g. by Domingo Cavallo, that the Peso would have appreciated against the Dollar if floated in 1997. See interview
<http://www.stern.nyu.edu/Sternbusiness/spring_summer_2003/argentina.html>.

exit was not seriously considered during these boom years. First, the fear that giving up the hard peg and moving to a milder peg (e.g., an adjustable peg, or an exchange rate band) or to a floating exchange rate would bring back inflation was still existent. Second, the ever higher degree of debt dollarisation in both public and private balance sheets founded fears of payment difficulties in the case of devaluation, which would probably have had to be expected, as a reflex of the current-account deficit, initially possibly worsened by overshooting. Third, there were hopes that the current-account balance would improve and turn to the positive due to a widely expected depreciation of the US-Dollar relative to the Yen and the European currencies, and that Argentina would continue to grow up to its potential, so that eventually a more comfortable exit opportunity would arise in the future[666]. Finally, again, the very necessity of an eventual exit was far from accepted. Both the Argentine government and the IMF (not to speak of the Argentine public which valued the Peso-Dollar parity and the growth it had brought very high), dazzled by the favourable experience with the Tequila crisis, had come to believe that the CBA was a viable long-term option for Argentina[667].

This belief obviously stood also behind the favourable market reactions to Domingo Cavallo leaving office in July 1996. The "self-styled guarantor of the famed Convertibility Plan" could leave office and nobody felt the CBA was endangered. "It appeared that the country had made the transition from sole reliance on the credibility of just a handful of officials to a deeper faith in the macroeconomic laws now governing Argentina's economy"[668].

### 5.3.3  Hard Exit after the External Shocks of the Late Nineties

Finally, there would have been the possibility to exit the CBA after the advent of the Asian, the Russian, and the Brazilian crises, when international capital started to shun Argentina. The potential costs of adjustment to external shocks with fixed exchange rates in place were well known; the rising difficulties to finance the fiscal and current account deficits could have given rise to contemplations of opening the

---

[666] Expectations that Argentina could keep up growing at seven percent per year in the long run, and eventually catch up with the first world, were widespread. With hindsight, these were fed by a collective, and officially nourished, overestimation of the situation. Opinion expressed by Daniel Heymann during an interview conducted by the author on November, 16th, 2004, in Buenos Aires.

[667] See Feldstein (2002), p. 13.

[668] Pastor/Wise (1999), p. 477.

door towards flexibilisation and devaluation in 1999/2000, or even until early 2001[669]. However, not even the Brazilian devaluation appeared to prompt the government, or the IMF, to seriously question the viability of the CBA. President De la Rúa, keen on demonstrating a difference to the 1980s, when hyperinflation had brought down the last Radical government, won the late 1999 elections on a pledge to maintain Convertibility.

Sticking to Convertibility seemed not only a laudable pose (the Tequila experience seemed to teach that it pays to stand firm) but, given the widespread currency mismatches in balance sheets, also a necessity if payment difficulties in the public and private sector, which devaluation would bring about, were to be avoided. To the credit of those responsible, an information problem also stood in the way of contemplating an exit: the true order of disequilibrium was not readily recognisable for a long time. The sluggish depreciation of the real exchange rate during the recession concealed the magnitude of necessary fiscal adjustment, and so the true distance from debt sustainability remained a matter of speculation, for policymakers and economists alike.

Yet, assuming the Alianza government had suspected both magnitude and necessity of fiscal adjustment, and chosen the way of, as well as found the backing for, floating the Peso in 2000 or even in early 2001[670]: what would have been different from the float actually experienced later? Very importantly, even in early 2001, there would have still been ample international reserves to smooth the overshoot of the exchange rate, the balance sheets in the financial sector would not yet have been so weakened by forced purchases of government bonds, and there would have been resources available from the IMF to bolster the transition. Above all, the independence of the central bank would not have been violated and policy credibility not so much eroded, which would have been an essential asset in the move towards a new monetary rule which could have aimed at either, again, the exchange rate (via exchange rate targets or some other variety of managed exchange rates) or inflation (via inflation or monetary targeting).

---

[669] See Pastor/Wise (1999), p. 494.

[670] It is likely that the government would have exposed "fear of floating", i.e. would, because of currency mismatches, fear of inflation, and/or concerns about credibility, not have allowed the peso to instantly depreciate all the way down to its equilibrium rate. Incomplete depreciation would have resulted in interest rates rising in expectation of further devaluation, with the concomitant real effects. "Therefore it is unclear that a more flexible exchange rate system would have successfully cleared the air in 2000." Calvo/Izquierdo/Talvi (2004), p. 38.

After floating the exchange rate, real wages and prices would have been reduced by inflation more rapidly and probably against less social resistance than that experienced after the "plan déficit cero", and inflation would have facilitated fiscal adjustment. The currency mismatches in corporate and financial sector balance sheets as well as on fiscal accounts would have in any case required remedial policies, and the restructuring of public debt would have most likely been unavoidable. However, all of this would have taken place on the background of a still less fragile economic and social environment. If coupled with a forced conversion of Dollar deposits and loans into Pesos[671], the devaluation would have implied the same abrogation of property rights, but would, to the degree that the realised devaluation would have been smaller than that incurred later, have entailed less factual economic harm and less distributional effects. To the extent that deposit freezes could have been reduced in extent or duration, or avoided altogether, public discontent would have been more limited.

It seems plausible to assume that such policies would have been feasible and in their consequences less hurting than what actually happened afterwards. The biggest appeal of such an "emergency exit" seems indeed that it would have prevented the excesses in political and social development that unfolded during 2001, done less economic harm, and possibly left the government in office. The comparison with solutions that would have avoided devaluation and the concomitant immediate balance sheet effects, however, is not so clear-cut.

### 5.3.4    Exit towards Full Dollarisation until 1999

Given the pervasive dollarisation of contracts in Argentina during the 1990s, the step from the CBA towards full dollarisation, i.e. the Peso's complete replacement by the Dollar, would have been a small one at virtually every point during the 1990s. Official dollarisation was indeed publicly considered by the Menem administration after the Brazilian devaluation, early in 1999[672]. After the elections of 1999, the new government explicitly rejected the idea. As indicated, the IMF staff team also considered the option to exit towards official dollarisation (combined, of course, with a comprehensive debt restructuring). Would full dollarisation have been desirable before, during, or after the crisis, or at any other point of time, for that matter?

---

[671] The "pesification" of deposits and loans was widely seen as unavoidable in the case of devaluation. See Schuler/Hanke (2002), p. 10.

[672] Talks with the US authorities about technical aspects of dollarisation had already taken place in 1998. See also Hanke (1999), and Schuler (2000).

Clearly, nothing would have changed the fact that Argentina by no means formed an optimal currency area with the US[673]. Full dollarisation was thus, viewed from the optimal currency criteria, as unsuitable for Argentina as was the CBA (but not more). And, clearly, full dollarisation, to be sustainable, would have required the same set of sustainable fiscal policies and institutional preconditions as required the CBA.

Thus, the only question is whether the gains of dollarisation per se, in terms of even more firmly "tied hands" and higher monetary credibility, would, at any point of time, have exceeded the costs of embarking on a monetary regime even more costly to exit[674], and of renouncing seigniorage income. Indeed, this trade-off would probably have ruled in favour of full dollarisation during the early nineties: full dollarisation would have prevented the speculative intermezzo of 1992 as well as the repercussions of the Tequila crisis, during which the Argentine CBA was put to a test. Thereafter, however, credibility of the peg was not the problem any more, so that Argentina, in the minds of its economic agents, was effectively "fully dollarised". So, a move towards official dollarisation would arguably have made not much difference after the successful mastering of Tequila until well into the crisis.

## 5.3.5    Dollarisation in the Midst of Crisis

Would full dollarisation, at par or at a previously devalued exchange rate, if introduced at some point during the crisis, have been preferable to, first, the factual outcome, and, second, to a conceivable "emergency exit" towards floating in time, as described above? As has been shown, the fiscal situation made sovereign default unavoidable since the failure of the "blindaje" in early 2001 at the very latest. Clearly, full dollarisation, until early 2001, would have avoided any meddling with the peg, and thus the massive credibility losses that translated into extreme rises of currency risk in spreads, the bank runs, and the capital flight evoked by the announcement of the switch to a basket peg. This alone would have been a clear advantage over the factual course of events, in preventing the acceleration down the road to catastrophe, and, as one can conjecture, much of public indignation and

---

[673] However: "The flaw with the theory of optimum currency areas is that economists presume to determine costs and benefits for consumers, rather than acknowledging that it is the evaluations of consumers that determine the costs and benefits economists must consider. If Argentines prefer to hold Dollars (and they do), it indicates that for them Argentina is part of an optimum currency area with the United States, no matter what economists may think." Schuler/Hanke (2002), p. 31.

[674] See Carrera et.al. (2002), p. 19.

probably even the government's dethronement. What is more, dollarisation at par would have prevented the breach of contracts incurred by devaluation and pesification, as well as the immediate balance sheet effects that led to rows of disorderly bankruptcies in the nontradables sector and to financial sector insolvency[675]. And it would have brought down interest rates and so helped the recovery. Again, as in the scenario of the "CBA rescued", full dollarisation, whether at par or not[676], would not have been the optimal long-term constitution for Argentina, all the more so after Brazil's move to floating. But the avoidance of the extreme economic, social, and political costs incurred with the breach of law could have outweighed much in the way of economic adjustment, plus the higher costs of a future exit from dollarisation[677].

One important qualification is key in comparing the options of floating versus dollarising. While dollarisation at par would have prevented the balance sheet effects of devaluation in the short run, it would not have done so in the long run, as the (then hypothetical) real exchange rate would nevertheless have needed to approach its equilibrium value, via a continuation of the deflationary process and the concomitant changes in relative prices. With the necessary relative fall in prices of nontradable goods, the increase in the real value of dollar debt would have entailed "creeping" balance sheet effects which, in the long run, necessarily would have equalled those incurred after a "once-and-for-all" devaluation[678]. It is only that portion of balance sheet effects which occurs as a reflex of the exchange rate's initial overshooting after a float that can be avoided altogether via full dollarisation (such overshooting, again, can be limited with the help of temporary capital controls). Moreover, even after a move towards full dollarisation, capital and exchange controls, including deposit freezes, might well have been unavoidable,

---

[675] See Schuler (2002).

[676] Dollarisation at par would have been feasible even after the run on reserves of late 2001: the central bank's foreign reserves as of late December 2001, complemented by domestic assets sold at market rates against Dollars, would have sufficed to change the monetary base into Dollars, and so would have allowed adhering to the Convertibility law. See Schuler/Hanke (2002), p. 14.

[677] Over time, the relative advantage of dollarisation will decrease, as every year of imported stability potentially increases the country's policy credibility and thus the relative costs of forgone seigniorage. See Alexander/von Furstenberg (2000), p. 219.

[678] While it can be argued that giving economic agents time to adjust to the necessary real depreciation occurring over time could smooth its negative effects, the counterargument is that the overall result could well be worsened by individuals' reactions to the expected fall in the relative prices of their goods, in terms of lower investment and output. See Roubini (2001), p. 13.

especially after the credibility-bashing policies after April 2001, as a run on reserves would have been the reflex of the severely damaged balance sheets of banks (packed with worthless government bonds on the assets side and non-performing loans on the liabilities side) even without the threat of devaluation[679]. Finally, without a seigniorage sharing agreement with the US, lost seigniorage would amount to an estimated 0.2 percent of GDP annually (with the respective seigniorage gains for the United States). While this opportunity cost is moderate because of low inflation and the low propensity to hold Pesos, it is higher than under the CBA where the bulk of Dollar reserves could be invested in interest-bearing assets[680].

The option of dollarising at a devalued exchange rate might seem relatively more appealing in that it would have confronted the economy with the unavoidable balance sheet effects largely once-and-for-all (provided a sufficient rate of devaluation) while avoiding the problems with overshooting. The caveat is that it would have entailed the same credibility losses and abrogation of property rights as those incurred with a move to a float. Being the less appropriate monetary constitution in the long run, dollarisation cum devaluation would thus have been plausibly inferior to the alternative of an "emergency exit" towards a flexible exchange rate, as sketched above[681], but possibly still superior to the events as they unfolded. The ranking in the comparison with dollarisation at par is not so clear-cut, and lastly depends on the time preference attributed to economic outcomes. If an immediate relative alleviation of adjustment costs is valued very high against potentially higher long-run costs, and if there is the expectation that the potential long-run costs can, in addition, be moderated in the course of time via an orderly and relatively favourable debt restructuring and subsequent apt fiscal and structural policies, a move towards dollarisation at par might seem superior to the dollarisation cum devaluation option[682].

---

[679] See Roubini (2001), p. 19.

[680] See Hanke/Schuler (1999). Alexander/von Furstenberg (2000), pp. 216 and 221, give a higher estimate, with 0.3 to 0.35 percent of GDP.

[681] "Since that credibility will be lost anyway by devaluation, why lock the country into an inappropriate currency regime?" Krugman (2001a).

[682] An appealing proposal of full dollarisation at par, designed to contain the long-run costs, has been made by Schuler/Hanke. According to this study, an exit towards official dollarisation would have been conceivable even at the turn of the year 2001/02. Among a variety of practical advice to model the move towards full dollarisation in the midst of chaos, a solution is given for the vexing problem of how to smooth further deflation and allow for recovery within the monetary

However, the question remains of whether Argentina would have been served well in the long run if surrendering its monetary autonomy to the US Federal Reserve, and renouncing any formal lender of last resort support[683]. With a view to Argentina's history, there is every reason to expect more responsible monetary policies even from an expansive-minded Fed, than from any conceivable Argentine central bank with a floating or intermediate exchange rate regime. The decisive question is whether, with official dollarisation, the additional hurdles in the way of an exit would have sufficed to provide the decisive push towards inescapably "condemning" the country to responsible fiscal and microeconomic policies, designed to grant sustainability and to smooth adjustment to external shocks. The experience with the CBA makes for anything but an optimistic answer[684].

Given, first, the fundamental inappropriateness of a monetary union with the US, second, the significant adjustment needs received as a legacy from previous political irresponsibility, and third, doubts of whether Argentina would be able bring forth better future policies, it was probably the better option for Argentina, from a long-run perspective, to take the exit from the CBA towards flexible exchange rates, although the move could have been done vastly better.

---

straitjacket of dollarisation: with a move towards free banking, i.e. the encouragement of competitive note issue by private banks (paper money denominated in Dollars, which would be, like traveller's cheques, not forced legal tender), overall liquidity would increase and exchange controls would be largely dispensable as confidence in the banking system could be regained quickly (after all: "Central banking is central planning in money, and central planning works as poorly in money as it does in agriculture and industry." Schuler/Hanke (1999), p. 411). Though too late to avoid sovereign default, full dollarisation would have "quarantined" the government's financial problems and so limited their damage to the rest of the economy; coupled with fiscal reform including comprehensive tax reductions these measures could have spurred economic growth. Moreover, as they argue, dollarisation would have encouraged Argentina to extend the liberalisation and reform processes it started in the 1990s. See Schuler/Hanke (2002). See also de la Torre et al. (2002) with their similar proposal of dollarisation to be followed over time by the introduction of greater flexibility, including through "pesification at the margin".

[683] The independence of the US Federal Reserve to conduct a nationally oriented monetary policy without having to react to liquidity pressures from dollarised countries is part of the very stability promise of dollarisation.

[684] See Eichengreen (2001b). The belief that economic reform remained insufficient because the CBA remained less than credible, and that dollarisation would decisively alter the framework in increasing credibility, fits ill with the overall evidence for high credibility (even claimed "excess credibility") of Convertibility in Argentina, especially during those years, after 1995, in which the bulk of economic, especially fiscal, policy legacies has its origin.

# 6 Conclusion

This treatise has focussed on this latest Argentine experience of exchange rate based stabilisation. To that end, it has explored the characteristics and dynamics of high inflations in general, and analyzed their manifestation in Argentina during the 1980s, the country's so-called "lost decade". After several failed stabilisation attempts and two bouts of hyperinflation, the currency board arrangement by which the government legally tied the domestic currency to the US-Dollar provided a consequential and highly effective stabilisation tool, which arguably was, short of official dollarisation, the only stabilisation option left. For the sake of foundation and complete understanding of the functioning of a currency board, the theory of currency boards has been expounded. The importance of complying macroeconomic, especially fiscal, as well as microeconomic policies accompanying a currency board has been deducted. Given the absence of the devaluation option as well as the restricted lender of last resort capacity, the dangers arising from irresponsible fiscal policies, on the one hand, and from external shocks, on the other, have become evident.

The analysis of the Argentine CBA's configuration has yielded its assessment as an institutionally highly credible, though in various aspects unorthodox CBA, which however, given the country's structural and trade characteristics, could not be considered an optimal long-term solution. The depiction of the economic reforms accompanying the "Plan Convertibilidad" has hinted at some of them staying badly insufficient and putting the CBA's sustainability at risk. Argentina's economic performance during the 1990s has been depicted with its spectacular stabilisation boom of the early 90s, the momentous Tequila crisis, the second expansionary phase, the deep recession activated by the series of external shocks of the late 90s, and the country's economic, political and social implosion accompanied by public default and the collapse of the CBA at the turn of the year 2001/02.

The analysis of the causes of the CBA's tragic collapse has yielded a complex picture of interacting factors, among them invaliding factors that had created multiple vulnerabilities over years, and triggering factors that unfolded their worst potential in meeting such vulnerable conditions. Chronic fiscal imbalances have been shown to stand at the centre of these vulnerabilities, having developed into a debt load unsustainable under other than very favourable conditions, and being responsible for much of the Peso's overvaluation. Among the various insufficient institutional reforms, accordingly, those stand out that failed to improve the fiscal performance, led by the unsatisfactory tax reforms and, above all, the still untackled federal fiscal relations with their highly perverse fiscal outcomes. Less immediately obvious, differential monetary policies within MERCOSUR, even before Brazil's devaluation in early 1999, have been shown to have undermined both countries' fixed exchange rate regimes, and to vastly increase Argentina's exposedness to external shocks. It has been argued that labour market rigidities, though eased too little and adding to the country's deeper vulnerabilities, often tend to be overemphasised in their responsibility for the crisis, while other institutional inadequacies, such as unsatisfactory industrial and privatisation policies as well as a lack of concern for education and social policies contributed as least as much to Argentina's lack of institutional insurance against adverse shocks. So, when the capital stop in the wake of the late 90s' emerging economies' crises, helped by the trade effects of Brazil's devaluation and the appreciating Dollar, hit Argentina, these vulnerabilities were unmasked, and the ensuing recession threatened to render public and private debt and/or the fixed exchange rate unsustainable – as held by the Sudden Stop thesis which condenses Argentina's vulnerabilities to its closedness, its indebtedness, and the currency mismatches in the balance sheets of much of its economy. It has been argued that, while default and devaluation could have been avoided through determined action, plausibly as late as in early 2001, politics proved unable to bring forward such action, and instead provided the ultimate triggers with some grave mistakes. Against these home-made blunders, reproaches directed towards the IMF or towards the "Washington Consensus", though in certain respects justified, are bound to pale. The contemplation of missed opportunities, i.e. of options for a less costly exit from the CBA, has yielded the sobering conclusion that almost any of these options would have been preferable to the exit actually undergone in early 2002.

### Some Lessons

The case of Argentina corroborates some important lessons. The first is about the dangers inherent in any exchange rate based stabilisation, and especially in a CBA: though more efficient than disinflation strategies that rely on a lengthy build-up of monetary credibility, in delivering credibility quickly and thus facilitating stable growth earlier, pegged exchange rates bear the potential of making themselves vulnerable by encouraging foreign indebtedness, currency mismatches, and overvaluation. Hence the wisdom that, if a CBA is adopted, it should remain a temporary arrangement, either aiming at an exit as early and "soft" as possible towards more exchange rate and thus policy flexibility, or else giving way to the utmost commitment in the shape of a monetary union or its unilateral variant of complete dollarisation. In failing to do either, an economy risks to buy stability against probable future instability. The more far-reaching implication of this wisdom, and of Argentina's and other countries' experiences with more or less hard pegs[685] (and a CBA contains, though it is often lumped together with official dollarisation, still only a peg to a stable currency, not a stable currency itself) is that the secular tendency of global exchange rate regimes "hollowing in the middle" [686] (i.e. moving ever more towards the speculation proof corner solutions of either freely floating or definitely fixed exchange rates in the form of monetary unions or official dollarisation) is likely to intensify with increasing global financial integration. The Argentine experience also substantiates the finding that, beyond the immediate stabilisation needs of extremely eroded high inflation economies, the choice of exchange rate is of second order importance to the development of good fiscal, financial, and monetary institutions in producing macroeconomic success in emerging market countries.

Thus, the second lesson from Argentina concerns the towering importance of a sustainable fiscal stance for emerging economies increasingly integrated in world financial markets, or, in other words, the necessity to run fiscal surpluses during upswings to potentialise non-debt financed countercyclical fiscal policies. The importance of sound fiscal policies is increasing with the rigour of the chosen exchange rate regime, i.e. with the distance from the option to devalue, reaching its extreme for a country forming part of a monetary union or being officially dollarised. The importance of lower overall debt levels is paramount for closed economies suffering from "original sin", i.e. unable to place local currency debt on international capital markets. Currency mismatches in fiscal and/or corporate balance sheets create a huge leverage to crisis when a real depreciation revalues debt in real terms. They are a recipe for disaster in case of devaluation.

Several other aspects add to the indispensability of a solid fiscal stance. For one, high indebtedness risks to exert at some point a pernicious influence on a country's liquidity position, so that a vicious circle develops which emanates from

---

[685] Empirically, intermediate exchange rate regimes have recorded more crises than extreme regimes. See Eichengreen (2001b).

[686] See, e.g., Fischer (2001), Alexander/von Furstenberg (2000), Edwards (2000), or Wagner (2000).

higher perceived credit risk reducing the maturities of new debt granted and which, with the deteriorating maturity structure, fires back on higher credit risk again. This vicious circle can only be avoided when a sustainable fiscal stance keeps credit risk sufficiently low so as to allow for the maintenance of a crisis proof maturity structure. In-crisis debt restructurings that trade short-term relief against higher future interest and capital payments only risk undermining the hoped-for medium-term recovery and offer no fundamental improvement.

The need for low public indebtedness receives further emphasis by the fact that fiscal consolidation under stress, i.e. in the midst of recession, is a precarious task to undertake. Although expansionary fiscal consolidation must not be an oxymoron but, on the contrary, the correction of a perceived unsustainable fiscal situation may bring down interest rates and increase demand (possibly helped by the Ricardian equivalence in reverse, i.e. by freeing demand from the suppressing expectations of higher future tax burdens), engineering such expansionary restriction is highly tricky. It depends on several preconditions, among them the reliance on expenditure cuts rather than on tax increases (which Argentina got wrong during Tequila and again with the "impuestazo" in 2000, and which it got right too late, with the "déficit cero" plan in mid-2001), and a strong political backing and high confidence in the maintenance of the fiscal slimming process[687]. Obviously, Argentina was unable to bring forth these requirements, of which, as has been argued, political factors were certainly more damaging than the rigid currency board framework per se: first, the lack of unanimity in tackling the fiscal malaise, and second, political meddling with the own commitments proved a mixture that stabbed the last chance of consolidation.

Moreover, the case of Argentina emphasises the importance of emerging economies' efforts to increase their openness to trade, i.e. to increase their share of exports relative to domestic absorption. When the latter is financed mostly from export revenues rather than from capital imports, the size of real exchange rate swings after a sudden stop is reduced. A higher share of tradables in output also reduces currency mismatches in private sector balance sheets, and so reduces the banking sector's exposedness to real exchange rate swings, thus limiting the probability and extent of necessary financial sector bailouts. The encouragement of FDI, the privatisation and streamlining of public enterprises and banks, and industrial policies aiming at increasing international competitiveness are still, and

---

[687] See Eichengreen (2001a), pp. 17f.

increasingly, desirable policies for any emerging economy. An important legacy of the late emerging markets' crises is that ideological blinders against capital controls aiming at reducing short-term capital inflows, and even against the idea of taxing foreign exchange transactions (the Tobin tax[688]), have been widely put off, and reducing speculative inflows has become a presentable endeavour.

Further lessons have to be drawn from the international financial institutions' experience with Argentina. Chronically torn between the options of either leaving a country's solvency problems to the markets (including leaving a big emerging market debtor to default, risking contagion, and endangering the global economy) or bailing it out (and thus fuelling moral hazard by letting capital markets collect risk premia without bearing the risk), the IMF hoped to be able to minimise the drawbacks of both options with the catalytic approach, which turned out to have failed in Argentina. The need for new approaches in international finance has been articulated since the late 1990s' crises, and several proposals have been made. One of them is the idea of a "sovereign Chapter 11", i.e. an internationally acknowledged standard sovereign bankruptcy procedure including the installation of a bankruptcy court for sovereign debtors that would shelter them from disruptive legal action of creditors until an orderly debt restructuring would be carved out[689]. A less ambitious, though easier to realise, approach is the adoption of collective action clauses in new bond issues so that creditors lose their right to sue individually, and the cost and duration of restructurings are reduced. Indeed, such collective action clauses are meanwhile standard in emerging-market sovereign bonds[690]. Still another idea is the Lerrick-Meltzer proposal according to which the IMF would, for a crisis government, ensure liquidity in the market for defaulted debt, in order to obtain a market conform reduction of debt to a sustainable level, and avoiding panic and contagion[691].

---

[688] See e.g. Frankel (1996), p. 156.

[689] See e.g. Krueger (2002).

[690] Argentina has included collective clauses in the bonds issued in the debt restructuring, as well as aggregated voting provisions which allow for amendments in key terms with the vote of a pre-defined majority of the aggregate principal amount outstanding. See Gelpern (2005), p. 6.

[691] See Lerrick/Meltzer (2001), but also the IMF Staff Note of April 2002, available at <http://www.imf.org/External/NP/psi/2002/eng/041002.htm>, and Schuler/Hanke (2002), pp. 34f, who propose an extension of the Lerrick-Meltzer proposal to assets of stressed banks.

## Argentina's New Challenge

Argentina today faces not much less of a challenge than it did 15 years ago. True, devaluation has opened a valve and removed overvaluation, and the "flexible" exchange rate (indeed, it is, at the time being, held intentionally undervalued) potentialises more degrees of, at least temporary, freedom in economic policy[692]. But, for the long run, such freedom depends on the very same fundamental preconditions that would have been required to keep the CBA sustainable[693].

Although four years after the CBA's collapse, export (especially the agrarian and tourism) sectors are booming, foreign reserves are flowing in, the pre-crisis GDP level has been reached again, unemployment is half of its peak level, and public as well as current accounts are comfortably in surplus, none of the microeconomic deficiencies inherited, few of the numerous breaches of contract caused by devaluation, and little of the serious derangements added through the government's crisis management have been tackled as yet. The crisis and its aftermath would have offered a chance to renegotiate the federal fiscal redistribution mechanism, and to convert the tax system towards a higher reliance on income taxation and higher tax compliance. However, little more than some questionable patchwork has been done in both fields[694].

The public debt to GDP ratio is, after the restructuring of over 100 billion Dollars of debt plus interest accrued, still dangerously high at 75 percent. The financial system is only slowly recovering from paralysis[695]. Long-term credit is still virtually non-existent. Most utility tariffs are still at their 2001 levels (while wholesale prices have risen by 80 percent since that time), covering operational costs with luck, but none of the big investments needed. With the capacity constraints increasingly felt, inflation is accelerating again: the annual inflation rate has surpassed the 10 percent mark in late 2005.

---

[692] See Frankel/Schmukler/Servén (2002), p. 31.

[693] "In general, it was not the exchange rate regime alone that was the fundamental source of precrisis vulnerability and of subsequent substantial damage. And changing the exchange rate regime will not automatically correct (although, [...], it may help ameliorate) these other critical problems." Mussa et al. (2000), p. 22.

[694] As to the federal fiscal redistribution, provincial revenues have been merely fixed at their 2003 revenue levels.

[695] "Since we didn't have money, we had to offer time." Alfonso Prat-Gay, the then central bank governor, cited after N.N. (2004), p. 10.

Monetary restriction is now the means to avoid a relapse into chronic high inflation. This means reining in monetary expansion (itself the result of the absorption of 6 billion Pesos of quasi monies, and continuously fed by incoming export revenue) and strapping growth, mostly by maintaining public, and increasing private, saving; the development of domestic capital markets is badly needed[696]. A more restrictive monetary stance may be imaginable as long as the economy is comfortably growing. It is anyone's guess where Argentine politics will turn to when the catch-up growth slows down and/or external conditions start to worsen[697].

Worryingly, Néstor Kirchner's policies, always fickle and difficult to interpret, have moved from outwardly populist, but economically mostly orthodox and arguably sensible in many instances, to a more factual left-leaning nationalist stance. Since the October 2005 congressional elections, Kirchner has not only changed to an even more provocative rhetoric vis-à-vis the IMF, the US, and foreign investors (which he regularly blames flatly for Argentina's crisis), but also increasingly fleshes his rhetoric with action. His sacking of the well-renowned economy minister Lavagna in November 2005 (and replacement by a low-profile crony), his demonstrative turning to the Venezuelan president with his ideas of a Bolivarian revolution re-issued, as well as his latest decree to pay back the IMF in full until the end of 2005 (yet another encroachment upon central bank independence), all bolster his demonstrative repudiation of the global economy's functioning principles. They not only leave little reason to expect politics bringing forward the central reforms necessary to facilitate sustainable growth in the long run, but also compromise Argentina's basic outward orientation, and further endanger its development prospects. Possible hopes attached to MERCOSUR and its potential to stimulate efficiency enhancing economic policies[698] have been frustrated also by the acceptance of Venezuela as a full member, which seems to redress regional solidarity towards mainly political ends while putting economic goals on hold (at least those running deeper than cheap oil or ready government credit). These recent developments do not leave much ground for hopes that

---

[696] See de la Torre et al. (2003), p. 27.

[697] The central bank is presently changing course from the quantitative targeting policy adopted after 2001 to inflation targeting, with the actual target band set between five and eight percent. See the BCRA's monetary programme for 2005, <http://www.bcra.gov.ar/pdfs/polmon/ProgMonPresenta2005.pdf>.

[698] See, e.g., Mussa et al. (2000), Hochreiter/Schmidt-Hebbel/Winckler (2002), or Belke/Gros (2002).

Argentina might, in the pursuit of economic sustainability, soon live up to the claim of getting the "serious country" its publicity experts want it to be. Nor does the worst expectation, a relapse into chronic high inflation, seem a completely absurd idea.

# Bibliography

Abramovitz, M. (1986): Catching Up, Forging Ahead, and Falling Behind, in: Journal of Economic History, 46, 2, pp. 385-406.

Alesina, A., and Barro, R.J. (2001): Dollarization, in: American Economic Association, Papers and Proceedings, 91, 2, pp. 381-385.

Alexander, V., and von Furstenberg, G.M. (2000): Monetary Unions – a superior alternative to full dollarization in the long run, in: The North American Journal of Economics and Finance, 11, pp. 205-225.

Altimir, O., and Beccaria, L. (2000a): Distribución del ingreso en la Argentina, in: Heymann, D., and Kosacoff, B. (eds.): La Argentina de los Noventa – Desempeño económico en un contexto de reformas, I. Buenos Aires, pp. 425-521.

Altimir, O., and Beccaria, L. (2000b): El mercado de trabajo bajo el nuevo régimen económico en Argentina, in: Heymann, D., and Kosacoff, B. (eds.): La Argentina de los Noventa – Desempeño económico en un contexto de reformas, I. Buenos Aires, pp. 331-424.

Andrade, J.P., Falcão Silva, M.L., and Trautwein, H.-M. (2005): Disintegrating effects of monetary policies in the MERCOSUR, in: Structural Change and Economic Dynamics, 16 (2005), pp. 65-89.

Artana, D., López Murphy, R., and Navajas, F. (2003): A Fiscal Policy Agenda, in: Kuczynski, P.-P., and Williamson, J. (eds.): After the Washington Consensus. Restarting Growth and Reform in Latin America, Institute for International Economics, Washington, D.C., March 2003, pp. 75-101.

Artana, D., Navajas, F., and Urbiztondo, S. (1998): Regulation and Contractual Adaptation in Public Utilities: The Case of Argentina. Washington, D.C., June 1998-No° IFM-115.

Baliño, Th.J.T., and Enoch, Ch. (1997): Currency Board Arrangements – Issues and Experiences, in: IMF Occasional Paper, 151.

Ball, L., and Romer, D. (1991): Sticky Prices as Coordination Failure, in: American Econmic Review, 81, June, pp. 539-552.

Begg, D. (2002): Growth, Integration, and Macroeconomic Policy Design: Some Lessons for Latin America. Paper prepared for the conference "Monetary Union: Theory, EMU Experience, and Prospects for Latin America" organized by the Oesterreichische Nationalbank, the University of Vienna, and the Banco Central de Chile, April 15-16, 2002.

Belke, A., and Gros, D. (2002): Monetary Integration in the Southern Cone:

Mercosur Is Not Like the EU? Study presented at the Conference "Towards Regional Currency Areas", Santiago de Chile, March 26-27, 2002, at the Conference "Monetary Union: Theory, EMU Experience, and Prospects for Latin America", April 15-16, 2002, and at the Conference "Exchange Rates, Economic Integration, and the International Economy", Ryerson University/Toronto, May 17-19, 2002.

Bennett, A.G.G. (1994): Currency Boards: Issues and Experiences. in: Baliño, T.J. (ed.): Frameworks for Monetary Stability. Washington, pp. 186-212.

Bernholz, P. (1995a): Currency Competition, Inflation, Gresham's Law and Exchange Rate, in: Siklos, P.L. (ed.): Great Inflations of the 20th Century – Theories, Policies and Evidence. Aldershot: Edward Elgar, pp. 97-124.

Bernholz, P. (1995b): Necessary and Sufficient Conditions to End Hyperinflations, in: Siklos, P.L. (ed.): Great Inflations of the 20th Century – Theories, Policies and Evidence. Aldershot: Edward Elgar, pp. 257-287.

Bernholz, P. (2003): Monetary Regimes and Inflation. Cheltenham (UK) and Northampton (USA), 2003.

Blanchard, O.J. (1997): Comment on "Stopping Inflations, Big and Small", in: Journal of Money, Credit and Banking, 29, 4, pp. 778-782.

Blejer, M.I. (1983): On the Anatomy of Inflation – The Variability of Relative Commodity Prices in Argentina, in: Journal of Money, Credit and Banking, 15, 4, pp. 469-482.

Bordo, M.D., and Jonung, L. (2001): A Return to the Convertibility Principle? Monetary and Fiscal Regimes in Historical Perspective: The International Evidence, in: Leijonhufvud, A. (ed.): Monetary Theory and Policy Experience. Chippenham, Wiltshire, pp. 225-283.

Broda, C. (2001): Coping with Terms-of-Trade Shocks: Pegs versus Floats, in: American Economic Association, Papers and Proceedings, 91, 2, pp. 376-380.

Burki, J., and Perry, G.E. (1998): Beyond the Washington Consensus: Institutions Matter. Washington, DC: Worldbank.

Cagan, P. (1956): The Monetary Dynamics of Hyperinflation, in: M. Friedman, ed.: Studies in the Quantity Theory of Money, Chicago, University of Chicago Press.

Cagan, P. (1989a): Hyperinflation, in: Eatwell, J., Milgate, M., and Newman, P. (Ed.): The New Palgrave: Money. London and Basingstoke, pp. 179-184.

Cagan, P. (1989b): Monetarism, in: Eatwell, J., Milgate, M., and Newman, P. (Ed.): The New Palgrave: Money. London and Basingstoke, pp. 195-205.

Calvo, G.A., and Mishkin, F.S. (2003):

The Mirage of Exchange Rate Regimes for Emerging Market Countries, NBER Working Paper 9808, <http://www.nber.org/papers/w9808>.

Calvo, G.A., Izquierdo, A., and Talvi, E. (2003): Sudden Stops, the Real Exchange Rate, and Fiscal Sustainability: Argentina's Lessons, NBER Working Paper 9828, <http://www.nber.org/papers/w9828>.

Canavese, A. (2001): Convertibilidad en Argentina: Funcionamiento de una Caja de Conversión Anclada al Dólar. Paper prepared for the Conference "Relaciones Económicas entre la Unión Europea y el Mercosur" organized by the Instituto de Economía Internacional (IEI), Universidad de Valencia (España), June 13-14, 2001.

Caprio, G.Jr. (1998): Banking on Crises: Expensive Lessons from Recent Financial Crises, in: World Bank, Country Economics Department, Working Paper 1979.

Caprio, G.Jr.., Dooley, M., Leipziger, D., and Walsh, C. (1996): The Lender of Last Resort Function Under a Currency Board. The Case of Argentina, in: World Bank, Country Economics Department, Working Paper 1648.

Carrera, J.E., Féliz, M., Panigo, D., and Saavedra, M. (2002): How Does Dollarization Affect Real Volatility? A General Methodology for Latin America, <http://www.isis.unlp.edu.ar>.

Catão, L. (1998): Intermediation Spreads in a Dual Currency Economy: Argentina in the 1990s, in: IMF Working Paper 98/90.

Choueiri, N., and Kaminsky, G. (1999): Has the Nature of Crises Changed? A Quarter Century of Currency Crises in Argentina, in: IMF Working Paper 99/152.

Cukierman, A.S. (1995): Rapid Inflation: Deliberate Policy or Miscalculation?, in: Siklos, P.L. (ed.): Great Inflations of the 20th Century – Theories, Policies and Evidence. Aldershot: Edward Elgar, pp. 125-182.

Davies, Glyn (2002): A History of Money. From Ancient Times to the Present Day. University of Wales Press Cardiff, 2002.

De la Torre, A., Yeyati, E.L., and Schmukler, S.L. (2002): Argentina's Financial Crisis: Floating Money, Sinking Banking, <http://www.nber.org/~confer/2002/argentina02/schmukler.pdf>.

De la Torre, A., Yeyati, E.L., and Schmukler, S.L. (2003): Living and Dying with Hard Pegs: The Rise and Fall of Argentina's Currency Board, <http://www.utdt.edu>.

Di Tella, R., and MacCulloch, R. (2004): Why Doesn't Capitalism Flow to Poor Countries?, <http://www.hbs.edu>.

Dolmas, S., and Zarazaga, C. (1996): Policy Rules and Tequila Lessons: Conclusions from an Economic Conference, in:

Federal Reserve Bank of Dallas, Southwest Economy, 6, 1996, <http://www.dallasfed.org/htm/pubs/swe/6_96.html>.

Dominguez, K.M.E., and Tesar, L.L. (2004): International Borrowing and Macroeconomic Performance in Argentina. Paper prepared for the NBER conference on International Capital Flows, December 17-18, 2004, in Santa Barbara, California.

Dornbusch, R. (2001): Fewer Monies, Better Monies, in: American Economic Association, Papers and Proceedings, 91, 2, pp. 238-242.

Dornbusch, R., Goldfajn, I., and Valdés, R.O. (1995): Currency Crises and Collapses, in: Brookings Papers on Economic Activity, pp. 219-293.

Edwards, S. (2000): Exchange Rate Regimes, Capital Flows and Crisis Prevention, Paper prepared for the NBER Conference on Economic and Financial Crises in Emerging Market Economies, held in Woodstock, October 19-12, 2000, <http://www.nber.org/~confer/2000/wisef00/edwards.pdf>.

Eichengreen, B. (1996): Vom Goldstandard zum Euro – Die Geschichte des internationalen Währungssystems. Berlin 1999, pp. 238ff.

Eichengreen, B. (2001a): Crisis Prevention and Management: Any New Lessons from Argentina and Turkey?
Background Paper for the World Bank's Global Development Finance 2002, <http://emlab.berkeley.edu/users/eichengr/POLICY.HTML>.

Eichengreen, B. (2001b): What problems can dollarization solve?, in: Journal of Policy Modeling, 23, pp. 267-277.

Eichengreen, B., Hausmann, R., and Panizza, U. (2003): Currency Mismatches, Debt Intolerance and Original Sin: Why They Are Not the Same and Why it Matters. NBER Working Paper 10036, <http://www.nber.org/papers/w10036>.

Ennis, H.M., and Pinto, S.M. (2002): Privatization and Income Distribution in Argentina, <http://www.be.wvu.edu/divecon/econ/pinto/Privatization%20in%20Argentina%20final.PDF>.

Enoch, C., and Gulde, A.-M. (1998): Are Currency Boards a Cure for All Monetary Problems?, in: IMF Finance & Development, 35, 4.

Enoch, C.E., and Gulde, A.-M. (1997): Making a Currency Board Operational, in: IMF Paper on Policy Analysis and Assessment, 97, 10.

Fanelli, J.M., and González Rozada, M. (1998): Convertibilidad, Volatilidad y Estabilidad Macroeconómica en Argentina, CEDES, Buenos Aires, 1998.

Feldstein, M. (2002): Argentina's Fall. Lessons from the Latest Financial Crisis, in:

Foreign Affairs, 81, 2, pp. 8-14.

Fischer, St. (2001): Exchange Rate Regimes: Is the Bipolar View Correct?, in: International Monetary Fund, Distinguished Lecture on Economics in Government. New Orleans, January 06, 2001.

Frankel, J., Schmukler, S.L., and Servén, L. (2002): Global Transmission of Interest Rates: Monetary Independence and Currency Regime, NBER Working Paper 8828, <http://www.nber.org/papers/w8828>.

Frankel, J.A. (1996): Recent Exchange-Rate Experience and Proposals for Reform, in: American Economic Review, Papers and Proceedings, 86, pp. 153-158.

Frenkel, R., and González Rozada, M. (1999): Balance of Payments Liberalization. Effects on Growth and Employment in Argentina, CEDES, Buenos Aires, 1999.

Freytag, A. (1998): Einige Anmerkungen zur Wahl der Reservewährung eines Currency Boards, in: Zeitschrift für Wirtschaftspolitik, 47, pp.3-19.

Fuhrmann, W. (1999): Zur Theorie des Currency Boards, in: Zeitschrift für Wirtschaftspolitik, 48, pp. 85-104.

Fuhrmann, W., and Richert, R. (1995): Ein Währungssystem mit einem Currency Board, in: WISU, 24, pp. 1035-1039.

Galiani, S., Gertler, P., Schargrodsky, E., and Sturzenegger, F. (2003): The Benefits and Costs of Privatization in Argentina: A Microeconomic Analysis, in: Inter-American Development Bank, Latin American Research Network, Research Network Working Paper R-454.

Galiani, S., Heymann, D., and Tommaso, M. (2002): Missed Expectations: The Argentine Convertibility. William Davidson Institute Working Paper no. 515.

Ganapolsky, E.J.J., and Schmukler, S.L. (1998): Crisis Management in Capital Markets: The Impact of Argentine Policy during the Tequila Effect, in: World Bank, Country Economics Department, Working Paper 1951.

Gelpern, Anna (2005): After Argentina, in: Institute for International Economics, Policy Briefs Number PB05-2.

Gerchunoff, P., and Aguirre, H. (2004): La Política Económica de Kirchner en la Argentina: Varios Estilos, una Sola Agenda, <http://www.realinstitutoelcano.org/documentos/122.asp>.

Ghosh, A.R., Gulde, A.-M., and Wolf, H.C. (1998): Currency Boards: The Ultimate Fix?, in: IMF Working Paper 98/8.

González Rozada, M., and Menendez, A. (2002): Why have Poverty and Income Inequality Increased so much? Argentina 1991-2002, <http://www.utdt.edu>.

Guidotti, P. (2004): Global Finance, Macroeconomic Performance, and Policy

Response in Latin America: Lessons from the 1990s, <http://www.utdt.edu>.

Gulde, A.-M., Kähkönen, J., and Keller, P. (2000): Pros and Cons of Currency Board Arrangements in the Lead-up to EU-Accession and Participation in the Euro Zone, in: IMF Policy Discussion Paper 00/1.

Hanke, St.H. (1999): How to Make the Dollar Argentina's Currency, in: The Wall Street Journal, February 19, 1999.

Hanke, St.H. (2000): The Disregard for Currency Board Realities, in: Cato Journal, 20, 1, pp. 49-59.

Hanke, St.H. (2002): Argentina's Blunders, in: National Post, January 5, 2002.

Hanke, St.H., and Schuler, K. (1999): A Monetary Constitution for Argentina: Rules for Dollarization, in: Cato Journal, 18, 3, pp. 405-419.

Hanke, St.H., and Schuler, K. (2000): Currency Boards for Developing Countries: A Handbook, in: International Center for Economic Growth, ICS Press, San Francisco 1994, updated June 2000.

Heymann, D. (2000): Políticas de reforma y comportamiento macroeconómico, in: Heymann, D., and Kosacoff, B. (eds.): La Argentina de los Noventa – Desempeño económico en un contexto de reformas, I. Buenos Aires, pp. 37-176.

Heymann, D., and Kosacoff, B. (2000): Comentarios generales sobre el comportamiento de la economía y temas abiertos al finalizar los noventa, in: Heymann, D., and Kosacoff, B. (eds.): La Argentina de los Noventa – Desempeño económico en un contexto de reformas, I. Buenos Aires, pp. 9-36.

Heymann, D., and Leijonhufvud, A. (1995): High Inflation. Oxford, 1995.

Hicks, J. (1967): Critical Essays in Monetary Theory. Oxford, 1967.

Hochreiter, E., Schmidt-Hebbel, K., and Winckler. G. (2002): Monetary Union: European Lessons, Latin American Prospects. Paper prepared for the conference "Monetary Union: Theory, EMU Experience, and Prospects for Latin America" organized by the Oesterreichische Nationalbank, the University of Vienna, and the Banco Central de Chile, April 15-16, 2002.

Hopenhayn, H.A., and Neumeyer, P.A. (2003): The Argentine Great Depression 1975-1990, <http://www.utdt.edu>.

Huber, E., and Solt, F. (2004): Successes and Failures of Neoliberalism, in: Latin American Research Review, 39, 3, pp. 150-164.

Humpage, O.F., and McIntire, J.M. (1995): An Introduction to Currency Boards, in: Federal Reserve Bank of Cleveland, Economic Review, 31, 2, pp. 2-11.

Humphrey, Th. M. (1998): Mercantilists and Classicals: Insights from Doctrinal History, in: Federal Reserve Bank of Richmond, Annual Report 1998,

<http://www.rich.frb.org/pubs/ar/1998/>.

IMF Independent Evaluation Office (2004): The IMF and Argentina, 1991-2001, IMF, Independent Evaluation Office. Washington, D.C., 2004.

IMF Staff Team (1999): Experimental Report on Transparency Practices: Argentina, in: IMF, Experimental Reports on Observance of Standards and Codes, April 15, 1999.

Ireland, P.N. (1997): Stopping Inflations, Big and Small, in: Journal of Money, Credit and Banking, 29, 4, pp. 759-775.

Joint Economic Committee (2005), Research Report # 109-7, May 2005, <http://www.house.gov/jec/publications/109/rr1097.pdf>.

Jonas, J. (2002): Argentina: The Anatomy of a Crisis, ZEI Working Paper B02-12, <http://www.zei.de>.

Keynes, J.M. (1920): The Economic Consequences of Peace, Macmillan Press, London.

Kiguel, M.A. (1989): Budget Deficits, Stability, and the Monetary Dynamics of Hyperinflation, in: Journal of Money, Credit and Banking, 21, 2, pp. 148-157.

Kiguel, M.A. (1992): La inflación en Argentina : política de « alto y siga » desde el Plan austral, in : Boletín del CMLA, 38, mayo/junio 1992, pp. 103-120.

Kiguel, M.A. (1999): The Argentine Currency Board, Universidad del CEMA, Sérias económicas, 152.

Kiguel, M.A., and Neumeyer, P.A. (1995): Seigniorage and Inflation: The Case of Argentina, in: Journal of Money, Credit and Banking, 27, 3, pp. 672-682.

Krueger, A.O. (2002): A New Approach to Sovereign Debt Restructuring, available at <http://www.imf.org>.

Krugman, P. (2001a):
Argentina's Money Monomania, <http://www.wws.princeton.edu/~pkrugman/>.

Krugman, P. (2001b): Notes on Depreciation, the Yen, and the Argentino <http://www.wws.princeton.edu/~pkrugman/>.

Laidler, D. (1989): The Bullionist Controversy, in: Eatwell, J., Milgate, M., and Newman, P. (Ed.): The New Palgrave: Money. London and Basingstoke, pp. 60-71.

Lanata, J. (2004): ADN – Mapa genético de los defectos argentinos. Buenos Aires, 2004.

Lavagna, R. (2004): Statement to the Executive Board Members from the Governor for Argentina, His Excellency Roberto Lavagna, on the IEO Evaluation of the Role of the Fund in Argentina, 1991-2001, in: IMF Independent Evaluation Office

(2004): The IMF and Argentina, 1991-2001, IMF, Independent Evaluation Office. Washington, D.C., 2004.

Leijonhufvud, A. (1990): Extreme Monetary Instability: High Inflations, in: Universität Hohenheim, Diskussionsbeiträge aus dem Institut für Volkswirtschaftslehre, 53.

Lerrick, A., and Meltzer, A.H. (2001): Beyond IMF Bailouts: Default without Disruption, in: Carnegie Mellon, Quarterly Economic Report, May 2001, pp. 1-4, <http://www.house.gov/jec/imf/gailliot.pdf>.

Logue, D.E., and Sweeney, R.J. (1981): Inflation and Real Growth: Some Empirical Results, in: Journal of Money, Credit and Banking, 13, 4, pp. 497-501.

López-Murphy, R., Artana, D., and Navajas, F. (2003): The Argentine Economic Crisis, in: Cato Journal, 23, 1, pp. 23-28.

Marshall, A. (2004): Labour Market Policies and Regulations in Argentina, Brazil and Mexico: Programmes and Impacts, in: Consejo Nacional de Investigaciones Científicas y Técnicas and Instituto de Desarrollo Económico y Social Buenos Aires, Employment Strategy Papers 2004/13.

McCallum, B.T. (1984): Are Bond-Financed Deficits Inflationary? A Ricardian Analysis, in: Journal of Political Economy, 26, 1, pp. 123-135.

Mussa, M. (2002): Argentina and the Fund: Fro Triumph to Tragedy, <http://www.iie.com/papers/mussa0302-1.htm>.

Mussa, M., Masson, P., Swoboda, A., Jadresic, E., Mauro, P., and Berg, A. (2000): Exchange Rate Regimes in an Increasingly Integrated World Economy, in: IMF Occasional Paper, 193.

Muth, J.F. (1961): Rational Expectations and the Theory of Price Movements, in: Econometrica 29, July, 315-335.

N.N. (1994): Back in the Saddle – A Survey of Argentina, in: The Economist, November 26, 1994.

N.N. (2004): The Long Road Back – A Survey of Argentina, in: The Economist, June 5, 2004.

Nunnenkamp, P. (1999): Latin America after the Currency Crash in Brazil – Why the Optimists May be Wrong, in: Kieler Diskussionsbeiträge, Institut für Weltwirtschaft Kiel, 337.

Oppers, S.E. (2000): Dual Currency Boards: A Proposal for Currency Stability, in: IMF Working Paper 00/199.

Pastor, M., and Wise, C. (1999): Stabilization and its Discontents: Argentina's Economic Restructuring in the 1990s, in: World Development, 27, 3, pp. 477-503.

Porzecanski, A. (2003): Argentina: The Root Cause of the Disaster,

<http://www.nber.org/%7Econfer/2002/argentina02/porzecanski.pdf>.

Pou, P. (2000): Argentina's Structural Reforms of the 1990s, in: Finance & Development, 37, 1, pp. 13-15.

Powell, A. (2002): Argentina's Avoidable Crisis: Bad Luck, Bad Management, Bad Politics, Bad Advice. Paper presented at the Brookings Trade Conference, Washington DC, May 2nd, 2002.

Reinhart, C.M., Rogoff, K.S., and Savastano M.A. (2003): Debt Intolerance. NBER Working Paper 9908, <http://www.nber.org/papers/w9908>.

República Argentina, Poder Ejecutivo Nacional (2001): Decreto 1311/2001, in: Boletín Oficial 26/10/2001 – ADLA 2001, E, 5556.

República Argentina, Poder Ejecutivo Nacional (2002): Decreto 401/2002, in: Boletín Oficial 05/03/2002 – ADLA 2002, B, 1678.

República Argentina, Poder Legislativo Nacional (1991): Ley 23928, in: Boletín Oficial 28/03/1991 – ADLA 1991 – B, 1752.

República Argentina, Poder Legislativo Nacional (1992): Ley 24144, in: Boletín Oficial 22/10/1992 – ADLA 1992 – D, 3892.

República Argentina, Poder Legislativo Nacional (1995): Ley 24485, in: Boletín Oficial 29/09/1995 – ADLA 1995 – E, 6957.

República Argentina, Poder Legislativo Nacional (2001): Ley 25445, in: Boletín Oficial 25/06/2001 – ADLA 2001 – D, 4043.

Rofman, A.B. (1997): Convertibilidad y desocupación en la Argentina de los '90 – Análisis de una relación inseparable. Buenos Aires 1997.

Rojas-Suárez, L. (2003): Monetary Policy and Exchange Rates: Guiding Principles for a Sustainable Regime, in: Kuczynski, P.-P., and Williamson, J. (eds.): After the Washington Consensus. Restarting Growth and Reform in Latin America, Institute for International Economics, Washington, D.C., March 2003, pp. 123-155.

Rose, A.K., and van Wincoop, E. (2001): National Money as a Barrier to International Trade: The Real Case for Currency Union, in: American Economic Association, Papers and Proceedings, 91, 2, pp. 386-390..

Roubini, N. (1998a): An Introduction to Open Economy Macroeconomics, Currency Crises and the Asian Crisis, <http://www.stern.nyu.edu/globalmacro/>.

Roubini, N. (1998b): The Case Against Currency Boards: Debunking 10 Myths about the Benefits of Currency Boards, <http://www.stern.nyu.edu/globalmacro/>.

Roubini, N. (2001): Should Argentina Dollarize or Float?
The Pros and Cons of Alternative Exchange Rate Regimes and their Implications for Domestic and Foreign Debt Restructuring and Reduction,

<http://www.stern.nyu.edu/globalmacro/>.

Saiegh, S.M., and Tommasi, M. (1999): Why is Argentina's Fiscal Federalism so Inefficient? Entering the Labyrinth, in: Journal of Applied Economics, II, 1, pp. 169-209.

Sanguinetti, P., Pantano, J., Posadas, J. (2002): Trade Liberalization and Export/Import Diversification in Argentina: The Role of Tariff Preferences and Economies of Scale. Paper prepared for the project "Patterns of Integration in the Global Economy: What Does Latin America Trade? What Do its Workers Do?" sponsored by the World Bank.

Sargent, Th.J. (1997): Comment on "Stopping Inflations, Big and Small", in: Journal of Money, Credit and Banking, 29, 4, pp. 776-777.

Schuler, K. (1998): Introduction to Currency Boards, <http://www.cato.org>.

Schuler, K. (2000): Basics of Dollarization, in: Joint Economic Committee Staff Report, July 1999, updated January 2000.

Schuler, K. (2002): Fixing Argentina, in: Cato Institute, Policy Analysis, 445, July 16, 2002.

Schuler, K., and Hanke, St. (2002): How to Dollarize Argentina Now, <http://www.cato.org>.

Schuler, K.A. (1992): Currency Boards. Fairfax, Virginia, 1992, <http://users.erols.com/kurrency/webdiss1.htm>.

Schumacher, L. (2000): Bank Runs and Currency Run in a System Without a Safety Net: Argentina and the "Tequila" Shock, in: Journal of Monetary Economics, 46, 1, pp. 257-277.

Schwartz, A.J. (1989): Banking School, Currency School, Free Banking School, in: Eatwell, J., Milgate, M., and Newman, P. (Ed.): The New Palgrave: Money. London and Basingstoke, pp. 41-49.

Setzer, R. (2001): Das optimale Wechselkurssystem für Argentinien. Stuttgart-Hohenheim, 2001.

Siklos, P.L. (1995): Hyperinflations: Their Origins, Development and Termination, in: Siklos, P.L. (ed.): Great Inflations of the 20th Century – Theories, Policies and Evidence. Aldershot: Edward Elgar, pp. 3-34.

Spahn, H.-P. (2001): From Gold to Euro. On Monetary Theory and the History of Currency Systems. Berlin, Heidelberg, 2001.

Stiglitz, J.E. (1998): More Instruments and Broader Goals: Moving toward the Post-Washington Consensus. United Nations University / World Institute for Development Economics Research, Helsinki.

Sturzenegger, F.A. (1994): Hyperinflation with Currency Substitution: Introducing an Indexed Currency, in: Journal of Money, Credit and Banking, 26, 3, pp. 377-395.

Vásquez, I. (1996): The Brady Plan and Market-Based Solutions to Debt Crises, in: Cato Journal, 16, 2, <http://www.cato.org>.

Végh, C.A. (1995): Stopping High Inflation: An Analytical Overview, in: Siklos, P.L. (ed.): Great Inflations of the 20th Century – Theories, Policies and Evidence. Aldershot: Edward Elgar, pp. 35-95.

Wagner, H. (2000): Which exchange rate regimes in an era of high capital mobility?, in: The North American Journal of Economics and Finance, 11, pp. 191-203.

Waisgrais, S. (2003): Wage Inequality and the Labour Market in Argentina: Labour Institutions, Supply and Demand in the Period 1980-1999, in: International Institute for Labour Studies, Discussion Paper DP/146/2003.

Walters, A. (1989): Currency Boards, in: Eatwell, J., Milgate, M., and Newman, P. (Ed.): The New Palgrave: Money. London and Basingstoke, pp. 109-114.

Williamson, J. (1995): What Role for Currency Boards?, in: Institute for International Economics, Policy Analyses in International Economics, 40.

Williamson, J. (2000): What Should the World Bank Think about the Washington Consensus?, in: The World Bank Research Observer, vol. 15, No. 2, pp. 251-64, <http://www.worldbank.org/research/journals/wbro/obsaug00/pdf/(6)Williamson.pd f>.

Williamson, J. (2002): Did the Washington Consensus Fail?, Outline of speech at the Center for Strategic & International Studies, Washington, DC, November 6, 2002, <http://www.iie.com/publications/papers/paper.cfm?researchid=488>

Williamson, J. (2003): Overview – An Agenda for Restarting Growth and Reform, in: Kuczynski, P.-P., and Williamson, J. (eds.): After the Washington Consensus. Restarting Growth and Reform in Latin America, Institute for International Economics, Washington, D.C., March 2003, pp. 1-19.

Wohlmann, M. (1998): Der nominale Wechselkurs als Stabilitätsanker: Die Erfahrungen Argentiniens 1991-1995, in: Göttinger Studien zur Entwicklungsökonomik, 5, Frankfurt am Main.

Zarazaga, C.E. (1995a): Can Currency Boards Prevent Devaluations and Financial Meltdowns?, in: Federal Reserve Bank of Dallas, Southwest Economy, 4, 1995, <http://www.dallasfed.org/htm/pubs/swe/4_95.html>.

Zarazaga, C.E. (1995b): The Tequila Effect, in: Federal Reserve Bank of Dallas, Southwest Economy, 2, 1995, <http://www.dallasfed.org/htm/pubs/swe/2_95.html>.

Zarazaga, C.E. (1995c): Argentina, Mexico, and Currency Boards: Another Case of Rules Versus Discretion, in: Federal Reserve Bank of Dallas, Economic Review, 4, 1995, pp. 14-24.

# Statistical Appendix

## Macro Indicators

### Figure 30: Argentine Real GDP Growth and its Components

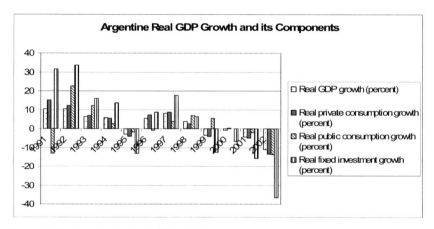

Source: IMF Independent Evaluation Office (2004), p. 10.

### Figure 31: Foreign Trade and Current Account Balance

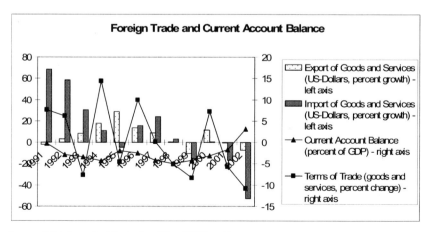

Source: IMF Independent Evaluation Office (2004), p. 10.

## Figure 32: Real Effective Exchange Rate and International Reserves

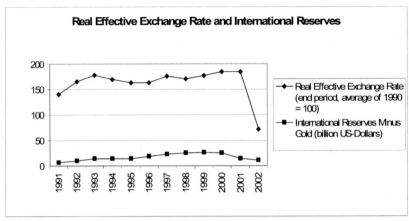

An increase in the real effective exchange rate indicates a Peso appreciation.
Source: IMF Independent Evaluation Office (2004), p. 10.

## Figure 33: Unemployment Rate

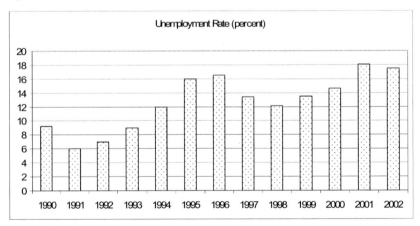

Source: Dominguez/Tesar (2004), p. 34, on data from IMF International Financial Statistics.

## Financial and Banking Indicators

## Figure 34: Inflation and Money Growth

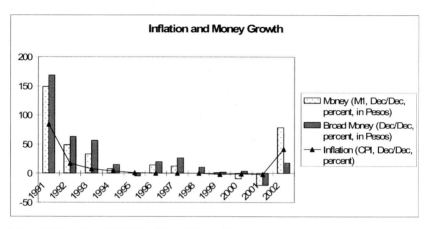

Source: IMF Independent Evaluation Office (2004), p. 10.

## Figure 35: Deflation

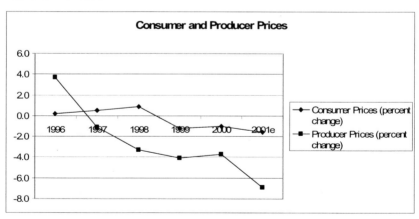

Source: Hanke/Schuler (2002), p. 4, on data from IMF, INDEC, MECON, BCRA, and J.P.Morgan.

## Figure 36: Money Market and Lending Rates

* Nov 30rd (last day of Peso interbank market): 689%
Source: Hanke/Schuler (2002), p. 4, on data from IMF, INDEC, MECON, BCRA, and J.P.Morgan.

## Figure 37: Interest Rate and Risk Spreads

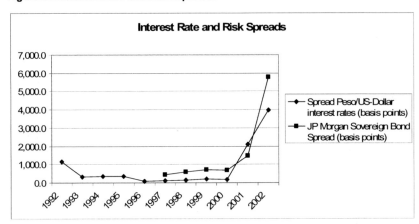

Source: Dominguez/Tesar (2004), p. 34, on data from Della Paolera/Taylor (2003), IMF International Financial Statistics, and Data Resources International.

## Figure 38: Peso Interest Rates

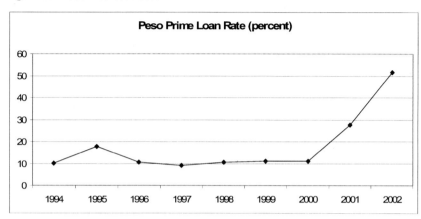

Source: Dominguez/Tesar (2004), p. 34., on data from Della Paolera/Taylor (2003) and IMF International Financial Statistics.

## Figure 39: Bank Lending to Public and Private Sector

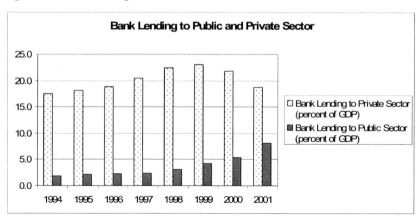

Source: Dominguez/Tesar (2004), p. 34, on data from BCRA.

**Figure 40: Peso and Dollar Bank Deposits**

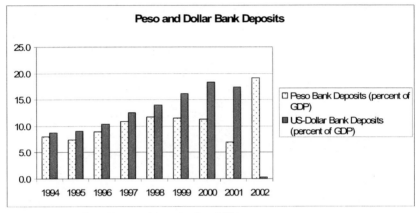

Source: Dominguez/Tesar (2004), p. 34, on data from BCRA.

**Fiscal Indicators**

**Figure 41: Public and External Debt**

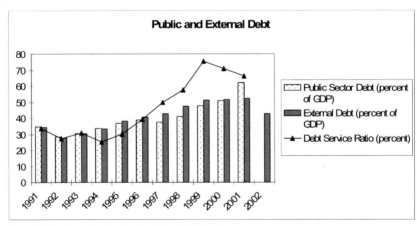

Source: IMF Independent Evaluation Office (2004), p. 10.

## Figure 42: External Debt as a Percentage of Exports

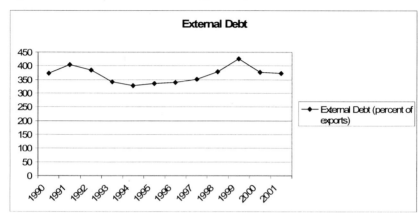

Source: Dominguez/Tesar (2004), p. 34, on data from Global Development Finance.

## Figure 43: Primary Government Balance

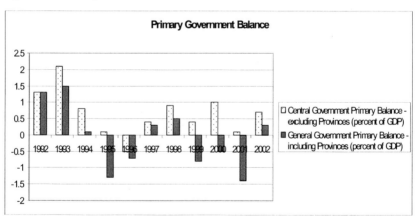

Source: IMF Independent Evaluation Office (2004), p. 10.

## Figure 44: Overall Government Balance

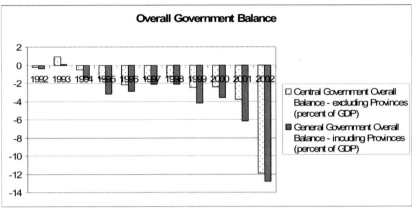

Source: IMF Independent Evaluation Office (2004), p. 10.

## Figure 45: Major Taxes in Argentina, as of December 2001

| Tax | Rate(s) (%) | Revenue (bn Pesos) | Remarks |
|---|---|---|---|
| **Federal** | | | |
| Social security taxes | 32.9 | 6.4* | Employees pay 11%, including 5% (down from 11% before Nov. 2001) to private pension funds; employers pay 21.9%. |
| Value-added tax | 21 | 11.9 | Main rate: 21%; special rates of 10.5% and 27%. |
| Income tax | 9-35 | 8 | Corporate rate: 35%; individual rates: 9%-35%, with top rate starting at 120,000 Pesos. |
| Fuel taxes | 50-60 | 2.5 | Rates vary, and were rejiggered in 2001. |
| Financial transactions tax | 0.6 | 1.9 | Imposed in April 2001 at 0.4%, increased in August 2001; paid on both bank credits and debits. |
| Excise taxes | various | 1.3 | Part of revenue shared with provinces. |
| Tariffs | 0-35 | 1.3 | Raised on many items March 2001. |
| Personal assets tax | 0.5, 0.75 | 0.5 | Bottom rate starts at total assets of 102,300 Pesos; top rate starts at 300,000 Pesos. |
| Presumptive minimum tax | 1 | 0.4 | Starts at assets of 300,000 Pesos. |
| All other revenue | various | 5.9 | |
| Total (including nontax) revenue | | 40.1 | Revenue for national nonfinancial sector, cash basis, Jan.-Sep. 2001. See notes. |
| **Provincial and local** | | | |
| Tax on gross sales | 1.0-4.9 | 3 | Averages 3%; many exemptions. |
| Property tax | various | 1 | |
| Motre vehicle tax | various | 0.5 | A common rate is 3%. |
| Stamp taxes | 1 | 0.4 | Most common rate is 1%. |
| All other revenue | various | 0.5 | |
| Total of these taxes | | 5.4 | Revenue for Jan.-June 2001. See notes. |

*: Plus 3.3 billion Pesos to priate pension accounts.
Capital gains tax for individuals and gift and estate taxes are zero, but real estate sales are subject to a 1.5% transfer tax.
The provincial governments receive considerable federal revenue sharing (about 12 billion Pesos over nine months).

Source: Schuler/Hanke (2002), p. 36, on data from Fundación Invertir Argentina, MECON, and Administración Federal de Ingresos Públicos.

## Distribution and Poverty Indicators

## Figure 46: Gini Coefficient

Note: A value of 0 indicates perfect equality of income, a value of 1 perfect inequality (where one household would earn the total of available income).
Source: Gasparini (2002), on data from EPH.

## Figure 47: People Living below the Official Poverty Line

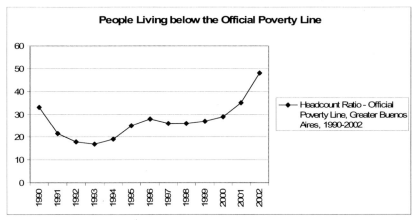

Source: Gasparini (2002), on data from EPH.

## Selected Data

## Figure 48: Key Economic Data

| | 1991 | 1992 | 1993 | 1994 | 1995 | 1996 | 1997 | 1998 | 1999 | 2000 | 2001 | 2002 |
|---|---|---|---|---|---|---|---|---|---|---|---|---|
| Real GDP Growth (percent) | 10.5 | 10.3 | 6.3 | 5.8 | -2.8 | 5.5 | 8.1 | 3.8 | -3.4 | -0.8 | -4.4 | -10.9 |
| Real Private Consumption Growth (percent) | 15 | 12.1 | 7.1 | 5.4 | -4 | 7.3 | 8.7 | 2.5 | -4 | 0.3 | -4.9 | -13.3 |
| Real Public Consumption Growth (percent) | -13.1 | 22.7 | 12.1 | 2.7 | -1.6 | -0.9 | 3.8 | 7.1 | 5.6 | -0.1 | -1.9 | -13.5 |
| Real Fixed Investment | 31.5 | 33.5 | 16 | 13.7 | -13 | 8.8 | 17.7 | 6.5 | -12.6 | -6.8 | -15.7 | -36.4 |
| Inflation (CPI, Dec.-Dec., | 84 | 17.5 | 7.4 | 3.9 | 1.6 | 0.1 | 0.3 | 0.7 | -1.8 | -0.7 | -1.5 | 41 |
| Money (M1, Dec.-Dec., percent, in Pesos) | 148.6 | 49 | 33 | 8.2 | 1.6 | 14.6 | 12.8 | 0 | 1.6 | -9.1 | -20.1 | 78.4 |
| Broad Money (Dec.-Dec., percent, in Pesos) | 167.9 | 63 | 55.9 | 14.9 | -4.3 | 20 | 26.9 | 10.3 | 2.3 | 4.4 | -19.7 | 18.3 |
| Current Account Balance (Billion US-Dollars) | -0.4 | -6.5 | -8 | -11.1 | -5.2 | -6.8 | -12.2 | -14.5 | -11.9 | -8.8 | -4.5 | 9.6 |
| Current Account Balance (percent of GDP) | -0.2 | -2.9 | -3.4 | -4.3 | -2 | -2.5 | -4.2 | -4.9 | -4.2 | -3.1 | -1.7 | 3.1 |
| Export of Goods and Services (US-Dollars, percent growth) | -2.1 | 3.4 | 8.5 | 17.8 | 28.9 | 13.6 | 9 | 0.7 | -10.5 | 11.6 | -0.5 | -7.4 |
| Import of Goods and Services (US-Dollars, percent growth) | 68.3 | 58.8 | 30.3 | 11.3 | -4.6 | 15.8 | 24.1 | 3.4 | -15.3 | 0.5 | -16.6 | -52.6 |
| Public Sector Debt (percent of | 34.8 | 28.3 | 30.6 | 33.7 | 36.7 | 39.1 | 37.7 | 40.9 | 47.6 | 50.9 | 62.2 | |
| External Debt (percent of | 34.5 | 27.7 | 30.5 | 33.3 | 38.4 | 40.6 | 42.7 | 47.5 | 51.2 | 51.6 | 52.2 | 42.9 |
| Debt Service Ratio (percent) | 33.6 | 27.5 | 30.9 | 25.2 | 30.2 | 39.4 | 50 | 57.6 | 75.4 | 70.8 | 66.3 | |
| International Reserves Minus Gold (billion US-Dollars) | 6.2 | 10.2 | 14 | 14.6 | 14.5 | 18.3 | 22.3 | 24.8 | 26.3 | 25.1 | 14.6 | 10.5 |
| Exchange Rate (Peso/US-Dollar, end period) | 1 | 1 | 1 | 1 | 1 | 1 | 1 | 1 | 1 | 1 | 1 | 3.4 |
| Real Effective Exchange Rate (end period, average of 1990 = 100) | 140.5 | 165.4 | 177.8 | 169.3 | 162.9 | 163.3 | 175.8 | 170.6 | 177.6 | 184.8 | 184.7 | 71.6 |
| Terms of Trade (goods and services, percent change) | 7.6 | 6.1 | -7.7 | 14.4 | -4.5 | 9.9 | 0.2 | -5.1 | -8.4 | 7.2 | -5.7 | -10.8 |
| Central Government Primary Balance (percent of GDP) | | 1.3 | 2.1 | 0.8 | 0.1 | -0.5 | 0.4 | 0.9 | 0.4 | 1 | 0.1 | 0.7 |
| General Government Primary Balance (percent of GDP) | | 1.3 | 1.5 | 0.1 | -1.3 | -0.7 | 0.3 | 0.5 | -0.8 | -0.5 | -1.4 | 0.3 |
| Central Government Overall Balance (percent of GDP) | | -0.2 | 0.9 | -0.5 | -1.5 | -2.2 | -1.6 | -1.3 | -2.5 | -2.4 | -3.8 | -11.9 |
| General Government Overall Balance (percent of GDP) | | -0.4 | 0.1 | -1.4 | -3.2 | -2.9 | -2.1 | -2.1 | -4.2 | -3.6 | -6.2 | -12.8 |

Source: IMF Independent Evaluation Office (2004), p. 10.

## Figure 49: Indicators of Economic Structure in Selected Emerging Market Economies

|  | Period | Argentina | Brazil | Chile | Average* |
|---|---|---|---|---|---|
| Gross savings/GDP | 1990-2001 | 14.8 | 18.6 | 21.9 | 24.1 |
| Exports/GDP | 1990-2001 | 9.4 | 9.3 | 30.7 | 34.2 |
| Domestic debt markets/GDP | 1992-2001 | 42 | 123.1 | 110.4 | 113.2 |
| External debt/GDP | 1990-2001 | 41.3 | 52.7 | 45.6 | 50.6 |
| External debt/exports | 1990-2001 | 368.2 | 322.4 | 143.3 | 176.4 |
| Short term external debt/foreign reserves | 1992-2001 | 110.3 | 79.9 | 37.4 | 80.6 |
| Foreign-currency-denominated debt/total public sector debt** | 1996-1999 | 89.2 | ... | 26.5 | 56.3 |
| General government overall balance/GDP | 1990-2001 | -2.5 | -3.5 | 0.2 | -1.6 |
| General government total revenue and grants/GDP | 1990-2001 | 22 | 28.9 | 21.7 | 22.2 |
| Central government total expenditure and net lending/GDP | 1990-2001 | 19.6 | 20.2 | 20.4 | 19.6 |

* Contains Argentina, Brazil, Chile, Colombia, Indonesia, Korea, Malaysia, Mexico, Philippines, and Thailand.
** Public sector debt for Argentina and central government debt for the rest of the countries. Argentina's debt includes the debt of the central bank and the government-guaranteed debt of public sector banks. Argentina's foreign-currency-denominated debt is the sum of bilateral and multilateral loans, and foreign-currency-denominated bonds and securities. It does not include foreign-currency-denominated loans from private banks.
Source: IMF Independent Evaluation Office (2004), p. 86.

# HOHENHEIMER VOLKSWIRTSCHAFTLICHE SCHRIFTEN

Band    1    Walter Deffaa: Anonymisierte Befragungen mit zufallsverschlüsselten Antworten. Die Randomized-Response-Technik (RRT). Methodische Grundlagen, Modelle und Anwendungen. 1982.

Band    2    Thomas Michael Baum: Staatsverschuldung und Stabilisierungspolitik in der Demokratie. Zur neoinstitutionalistischen Kritik der keynesianischen Fiskalpolitik. 1982.

Band    3    Klaus Schröter: Die wettbewerbspolitische Behandlung der leitungsgebundenen Energiewirtschaft. Dargestellt am Beispiel der Fernwärmewirtschaft der Bundesrepublik Deutschland. 1986.

Band    4    Hugo Mann: Theorie und Politik der Steuerreform in der Demokratie. 1987.

Band    5    Max Christoph Wewel: Intervallarithmetische Dependenzanalyse in der Ökonometrie. Ein konjekturaler Ansatz. 1987.

Band    6    Heinrich Pascher: Die U.S.-amerikanische Deregulation Policy im Luftverkehrs- und Bankenbereich. 1987.

Band    7    Harald Lob: Die Entwicklung der französischen Wettbewerbspolitik bis zur Verordnung Nr. 86-1243 vom 01. Dezember 1986. Eine exemplarische Untersuchung der Erfassung der Behinderungsstrategie auf der Grundlage des Konzepts eines wirksamen Wettbewerbs. 1988.

Band    8    Ulrich Kirschner: Die Erfassung der Nachfragemacht von Handelsunternehmen. Eine Analyse der ökonomischen Beurteilungskriterien und der wettbewerbsrechtlichen Instrumente im Bereich der Verhaltenskontrolle.1988.

Band    9    Friedhelm Herb: Marktwirtschaftliche Innovationspolitik. 1988.

Band   10   Claus Schnabel: Zur ökonomischen Analyse der Gewerkschaften in der Bundesrepublik Deutschland. Theoretische und empirische Untersuchungen von Mitgliederentwicklung, Verhalten und Einfluß auf wirtschaftliche Größen. 1989.

Band   11   Jan B. Rittaler: Industrial Concentration and the Chicago School of Antitrust Analysis. A Critical Evaluation on the Basis of Effective Competition. 1989.

Band   12   Thomas Märtz: Interessengruppen und Gruppeninteressen in der Demokratie. Zur Theorie des Rent-Seeking. 1990.

Band   13   Andreas Maurer: Statistische Verfahren zur Ermittlung von oligopolistischen Strukturen. 1990.

Band   14   Peter Mendler: Zur ökonomischen und politisch-institutionellen Analyse öffentlicher Kredithilfen. 1992.

Band   15   Heinrich J. Engelke: Die Interpretation der Rundfunkfreiheit des Grundgesetzes: Eine Analyse aus ökonomischer Sicht. 1992.

Band   16   Thomas Fischer: Staat, Recht und Verfassung im Denken von Walter Eucken. Zu den staats- und rechtstheoretischen Grundlagen einer wirtschaftsordnungspolitischen Konzeption. 1993.

Band   17   Stefan Elßer: Innovationswettbewerb. Determinanten und Unternehmensverhalten. 1993.

Band   18   Reinhard Scharff: Regionalpolitik und regionale Entwicklungspotentiale. Eine kritische Analyse. 1993.

Band   19   Karin Beckmann: Probleme der Regionalpolitik im Zuge der Vollendung des Europäischen Binnenmarktes. Eine ökonomische Analyse. 1995.

Band 20  Bernd Nolte: Engpaßfaktoren der Innovation und Innovationsinfrastruktur. Eine theoretische und empirische Analyse für ländliche Wirtschaftsräume in Baden-Württemberg. 1996.

Band 21  Klaus-Rainer Brintzinger: Die Nationalökonomie an den Universitäten Freiburg, Heidelberg und Tübingen 1918 - 1945. Eine institutionenhistorische, vergleichende Studie der wirtschaftswissenschaftlichen Fakultäten und Abteilungen südwestdeutscher Universitäten. 1996.

Band 22  Steffen Binder: Die Idee der Konsumentensouveränität in der Wettbewerbstheorie. Teleokratische vs. nomokratische Auffassung. 1996.

Band 23  Alexander Burger: Deregulierungspotentiale in der Gesetzlichen Rentenversicherung. Reformnotwendigkeiten versus Reformmöglichkeiten. 1996.

Band 24  Burkhard Scherer: Regionale Entwicklungspolitik. Konzeption einer dezentralisierten und integrierten Regionalpolitik. 1997.

Band 25  Frauke Wolf: Lorenzkurvendisparität. Neuere Entwicklungen, Erweiterungen und Anwendungen. 1997.

Band 26  Hans Pitlik: Politische Ökonomie des Föderalismus. Föderative Kompetenzverteilung im Lichte der konstitutionellen Ökonomik. 1997.

Band 27  Stephan Seiter: Der Beitrag Nicholas Kaldors zur Neuen Wachstumstheorie. Eine vergleichende Studie vor dem Hintergrund der Debatte über den Verdoorn-Zusammenhang. 1997.

Band 28  André Schmidt: Ordnungspolitische Perspektiven der europäischen Integration im Spannungsfeld von Wettbewerbs- und Industriepolitik. 1998.

Band 29  Bernd Blessin: Innovations- und Umweltmanagement in kleinen und mittleren Unternehmen. Eine theoretische und empirische Analyse. 1998.

Band 30  Oliver Letzgus: Die Ökonomie internationalen Umweltschutzes. 1999.

Band 31  Claudia Hafner: Systemwettbewerb versus Harmonisierung in Europa. Am Beispiel des Arbeitsmarktes. 1999.

Band 32  Jürgen Kulle: Ökonomie der Musikindustrie. Eine Analyse der körperlichen und unkörperlichen Musikverwertung mit Hilfe von Tonträgern und Netzen. 1998.

Band 33  Michael Ganske: Intertemporale Aspekte von Staatsverschuldung und Außenhandel. 1999.

Band 34  Margit Ströbele: Die Deregulierungswirkungen der europäischen Integration. Das Beispiel der Sondermärkte. 1999.

Band 35  Marion Benesch: Devisenmarktinterventionen in Theorie und Praxis. Eine umfassende Analyse ihrer Zielsetzungen, Wirkungsweisen und wirtschaftspolitischen Bedeutung. 1999.

Band 36  Torsten Gruber: Unterschiedliche geldpolitische Transmissionsmechanismen und Stabilitätskulturen als mögliche Ursachen geldpolitischer Spannungen in der Europäischen Währungsunion. 2000.

Band 37  Bertram Melzig-Thiel: Arbeit in der Informationsgesellschaft. Chancen und Risiken neuer Informations- und Kommunikationstechnologien für die Beschäftigung. 2000.

Band 38  Annette Fritz: Die Entsorgungswirtschaft im Spannungsfeld zwischen Abfallpolitik und Kartellrecht. Eine industrieökonomische Branchenstudie. 2001.

Band 39  Harald Strotmann: Arbeitsplatzdynamik in der baden-württembergischen Industrie. Eine Analyse mit amtlichen Betriebspaneldaten. 2002.

www.peterlang.de